Seduced, Abandoned, and Reborn

EARLY AMERICAN STUDIES

Daniel K. Richter and Kathleen M. Brown, Series Editors

Exploring neglected aspects of our colonial, revolutionary, and
early national history and culture, Early American Studies reinterprets
familiar themes and events in fresh ways. Interdisciplinary in character,
and with a special emphasis on the period from about 1600 to 1850,
the series is published in partnership with the McNeil Center for
Early American Studies.

A complete list of books in the series is available from the publisher.

Seduced, Abandoned, and Reborn

Visions of Youth in Middle-Class America, 1780–1850

Rodney Hessinger

PENN

University of Pennsylvania Press
Philadelphia

Copyright © 2005 University of Pennsylvania Press
All rights reserved
Printed in the United States of America on acid-free paper

10   9   8   7   6   5   4   3   2   1

Published by
University of Pennsylvania Press
Philadelphia, Pennsylvania 19104-4112

Library of Congress Cataloging-in-Publication Data

Hessinger, Rodney.
  Seduced, abandoned, and reborn : visions of youth in middle-class America, 1780–1850 /
Rodney Hessinger.
    p. cm. — (Early American studies)
  Includes bibliographical references and index.
  ISBN 0-8122-3879-6 (cloth : alk. paper)
  1. Youth—United States—History—18th century.   2. Youth—United States—History—19th
century.   3. Youth—Books and reading—United States—History.   4. Social control—United
States—History.   5. Moral education—United States—History.   6. United States—Social
conditions—18th century.   7. United States—Social conditions—19th century.   8. United
States—Moral conditions.   I. Title.   II. Series

HQ796.H465 2005
305.235'086'220973—dc22   2005042228

In memory of Frank Hessinger, Jr.

Contents

Introduction

Recording his famous impressions of America in the 1830s, Alexis de Tocqueville expressed surprise at the pervasiveness of American democracy. Its spirit had reached far beyond the realm of politics, extending even into the traditional institution of the family. Commenting on the relations between parents and children, the French aristocrat and traveler observed that while "vestiges" of parental authority remained, they were exercised only during the "first years of childhood." Adults rapidly released restraints on the young: "As soon as the young American approaches manhood, the ties of filial obedience are relaxed, day by day." Youth were soon wholly independent: "at the close of boyhood the man appears and begins to trace out his own path." In America, Tocqueville concluded, there was "strictly speaking, no adolescence."[1] His words were both perceptive and prophetic. Youth did largely stand as adults in the early American republic. The modern notion of adolescence, conceived as a period of protected dependency following childhood, would not take shape until the end of the nineteenth century.[2]

How had this occurred? Patriarchal control over youth had eroded to an unprecedented extent in the early American republic. To be sure, adults have always had some trouble ruling the young. Colonial America was no exception. By the late seventeenth century, ministers in New England already felt their grasp slipping, finding themselves delivering sexually suggestive sermons just to capture the attention of youth.[3] Yet powerful influences were at work to uphold patriarchy in the colonial era. In subsistence farm communities, parents relied heavily on the labor of their sons and daughters. For this reason, parents were slow to give their children the means to establish their own families. With a highly restricted land market and few opportunities for wages, children had no choice but to wait patiently for parents to bestow property on them before they could set up on their own. In addition, village churches and courts steered the courting behavior of young adults. Puritan elders whipped youth for fornication, while Quaker men and women investigated young couples through committees of their

Monthly Meetings. Not all youth were subjected to such patriarchal conventions or community control. Those young adults who arrived on their own in the New World had to worry less about parental interference, though they usually did have to serve out an indenture or apprenticeship before they could strike out alone. In the plantation economies of the South, parents could be indulgent with youth, for children's labor was dispensable when slaves were on hand. For the North, however, especially in stable communities beyond the seaboard, extended dependency was the common lot.[4]

A number of factors made the early republic a particularly challenging era for patriarchy. Accepting the lessons of the Revolution, most Americans in the late eighteenth century came to believe that stern patriarchal rule was inappropriate in a democracy. Self-determination over major life choices, like choosing a marriage partner, would belong to the young, not their parents. In the early nineteenth century, the power of elders was further undermined. In the urban Northeast, a cultural marketplace for the attention of youth emerged. The Market Revolution, the rapid expansion of capitalist enterprise and industry, was critical to opening choices for the young. They would be empowered consumers, as elders competed for influence. In the case of publishing, for example, writers began to produce a steady stream of books for young adults. The market for youth went beyond what was being hawked in the storefronts of burgeoning cities. In colleges and churches alike, adults scrambled to gain hold of youth. In the midst of this fight, conservative moralists had to compromise their messages, but they did win various struggles. In fact, their voices would shape generations to come. Bourgeois Americans, those aspiring people who sought to improve themselves and those around them, would simultaneously create and absorb their lessons.

If youth were to be largely independent in America, how could elders hope to guide their actions? This became a central dilemma in emerging bourgeois culture. Persuasion, rather than coercion, became the main means to direct youth. That is, guardians tried to entice youth to listen to them. The challenge was not easy because others were competing for influence. Peers and corrupt elders could lead youth astray, indulging dangerous impulses in the young. To better comprehend this difficulty, consider briefly the world through the eyes of Ashbel Green. A conservative theologian and educator, this Presbyterian minister and president of the College of New Jersey (known today as Princeton) had seen his college wracked by riots and disorder in the early nineteenth century. He wished to reassert control over his institution. In a report to the board of trustees in 1816, Green observed how students could easily corrupt one another. "The new comers," he warned, "are not yet trained to the discipline of the house and are therefore fit materials to be seduced and converted into cat's paws" by devious older students.[5] Presumably, entering students would want to earn the esteem of their peers and therefore were easily convinced to help carry out troublesome plots. Green's fear that students might be "seduced" into wrongful behavior was a major refrain in late eighteenth- and early nineteenth-century America. How could Green earn the allegiance and obedience of incoming students? Ironically, Green too would have to enter the business of seduction.

Green's tough rhetoric about the "discipline of the house" was misleading. It belied the weak position of professors at his school. On the occasion of Green's inauguration, he had also blustered that he would not indulge youth: "Now a coaxing system, is exactly the worst kind of a thing that can be called government." He insisted he would not bend: "No in every deed—I shall coax no one—I shall thank no one for doing his duty— Why should I?" And yet already one could see cracks in his front. He quickly admitted, "every one who shall do well will be made happy," while "every one who shall excel shall be honoured."[6] Alluding to his willingness to grant awards to students, Green was already prepared to rule with the carrot, not just the stick. It was a difficult balancing act. At what point did one bend too far? Like corrupt peers, professors had to persuade, perhaps even seduce, youth into following them. The danger in this was that it forced instructors to pander to the young. Fearing this problem, Green instructed his faculty that an "evil to be avoided" was the "undue desire of obtaining popularity among our pupils." Professors were failing to correct the young and instead were seeking to gain "their esteem and applause." This, in his view, was a mistake. It was sure to cause the "most lasting injury" to the school. In fact, Green was certain that professors' efforts to please students was "among the most prolific causes" of a recent "rebellion" suffered by the college. While winning the favor of the young might yield a professor temporary rewards, ultimately he would be "degraded into contempt."[7] Students would come to understand they held the reins.

This dilemma was not simply a problem in the somewhat rarefied world of the early nineteenth-century college. After Ashbel Green left the College of New Jersey, he would face similar developments in religion. In churches, as in schools, adults were pandering to the young. As editor of Philadelphia's Old School Presbyterian journal, *The Christian Advocate*,

Green would publish searing critiques of revivalists who were exciting and flattering youth. Green did not struggle alone. In fact, he was one among a large number of outspoken adults who tried to fight the shift in power to young adults. While young men, more than young women, would see their horizons expand in the early republic, both were granted a greater range of choices in the late eighteenth and early nineteenth centuries. In a wide array of arenas, those who wished to guide youth had to compete with those who would seduce them. A surprisingly broad range of writers, people from disparate backgrounds and occupations, spoke in unison of the need to restrain, as well as guard, the young. Didactic novelists seeking to guide young women through courtship warned against the seductive ploys of male libertines. Writers on the dangers of masturbation battled the purveyors of pornography. Orthodox ministers struggled against the emotional appeals of evangelical firebrands. Ultimately, the voices of respectability were forced into the same pandering game. The line between guardian and seducer became blurred.

*   *   *

This book traces the story of Americans' reaction to the freedoms granted youth in the early republic. It demonstrates how the perceived social disorder of young adults helped shape the identity of the emerging middle class, particularly in the central sites of bourgeois cultural production: cities, schools, and presses. Regionally, it will concentrate on the urban Northeast, particularly the city of Philadelphia. In these centers of bourgeois cultural formation, elders coming to terms with troublesome youth crafted new values that would come to infuse middle-class society. The moralists who performed this cultural work did not set out to craft new ideologies, much less a new set of social relations. The challenge they faced, and the response to it with which this text is ultimately concerned, was to guide the next generation into stable and respectable stations in their families and communities. Their concern was not to secure status for youth in a material sense, so much as to transmit values that would keep them in good stead in an ever-changing society. Guiding the young was a vexing task in an age in which patriarchy had declined and youth could choose freely from a wide array of cultural vendors. Many of the values that advisors tried to impart had deep roots in the past. Chastity, virtue, piety, respect for elders, and hard work had all been important to colonial elders. But in the past one could rely on the broad support of a wider community to enforce these principles. Now these values had to be more deeply etched within the self, particularly for those seeking middle-class respectability. Freed from patriarchal constraints, empowered youth provoked the formation of bourgeois identity.

The stakes were high in trying to guide the young. The fact that the American population was demographically skewed toward youth in these years made the challenge for elders all the greater. Early American society was less age-graded than our own, so fixing definitive ages for the category of youth is tricky. The term was an open one, often used interchangeably with the phrases "young man" or "young woman." As a life stage, youth sat between childhood and adulthood. Rhetorically, it ended when one took on all the responsibilities of adulthood, such as a marriage and an occupation. As a loose guideline, however, we can see in the records of this era that early Americans generally considered the stage of youth as beginning in one's teens and lasting well into one's twenties. Given this, we can see that many Americans in this era fell into the category of youth. The historian Burton Bledstein has found that while the number of children under fifteen actually declined as the nineteenth century unfolded, the number of youth did not, with close to 30 percent of the population falling into the fifteen-to-twenty-nine age bracket.[8]

In a symbolic sense, the challenge was even bigger than these numbers suggest. If traditionally the life stage of youth ended when one was settled into a permanent station in life, in a bourgeois society, a world in which people are always striving to get ahead, most everyone could be said to be a youth.[9] Middle-class Americans never settled in a station, jumping from job to job and town to town. Geographic and occupational mobility characterized the bourgeoisie, so it should not be surprising that the words penned for youth in this era would come to define their class.

The cultural relationship between elders and youth underwent important changes over the course of the early republic. The chronology of this journey can be graphed as two intimately entwined trajectories. One pattern is the series of challenges offered by youth. The other is a corresponding series of responses by reformers. Ultimately, it is the second model we will privilege as this study progresses, for the goal of this book is to illuminate reformers' perceptions of, and reactions to, youth, more than it is to explore the lived social experiences of the young. Nonetheless, to illuminate the dynamic, to see how expanding freedoms for the young might have informed the cultural reactions of elders, it will be helpful for us to survey the changing lives of young adults in the early republic in some greater detail.

Youth seized a widening range of freedoms and choices in the early republic. If they did not often voice outright rebellion in the late eighteenth and first half of the nineteenth centuries, their growing boldness nonetheless greatly worried elders.[10] As noted, the revolutionary era witnessed expanding courtship choices for youth. The trend actually predates the late eighteenth century, for growing land scarcity in the long-settled regions of the Northeast had already weakened the leverage of parents over children as the century unfolded.[11] As the Revolution arrived, many Americans accepted growing freedom for youth vis-à-vis adults. Patriarchal authority exerted over youth, more so than that exercised over other dependents like slaves, was criticized as an unjust form of tyranny like that wielded by the British king over his subjects.[12] Shrinking parental control was tied to declining community influence. In the colonial past, tightly bound religious communities had regulated the courting and sex life of youth through churches, courts, and neighborhoods. Both verbal and physical chastisement had been used to prevent premarital sex and to pressure youth into marriage. As religious fervor waned and families sought privacy, however, the community decreasingly interfered in courtship and sexual life. By the end of the eighteenth century, both parents and community were less involved in the negotiation of marriage. At the same time, youth embraced more sexual freedom, especially having more sex out of wedlock, producing what one historian has called a "sexual revolution" in the young nation.[13]

Youth also took advantage of growing freedoms in colleges and churches. Both developments, most fully realized in the second and third decades of the nineteenth century, like changes in courtship, can be linked to an extension of democratic ideals. Certain market conditions, however, made their expression more fully possible. Exciting new religious choices appeared for youth in urban America in the early nineteenth century.[14] There was, to be sure, tremendous religious diversity in cities like Philadelphia before these years, but the resurgence of evangelical forces at this time drew more distinct lines both between and within churches, lines that demarked real differences in attitudes toward youth. Some preachers openly courted the young, encouraging them to break from the churches of fellow pastors.[15] Similarly, colleges faced new market pressures in these years. By the 1810s and '20s colleges had proliferated tremendously, leaving youth with the preponderance of negotiating power in their struggles with educators. Youth found themselves increasingly cherished as consumers by schools that had to fight with one another for their very survival. In addition, colleges provided an environment where youth could band together in ways unimaginable elsewhere in American society. It is not surprising, therefore, that colleges would struggle with many student disturbances in these years.[16]

By the 1830s and '40s unprecedented urban opportunities opened for the young. The Market Revolution cut many male youth loose from their families. As business and industry expanded, some apprentices faced declining prospects, slipping into the working class. Nonetheless, many other youth found economic opportunity as clerks and bookkeepers in the expanding storefronts and shops that lined city avenues. Young men also had growing options about how to spend their newly earned salaries and wages. Living in boardinghouses, away from parents and employers in anonymous cities, male youth were less accountable than ever. Many competing cultural vendors awaited the young as they entered the urban world. Gambling houses, taverns, brothels, and theaters opened their doors to youth.[17] Booksellers also plied their wares. Fueled by important new technological advances in printing, the publishing industry boomed, offering a wide range of reading fare for the young. The most disturbing result of these changes was an increasingly visible youth culture that celebrated licentiousness.[18] Young men who indulged in this so-called rake culture could procure pornography and revel in seduction as they read a seamy new brand of literature that guided them through the urban underworld.

These, then, were the changes that the self-anointed reformers of youth were battling in the early republic. But not all the problems imagined by the reformers were real. It is fully plausible that moralists may at times have conjured up more difficulties than existed. The saga of student disorder at the University of Pennsylvania, a story taken up in Chapter 3, provides an example. At Penn in the early nineteenth century, student disorder never seemed to reach greater heights than silly pranks and surliness toward professors. Yet the provost, Frederic Beasley, was so worried by the very real riots and disorders he saw plaguing other colleges that he perceived his school to be on the precipice of disaster. His perception, accurate or not, drove his actions. In cultural history it is a truism that perception is more important than reality. Still, in the case of youth in the early republic, the two often *did* correspond to one another. While some reformers did have overactive imaginations, at this point historians have assembled enough evidence, to which this study will contribute more, to establish that substantial new freedoms and opportunities were available and being seized by the young in the early republic.

So how did reformers respond? The path moralists forged in their effort to contain youth began with novels and periodical fiction. As the literary critic Cathy Davidson has discussed, the birth of the American republic was intimately bound up with the rise of the American novel.[19] The novel seems a curious place from which to stage a reform campaign. The literary theorist Mikhail Bakhtin has famously argued that the very hallmark of the novel is its dialogism, its ability and tendency to voice competing perspectives from society. Different passages and sentiments, he insists, will resonate distinctly with each reader. Context, rather than text, determines meaning.[20] Writers in the early republic actually understood some of these difficulties with the novel. They nonetheless had high hopes for its potential for moral influence.

Because the novel mixed entertainment with instruction, it had the ability to lure readers who might ignore straight didacticism. American writers did their best to contain the mutable character of fiction. The narratives that late eighteenth-century Americans composed and imported had a distinctive reformist cast. Showing a decided preference for the didactic strains of the eighteenth-century British novelist Samuel Richardson over the worldly satire of fellow Briton Henry Fielding, Americans saw great promise in the novel as a tool of moral instruction.[21] Seduction tales, narratives that warned young women to avoid the dangerous sexual ploys of men, proved most attractive of all. While certainly there was a lingering distrust of fiction, a range of writers saw novels as a persuasive means to discourage the young from illicit sex. American writers did their best to ensure that readers did not misconstrue their messages.

Convinced by and impressed with the moral lessons of seduction fiction, Philadelphia reformers in 1800 decided to carry their moral reform vision into brick and mortar. The Philadelphia Magdalen Society asylum, an institution meant to rescue young prostitutes from the consequences of male treachery, was a logical extension of seduction fiction. It was founded by paragons of the Philadelphia community, men such as Bishop William White, head of the Episcopal Church in Pennsylvania. The essential agreement of these reformers with Susanna Rowson, a novelist and playwright (occupations more suspect in this age), suggests a surprisingly broad consensus about the dangers facing youth at the turn of the century. And yet as the nineteenth century unfolded, the meaning of seduction fiction began to unravel. The operators of the Philadelphia Magdalen Society would witness this firsthand.

The novel proved untrustworthy as a vehicle for moral lessons. Encouraged by the managers of the Magdalen Society, Philadelphia prostitutes began to read their own past into seduction tales. The dialogue between their lurid pasts and the stock seduction narrative, which positioned women as pure victims, pulled at the seams of the narrative. Increasingly the seduction tale was stretched to cover and excuse behavior that was shocking to bourgeois moralists. In New York the notorious prostitute Helen Jewett draped her sexual improprieties in stories of violated innocence.[22] Similarly, several famous early nineteenth-century courtroom trials concerning seduction inspired vigorous celebrations of homicide in print, justifying murder as a response to seduction.[23] In 1804 a Presbyterian minister, Samuel Miller, accused the novel of framing "an apology for suicide, adultery, prostitution, and the indulgence of every propensity for which a corrupt heart can plead an inclination."[24] If his warnings seemed overzealous at the turn of the century, by midcentury many more would have found his sentiments persuasive.

As society tested and strained the meanings of moralistic seduction fiction, the ability of the novel to support reform collapsed. The didacticism of the late eighteenth-century novel gave way to two new novelistic forms, both ill-suited for advancing moral campaigns. Sensationalism and sentimentalism dominated the world of early nineteenth-century fiction. Both strains ostensibly pursued moral aims, but the performance was unconvincing. Writers of sensational fiction like George Lippard inveighed against seduction, but he simultaneously aroused sexual desire with erotically charged descriptions of female bodies and violence.[25] Sentimentalists seemed the more natural heirs of the didactic form. Promoting causes such as temperance and abolitionism, sentimentalist authors did not wholly abandon the world. Still, the fundamental impulse of sentimental fiction was inward toward the self, not outward toward society.[26] Sentimental scenes of suffering in novels were more apt to inspire delicious tears rather than principled institution building. Reformers did not give up on the power of the press, far from it—but as we will see, when they took up publishing again with renewed vigor in the 1830s and '40s, they moved to surer footing. By this point, advice literature, a more pure form of didacticism, had replaced the novel as the major means for influencing youth in print.

In the intervening years, reformers had taken to building institutions, especially colleges and Sunday schools, to guide the young. Colleges were initially inspired by republican dreams. Educators probably did not believe that all youth would attend college, but they did hope that those who did could form a virtuous leadership that would guide the country into the future. Riots and disorders dashed such hopes. Students were more inclined to mock and challenge professors, showing little concern for educators' goals. By the Jacksonian era, few could have hoped that struggling colleges would direct the country on a path of virtue. New reform strategies, however, were simultaneously being born in the fervor of evangelical revival.

The Second Great Awakening inspired the rapid founding of voluntary societies meant to save the souls of youth. Quickly, however, elders discovered the disruptive potential of evangelical religion. Fighting to save their own congregations, conservative Presbyterian ministers had to rebuff the inroads made by upstart groups like the Methodists. Matters became more alarming when evangelical flames began to engulf their own churches. In response, conservative churchmen created new institutions that absorbed some of the energy of the evangelical voluntary forms but preserved their own sense of hierarchy and order. The Sunday school embodied this compromise between old and new. Something else the Sunday school movement learned to harness was the power of new printing technologies. Reform writers would quickly apply this lesson in the Jacksonian era.

Reformers began to write two new major forms of advice literature in the 1830s and '40s. One new genre was the advice book written for the young man launching his career in the city. Despite their ostensibly secular purpose, these texts carried an unmistakable evangelical tone. According to these books, dangerous temptations lurked around every corner, as various seducers tried to take advantage of young men. In light of such dangers, writers insisted that success was predicated more on character and conscience than on business acumen. In the anonymous world of the city, they insisted, morality had to be inculcated in the self. The second major form of advice literature was the anti-masturbation text. Also indebted to evangelicalism, writers of these books replaced the sentimental appeal of seduction fiction with heavy-handed warnings against dabbling in sin. These midcentury sex reformers used language and metaphors that paralleled the work of other evangelical reformers. Temperance writing was a clear inspiration. If one sip of alcohol could lead one on a rapid downward slide towards alcoholism and degeneracy, for sex reformers one touch led a young man to sexual addiction. While this literature had jettisoned the ambiguities of fiction, it quickly revealed scandalous potentialities of its own by scaring audiences with grisly descriptions of sexual disease. Ultimately, the writers of this literature would serve order by calling on doctors and guardians to watch over youth who were incapable of controlling themselves.

From a bird's eye view we might see an evolving strategy of reform, one that starts with fiction, moves to institution building, and then finally revisits literature, but of a more pure didactic form. But such a summary would erroneously suggest a deliberate progression. The moralists who reacted to youth were a diverse group. They probably would not have recognized many of their compatriots as their own. In fact, they really should be seen as various discrete camps of reformers, only occasionally overlapping in thought and personnel. Didactic novelists, asylum directors, college educators, Sunday school proponents, advice writers, and sex-reform authors—all pursued their own unique visions. Princeton president Ashbel Green would probably have had little to do with novelist Susanna Rowson. But, there is real reason to examine them together. All agreed about the essential nature of the problem they faced. And all gradually worked toward fundamentally similar solutions to resolve them. To better understand the answers they devised we must place their work in some broader theoretical context.

*   *   *

To frame the problem faced by moralists slightly differently, to more fully comprehend the dialectic that developed between youth and elders, we might say that Americans in the early republic were forced to come to terms with the logic of John Locke's pedagogy on an unprecedented scale. The English philosopher's 1693 text, *Some Thoughts Concerning Education*, anticipated with remarkable clarity the dilemmas faced by the guardians of youth in the early American republic.[27] The overlap between Locke's ideas and those of other thinkers such as the Scottish moral sense writers makes it nearly impossible to draw lines of influence, especially since moral philosophy was most often popularized in fiction, not in philosophical treatises. Ultimately this book will not demonstrate the direct impact of Locke, but rather the maturation of a Lockean paradigm; it will highlight the development of strategies for influencing youth who were granted a larger share of freedom in society. Locke explored closely the challenges of rearing children who desired and possessed freedom.[28] The solutions he proffered were echoed in the choices made by writers and guardians in the early republic. Whether groping to Lockean solutions on their own or finding inspiration in his writings, moralists in the early republic elaborated a range of Lockean strategies to shape the behavior of the young.

To understand the dynamics of the young republic, then, it should be instructive to briefly explore Locke's pedagogical thought through a close reading of his *Some Thoughts Concerning Education*. In it one can see the interplay between the twin impulses to indulge, but simultaneously direct, the young. One important starting point for Locke's child-rearing theory was the desire for liberty in the young, a craving he believed present in mere infants. "We naturally," he insisted, "even from our Cradles, love Liberty, and have therefore an Aversion to many things for no other Reason but because they are enjoin'd us."[29] While he did advocate extending freedoms to youth as they aged, his first goal was to teach parents how to govern. The one instance for which Locke reserved corporal punishment as a "last Remedy" was when children showed an "*Obstinacy*," or "manifest *Perverseness* of the Will*," that is, when they openly defied the authority of their parents.[30] While Locke believed that children should conform to the will of parents, he recommended a range of noncoercive strategies that would prevent any counterproductive clashing of wills. Rather than commanding children to do things as an act of obedience, Locke believed parents should persuade children to listen to them. At some level, then, Locke was already accommodating children's desire for liberty.

Parents might be able to persuade by manipulating young children's perceptions of the world. Learning to read, for example, instead of being presented as a duty, might be "made a Play and Recreation." Parents could cultivate a "desire to be taught" if learning "were proposed to them as a thing of Honour, Credit, Delight, and Recreation, or as a Reward for doing something else."[31] As children aged, reason was increasingly to be used as a tool of persuasion. Once grown, he instructed, children would have to monitor their own behavior according to reason rather than desire.[32] It therefore behooved parents to spell out the logic of the demands they made on children. Similarly, Locke also urged the power of example over precept. The force of example could be pressed in two ways. Parents were to comment on the behavior of others, as well as model proper behavior for their children.[33] If parents took unwarranted liberties and then chastised a child for doing "what he sees you practice yourself," the child would resent the parent. He would think the punishment proceeds from "Peevishness and arbitrary Imperiousness."[34] According to Locke, the son naturally feels deserving of the same liberties indulged in by the parent. Parents therefore had to be careful to regulate their own behavior before the young. Here we can see that children's desire for liberty made real demands on elders.

The most "powerful Incentives to the Mind" of children, Locke insisted, were the persuasive tools of "*Esteem* and *Disgrace*." Parents were to praise children for good behavior and express shock, disappointment, or simply ignore children when they erred. If parents could get children to possess a "Love of Credit" and an "Apprehension of Shame and Disgrace," the major work for child rearing had been accomplished. The effectiveness of this approach was predicated on affectionate bonds between parents and children. Because children "find a Pleasure in being esteem'd and valu'd, especially by their Parents," they were quite malleable to reinforcement tactics.[35] This means of persuasion became particularly vital as children matured. Young adults were not easily intimidated into performing their duty.

As the child grew older, filial bonds were to be cemented by an extension of familiarity and friendship. The discipline of children, Locke insisted, was to be relaxed "as fast as their Age, Discretion, and good Behavior could allow it." Rather than talking sternly to a youth, a father would do well to "*talk familiarly*" with him. The "sooner you *treat him as a Man*, the sooner he will begin to be one." Similarly, he suggested that youth were to be admitted into the "*Friendship*" of parents. Welcomed into more egalitarian relations, a youth would find "himself happy under the Management of so favorable a Friend and so careful a Father."[36] It would be foolhardy to treat them otherwise: "We would be thought rational Creatures, and have our Freedom," Locke observed, "Whosoever has such Treatment when he is a Man, will look out other Company, other Friends, other Conversation, with whom he can be at Ease."[37]

Overall, Locke promoted a child-rearing strategy that sought to accommodate the desire for freedom in children and indulged the desire for liberty in youth. Success was predicated on the development of reason and the internalization of parental values. In Locke's scheme coercive strategies such as corporal punishment or the threat of disinheritance had limited applicability. Compulsion would only work so long as parents were present. Threats of punishment had diminishing returns as youth began to move in wider circles: "Every Man must some Time or other be trusted to himself and his own Conduct; and he that is a good, a virtuous, and able Man, must be made so within." Threats created only a temporary restraint, for a youth could easily put on a "counterfeit Carriage, and dissembled Outside" to "avoid the present Anger of a Father who perhaps may disinherit him."[38] The mask of virtue could be easily dropped when beyond the view of parents. To truly change the hearts of youth, elders would have to turn to persuasion over coercion.

The era of the early republic was an age made for Lockean child-rearing strategies. The decades at the close of the eighteenth century and start of the nineteenth century would extend and exaggerate some important patterns already underway at the time of the American Revolution. As we have seen, in the decades following American independence, youth would enjoy an expanding range of freedom, a growing range of choices in courtship, religious affiliation, and occupation. If moral guardians wished to direct the young, they therefore would have to persuade youth to buy into their ideals and values. As noted, one new means available for persuasion from the revolutionary era forward was the novel. Locke himself seemed to anticipate this powerful form. Locke had recommended parables as an important means for imparting values. Parables, he said, could teach lessons in an attractive form. They could "delight and entertain" children, especially if accompanied with illustrations. Parents thus could "tempt" children into virtue.[39] Late eighteenth-century American novels resembled parables. Drawing portraits grounded in true stories, purposely blurring the boundaries between fact and fiction, writers tried to inspire readers to learn lessons from the experiences of characters.

Other instructors of youth would turn to different Lockean means. In colleges educators would increasingly see promise in Lockean reinforcement techniques. Frustrated by youth who cared more about the opinion of their peers than that of their professors, educators tried to develop ways to earn the loyalty of students. By conferring esteem and disgrace through grading, they hoped to inspire youth to excellence. Writers of advice literature for the young man entering the business world also used Lockean techniques. Striking the Lockean pose, they always insisted that they were friends to the reader. The young should follow their friendly counsel, they insisted, because of their deep affection for them. Eventually, all would find themselves accommodating youth in one way or another, seemingly endangering their own endeavors.[40] Such indulgence, however, was unavoidable in an age when youth held an increasingly better bargaining position. It also was a dynamic inherent in the act of persuasion.

We might even more fully comprehend this dynamic between advisors and youth if we briefly view their relation through one other theoretical lens, that of Michel Foucault. This book explores some of the same historical terrain probed by this famous late twentieth-century philosopher. Using Foucault's terminology, especially as he develops it in *The History of Sexuality*, volume 1, and *Discipline and Punish*, one might say this book tracks the deployment of new technologies of power. In more straightforward terms, this book looks at the development of new means of regulating behavior in bourgeois society and in young adults in particular. We will see how reformers devised new methods of evaluating, organizing, and watching youth in the early American republic, all key mechanisms, according to

Foucault, in the spread of disciplinary power. Foucault argues that in the emerging bourgeois societies of the West in the eighteenth and nineteenth centuries, there was a fundamental shift away from externally imposed sanctions and toward the incitement of internalized measures of self-control.[41] In other words, people learned to police themselves. This, in essence, is the goal of Lockean pedagogy. Thus this study can add a new ideological dimension to Foucault's schema by describing the spread of Lockean techniques. With its emphasis on using persuasion rather than coercion to direct behavior, Lockean child rearing promoted the internalization of values.

This study departs from Foucault, however, in at least one important respect. Foucault's notion of power has been critical in academic circles because he has shifted focus away from the obvious, and in his view, less effective, forms of power such as the apparatus of the state, and toward more hidden but more tenacious forms of power that move, as if along capillaries, through the individuals that constitute societies. While this book by no means seeks to displace Foucault's formulations on power, it should import a sense of human agency and negotiation that is often absent from his work.

Foucault's notion of power sometimes operates as if it were a disembodied force that has a will of its own. With research closer to the ground, however, the interplay of historical actors who helped form bourgeois values becomes more apparent. Foucault suggests that knowledge and power were more hierarchically organized over the course of the eighteenth and nineteenth centuries. Atop this hierarchy were the expert ranks of the bourgeoisie: reformers, psychiatrists, educators, and physicians. Because power does not reside in their actual persons but is distributed throughout society, the hierarchy seems quite formidable and resilient. Resistance to power in Foucault often seems futile and even counterproductive, almost as if those who were subject to its operations were trying to wrestle free from a glue trap; every effort to resist catches one more fully in its grip.[42] In this book, we will witness closely the troubles of bourgeois reformers in the early American republic who were trying to direct youth. Their tenuous hold on young adults is palpable. Working hard to woo young adults to their messages, they are sometimes forced into compromising positions. In Foucauldian terms, the demanding cultural marketplace of the early American republic resisted the normalizing judgment of experts. In other words, disorderly youth exposed the weaknesses of the emergent bourgeois order.

* * *

If the primary goal of this book is to elucidate the efforts of reformers to instill self-control within youth, its secondary aim is an analysis of the formation of the middle class. Concentrating on a Northeastern urban cultural milieu, this book will put greater emphasis on print culture and transatlantic ideologies than previous studies of the creation of the American bourgeoisie have done.[43] By giving what the British historian G. J. Barker-Benfield has called the "culture of sensibility" a more prominent role in emerging conceptions of gender, this book aims to better capture the cosmopolitan origins of the middle class.[44] Laying witness to competing print forms in urban America, it will demonstrate that cultural conservatives were forced to weaken their messages to win popular support. The theme of cultural competition will be applied to arenas outside the world of print. Taking its cue from many of the outstanding new studies of the early republic, this book will apply notions of market competition to the arena of college education, as well as religion.[45]

This text will focus particularly on the city of Philadelphia. Quickly exited off the historiographic stage after the revolutionary era, Philadelphia has long been neglected, certainly in comparison to New York City, by students of the early republic. It deserves a much more central place in the narrative of the young nation. Bruce Dorsey has recently taken some steps to amend this negligence. Noting that Philadelphia gave birth to "almost every kind of benevolent and reform society," he makes a convincing case that Philadelphia both led and mirrored reform movements across America.[46] For this study, Philadelphia's leadership in prostitution reform and Sunday schools is of greatest concern. Even Philadelphia's failures should prove instructive to historians. The fact that the booming young city could not adequately fill the University of Pennsylvania with students reveals much about the state of higher education in this era. As the cultural center of the young nation until at least the 1830s, Philadelphia set many standards for Americans in smaller market centers. Building on various studies of New York City, this book aims to situate the formation of the bourgeoisie in the urban East.[47]

Some precise definitions are in order. As already noted, youth was a decidedly amorphous stage of life sitting between childhood and adulthood. While the matter of age can, and in fact should, be left relatively open, we should pin down more precisely in terms of class, race, and geography *which* youth we are considering. In the early republic a certain group of youth would arrest the attention of moralists more than any other.[48] Concerned with the reactions of reformers to youth, we must replicate their preoccupations. Our subject will be the youth whom Jared Waterbury, an advice writer, had in mind. In opening one of the many volumes penned for youth in the early American republic, this writer and minister identified the intended audience for his work. "The class of individuals to whom this work is inscribed," Waterbury wrote, are "those who belong to our principal cities and colleges." He did not say so explicitly, but Waterbury might have added he was most interested in white, middling youth, in particular. For Waterbury, such youth represented the "hope of the country"; they embodied the "influence which is destined to sway the moral and political interests of the nation."[49] These youth did in fact "sway" the future of America, although perhaps not in the way Waterbury had in mind. He was as much open to the influence of youth as they were to his influence, possibly more. Waterbury's youth were most liable to the twin influences of ideological and economic change that disrupted age relations in this era. Changing ideologies about governance and authority were felt strongly at the seats of learning. Northern cities were central sites for market growth. Printing presses issued their products from urban centers. Youth in such locales became quite conspicuous. Although this work cannot account for the experiences of all youth, it explores the impact of a select and influential group of youth on American culture.

The American bourgeoisie also requires definition. The creation of the American middle class is a relatively neglected topic.[50] The formation of the working class has garnered much more attention from students of the early American republic.[51] Following the lead of the British labor historian E. P. Thompson, historians of the American working class have paid close attention to expressions of class conflict in their subjects. After demonstrating a growing material divide separating the laboring population from the bourgeoisie, historians of the American working class have looked for the growth of values in their subjects that approached class-consciousness. The closest scholar of middle-class formation, Stuart Blumin, has largely followed the lead of historians of the working class, providing a materialist reading of the emergence of the middle class. While Blumin opts for the slightly softer concept of "class awareness" over class-consciousness, he ties bourgeois identity to specific material practices, artifacts, and spaces. The divide between manual and nonmanual labor, specialized spaces for work, shopping and consumption, expensive row homes with parlors and pianos—these, for Blumin, are the things that made the middle class. Undoubtedly they did, but there was also more. Such a reading of the middle class largely neglects the realm of the shared values that came to characterize the bourgeoisie. Respectability could be achieved not only by what one wore or the home one lived in but also by what one said and did in company.

Class formation cannot be reduced to the material world alone.[52] In an important study of the creation of the British middle class, Dror Wahrman has persuasively argued that considerable space exists between the social reality of class and its cultural representation or recognition.[53] While Wahrman traces the deployment of a highly specific language of self-identification by class, this book will use a more open definition of class formation, perhaps more appropriate for a study of the American bourgeoisie. As Wahrman himself observes, Americans, in comparison to British citizens, very infrequently used the category of middle class to identify a particular sector of their society.[54] If bourgeois Americans did not self-identify themselves as a distinct class, this does not exclude the possibility that they forged a distinct bourgeois ethic in their society. For Americans, it was the simultaneously more elusive and more accessible goal of achieving respectability that motivated the would-be bourgeoisie. It was elusive because it was more open to interpretation and contestation; it was nonetheless more accessible and expansive because it was more easily claimed by aspirants.[55] In a society in which battles did not have to be pitched against an aristocracy for core political rights like voting, middling Americans had much less cause to rally one another to form a self-described unit.[56]

In several respects, a state of détente and amalgamation developed between elite and middling Americans in the decades following the Revolution. Those Americans rising in the social order paid homage to the old elite by adopting many of their refining manners and artifacts.[57] Meanwhile, aristocratic Americans deferred to the emerging bourgeoisie in public life. Culturally discredited by a revolution against monarchy, the old aristocracy withdrew from the public stage in the early republic. Reform crusades were not the province of a withering and displaced elite, as historians once supposed. Rather, efforts to forge social order were driven by rising men of middling and upper status, many enjoying new-won wealth.[58] Certain old elites did serve as figureheads for some prominent voluntary societies, but they never formed the core group of such agencies. Identifying individual moralists as belonging to a certain class position is in fact of little consequence to this project. Instead, the nature of social bonds within Northern American society will be our concern.

The term "bourgeois" will be used more to capture a social dynamic than a specific group of people.[59] Americans were moving away from a world where one's status was ascribed, inherited by birth, and toward one where status was self-determined and voluntarily negotiated. Bourgeois values embodied the hope of self-determination and upward mobility in an open social world. In economic and educational institutions, this meant competition and achievement based on merit. This was as much constricting as liberating. Hard work, self-discipline, and even respect for elders became necessary to success. Seemingly more private spheres of action, such as the home and church, sponsored bourgeois values too. Here one can think of the work of the historians Leonore Davidoff and Catherine Hall, who situate the formation of the English middle class in the nexus of gender and evangelical religion.[60] Young Americans would have more choices to make about affiliation both in courtship and in places of worship. Again, however, freedom of choice came with responsibilities. One might easily be seduced into disreputable matches, so moral instructors warned youth against flights of passion.

In brief, we will explore the formation of bourgeois notions of meritocracy, chastity, domesticity, and a settled and sentimental piety. Each of these core components of bourgeois identity emerged in the effort to guide the young into respectable stations. Such notions certainly could help codify class categories too. In Europe, according to scholars such as Ian Watt and Isabel V. Hull, studying England and Germany respectively, the emerging bourgeoisie rhetorically measured its sexual modesty and self-control against the licentiousness of the aristocracy.[61] Even in America, bourgeois values could be used to draw class lines. If an aristocracy was conspicuously absent in the early republic, Americans still could use the European aristocracy as an important referent, pitting republican simplicity against aristocratic decadence.[62] As the nineteenth century progressed, the American bourgeoisie would also increasingly draw a line between themselves and those beneath them, contrasting working-class degeneracy with middle-class decorum. Still, for the period of our study, it was middling youth who most preoccupied bourgeois moralists. Fears of a dangerous working class were certainly important in shaping American bourgeois values as well, but this interpretation has been overstated.[63]

As a corollary to this cultural definition of the middle class, it should be emphasized that Americans did not always live up to their own espoused values. Historians have been discovering, for example, that many women were not confined to the home in the ways dictated by the ideology of domesticity.[64] Nonetheless, it is equally clear that the notion of a private separate sphere for women was an important cultural prescription that was intoned regularly by the voices of bourgeois respectability.[65] In other words, domesticity was an important cultural standard against which behavior was judged, even if behavior sometimes violated it. Similar observations could be offered about the other bourgeois values explored in this book. The goal is to see why bourgeois Americans came to imagine themselves as they did, not whether they always fulfilled these representations. The problems presented by youth in the early republic helped forge those values that became cultural markers of the emerging middle class.

*   *   *

This study opens with an analysis of seduction tales. This fiction voiced concerns about dangers facing young women in courtship. In late eighteenth century novels and periodicals, readers repeatedly encountered the plot line of a young innocent woman being seduced and abandoned, often with child, by a male rake. This plot line had special resonance for American readers who were witnessing booming rates of premarital pregnancy and bastardy in their communities. This fiction was a critically important cultural site for working out new responses to the courting freedom of young adults. These tales would fix new notions of gender and virtue that would become central to bourgeois thinking. In Chapter 2 we will view the reception of seduction fiction in the early nineteenth century through the experience of the Philadelphia Magdalen Society. This institution aimed to address the problem of prostitution, which it largely attributed to the machinations of young male seducers. Up to this point, historians of prostitution have been familiar with the New York Female Moral Reform Society, a group formed in the 1830s that loudly denounced men for the exploitation of women. The Philadelphia group, founded in 1800, actually seems a better vehicle for understanding larger cultural developments. Given their growing skepticism toward victimized women, we will see that the Magdalen Society led and reflected larger American dialogues about class and virtue.

If guiding the sexual development of youth proved challenging, so too did efforts at education. In Chapter 3 we will look at college troubles in the early nineteenth century through the lens of the University of Pennsylvania. Beset with riots and disorders, but also desperate to hang on to coveted students, college authorities moved slowly. Gradually, however, they devised important new strategies to control youth. To illustrate this, we will witness the intellectual journey of Penn's provost Frederic Beasley as he applied the insights of John Locke to his own college troubles. Beasley, like other college leaders at this time, sought a way to divide and rule his students. We will see that as educators developed new solutions, notions of competition and meritocracy became central to their pedagogy.

At the same time that colleges were struggling with disorderly students, ministers were increasingly confronted with righteous youth. Chapter 4 explores important transformations in mainline religion inspired by efforts to keep hold of and direct the young. Religious revival activity visited the urban East in the early nineteenth century but was not as triumphant there as farther west. Revivalists like Philadelphia pastor James Patterson challenged age hierarchy with fervent Christianity. Patterson empowered both male and female youth to spread the gospel and criticize seemingly impious elders. In response, orthodox ministers and laymen developed an important counteroffensive to the disruptions of revivalists who pandered to the passions of youth. We will see how and why in the 1820s and '30s conservative and moderate leaders embraced Sunday schools. In Sunday schools, potentially disruptive youth were turned into dutiful agents for the replenishment of established churches. We will see how notions of religious decorum and even theology were reworked in this effort to guide the young.

By the Jacksonian era, urban economic opportunities were increasingly a beacon for aspiring youth. Rather than leaving the young man to stake out a path wholly on his own, many bourgeois writers wrote self-help manuals to mentor male youth through the perils of the marketplace. Chapter 5 considers the product of their efforts. These writers were the beneficiaries of new advances in printing technologies, but they also had to counter the results of a newly flooded book market. Their books reveal an ambivalent embrace of market values that ultimately pointed bourgeois Americans toward the ideology of the self-made man. While these writers did accept self-interest as a means to motivate human behavior, the endorsement of market values did not come easily. Promoting self-interest required Jacksonian advice writers to explicitly and deliberately subordinate earlier notions of publicly crafted virtue and privately cultivated conscience that conflicted with the ideal of the self-made man.

Cities and presses loomed as dangers for sex-reform writers as well. The final chapter of this book considers the effort to control the sexual lives of young men that emerged in the Jacksonian era. Problems with promiscuity seemed more intractable than ever. Visible coteries of young men assembled around brothels in cities. Some authors took to celebrating their licentious lifestyles. In response, reformers began to revisit their conceptions of male youth. Because reformers of all stripes believed that addiction to sin flowed inevitably from even minor offences, sex reformers became convinced that they had to warn youth against masturbation. Ironically, these writers soon found they were open to the charge of inciting, not discouraging masturbation. We will see that the tortured relationship of the bourgeoisie to sex, their simultaneous revulsion and obsession with it, was played out in their talk about youth.

The difficulty of governing youth left a large imprint on an emerging middle class. Advisors would enjoy only partial success in their efforts to shape youth. Still, they did discover means to persuade and discipline them. By the mid-nineteenth century adolescent dependence was clearly in the offing. Even more importantly, bourgeois propriety was awaiting youth as they grew into adulthood.

Chapter 1
"Victims at the Shrine of Libertinism": Gender in the Seduction Tales of the Late Eighteenth Century

In January 1801 the *Lady's Magazine and Musical Repository* presented the following song. Entitled "The Men are all Rovers alike," it was sure to strike a familiar chord with its readers:

To me yet in teens Mamma would oft say,
That men were deceivers and sure to betray;
This lesson so strongly she painted to me,
That lovers I thought all deceivers must be
    And that men are all rovers alike.
Young Collin is handsome, good humor'd beside,
With artless kind offer, would make me his bride;
Mamma was mistaken I plainly can see,
And I doubt if all rovers deceivers must be,
    Or that men are all & c.
Thus sung the fair damsel, when Collin appear'd
Her doubts now all vanish'd, no danger she fear'd
To join in sweet wedlock, the lovers agree,
Was Miss in the wrong, that hereafter you'll see,
    For the men are all & c.[1]

We cannot know for sure if, or how far, tongue was placed in cheek by the writer of these lyrics. To the modern reader, at least, there appears to be an almost playful tone in its lines. We can know, however, that the potential for humor in such a song would depend on the readers' acquaintance with the themes it explores.

In the years following the Revolution, American popular novels and periodicals began to define manhood as inherently immoral. The seduction and abandonment of young women by young male predators was a plot line that late eighteenth-century American readers knew quite well. The regularity with which this theme was explored and the seriousness of tone used in such investigations suggest that there was a very real fear underlying these stories. Seduction fiction depicted the difficulties facing young women who had gained more freedom from parents and community but as a result were exposed to greater exploitation at the hands of mobile and unrestrained young men. While seduction fiction may be important as a window into late eighteenth-century American society—its northern and older regions in particular—it is of even greater significance because of the formative role it had in shaping American culture. Such fiction not only depicted the seduction and abandonment of young women; it offered solutions to this perceived problem.

A variety of cultural strategies were explored in seduction literature to resolve the problem of unaccountable male youth. Some writers held up an ideal of manhood that was steeped in the culture of sensibility. Young men were encouraged to be men of feeling who were not ashamed to shed a tear or to assist a vulnerable woman. Similarly, writers asked men to listen to their internal monitors or their consciences. Both concepts were gaining wider cultural currency, registering an ideological shift from more coercive patterns of social control. However, writers were not reluctant to double their chances by appealing to coercion as well. Visions of otherworldly punishment for male seducers populated seduction tales. Some writers also gave a measure of blame to women and asked them to avoid coquettish behavior that attracted suspect males.

These cultural strategies of controlling men, however, did not prove popular because, in part, at least, they contradicted the logic of the most popular message to emerge from the seduction tales. Above all else, these tales insisted that young men were immoral and that, as a result, young women would need to seek the protective guidance of parents in seeking prospective partners. It was to young women that these tales were most often addressed. This female audience was increasingly told that they were by nature virtuous and chaste.[2]

While scholars have fully explored the process whereby womanhood was redefined as virtuous, the transformation of the definition of manhood deserves closer attention. The historian Ruth Bloch has described how in the late eighteenth century the ideological forces of evangelicalism, moral philosophy, and sentimental literature, when combined with a transmuting philosophy of republicanism, conspired to characterize womanhood as virtuous while removing virtue from the male-dominated public sphere.[3] There are some important limitations to this sweeping intellectual history

that need to be observed. First, it is clear that similar ideological developments were unfolding in England despite the relative absence of a corresponding republican discourse.[4] Second, notions of female virtue had important class and race limits. As scholars such as Kathleen Brown and
Cornelia Hughes Dayton have demonstrated, Americans had elevated prop-
ertied white women's sexual honor and bodily integrity above that of servants, African Americans, and other marginal peoples, long before the post-
revolutionary years.[5] Even if we restrict our analysis to white women of
property, however, important questions remain. As Bloch herself admits,
the public sphere did not immediately assume the shape given to it by later
writers on domesticity as an immoral place for worldly men. Most American political theorists believed that the rational pursuit of self-interest
would benefit the public at large. Rather than immoral, the public sphere
seemed at worst morally neutral. The dissociation of virtue from the public
sphere might have helped men look less moral, but it appears that something more was needed to drive home the association of men with immorality. Seduction tales helped forge that association.

As historians have long recognized, the nineteenth-century ideology of
domesticity relied upon the creation of two opposing poles or spheres, each
assigned to a gender.[6] One of the central tenets of domesticity was the superior morality of women. As the above discussion has suggested, this notion
of female virtue was advanced with particular fervor at the end of the eighteenth century and sentimental fiction was one of the primary sites of its
popularization. Women had long suffered under the opprobrium of being
the lusty daughters of Eve, the original temptress in the Garden of Eden.
Coupled with this biblical imagery was the conventional medical perspective on female desire. In the early modern Western world, female lust was
accepted as a necessary evil, for women were thought unable to conceive
without orgasm.[7] Passion in women, less controlled by reason than it was
in men, made them more morally suspect. While racial distinctions did
help elevate white women's sexual honor in the colonies, even they were
treated by the courts as morally untrustworthy in the eighteenth century.[8]
Building on eighteenth-century gains in moral estimations of women, seduction tales took notions of female virtue to new poetic dimensions. These
stories may have been crucial in creating a structuring cultural dichotomy,
by providing a pole of male immorality counterpoised to female virtue and
chastity. Seduction tales were insistent in their notion of female innocence
and largely blamed men for the scenes of seduction they described. One
must consider the costs of such portrayals.

Nancy Cott has ably argued that by assuming a posture of morality and passionlessness, some women were able to advance their position within society and protect themselves from male aggression.[9] Cott asserts that this strategy represented the best possible option available to them at the time. Where this argument fails is in its assumption that solutions to female vulnerability were only available within characterizations of womanhood. Building on Cott, we might step back and look at the negotiation of gender more fully to discover other remedies for vulnerable womanhood. In seduction fiction we will find possible responses to female vulnerability, such as appeals to male sensibility or conscience, or warnings to men about the consequences of their actions. Yet seduction fiction writers ultimately eschewed attempts at reforming men and decided primarily to respond to female vulnerability by defining men as evil and by urging women to seek protection. Faced with the monsters of their own construction, these authors turned to sheltering women. In making such decisions, they foreclosed the possibility of building a model of manhood that stressed male accountability, and instead used images of predatory manhood to fix one pole of an emerging gender dichotomy.

*   *   *

Seduction fiction proved immensely popular in the young nation. The novels *The Coquette* and *Charlotte Temple* captivated American readers not only when first printed but for many years thereafter. *The Coquette* was a best-seller in 1797 and was often reprinted in the nineteenth century. The grave of Elizabeth Whitman, the woman who was presumed to be the real-life counterpart to the novel's heroine, Eliza Wharton, became a veritable shrine for young readers. *Charlotte Temple*, the first American best-seller, published in 1794, was the most popular novel in America until the publication of *Uncle Tom's Cabin* in 1852; it has been reprinted probably over two hundred times.[10] If not quite as well documented, the popularity of seduction tales in periodicals is certain and impressive. One close scholar of eighteenth-century periodical fiction noted that the theme of seduction outstripped all other topics in these magazines. Stories and didactic essays on seduction also recurred in almanacs, pamphlets, broadsides, and newspapers.[11] Those Americans who read widely could encounter in advice literature many of the same lessons taught in seduction tales. Late eighteenth-century manners books mirrored the fiction of the period, often advising female readers that they needed to protect themselves against the advances of aggressive males.[12]

As such literature appeared, there was a growing audience to receive it, since literacy rates boomed over the eighteenth century. Historians have found that younger women in New England had acquired near-universal literacy (thus catching up with men) by the end of the century.[13] High book prices and limited printing technologies, however, did put a cap on availability. Compared to those of the 1820s and '30s, print runs in the late eighteenth century were small. A large print run in the 1790s would have been fifteen hundred, whereas some novels in the 1830s were produced in runs of thirty thousand.[14] Still, seduction tales reached many more readers than their total sales and printings would suggest. The number of lending libraries increased rapidly in the final years of the eighteenth-century, making fiction available to many nonpurchasers.[15] Also, the colonial tradition of reading literature aloud to assembled groups, such as women at work in the household, persisted into the early national period.[16] While most northern white young adults could read by the end of the eighteenth century, it was not necessary to have access to the printed word to encounter seduction tales. Seduction was being explored on the theatrical stage from the late eighteenth century forward. In fact, the first professional play in America, *The Contrast*, in 1787 unveiled a villain who reveled in seduction.[17]

Seduction tales resonated with readers because they addressed real developments in the American marriage market. Enjoying more courting freedom, young women could no longer count on the protective guidance of parents and community. Over the course of the eighteenth century, young adults had gained more control over their lives, and over the selection of mates, in particular.[18] The trend of declining patriarchy was exacerbated by the ideological shifts of the revolutionary era.[19] Cultural expectations for a more democratic American family corresponded to economic and geographic changes; male youth often relocated in search of occupations in a transitional economy in which inheritance was uncertain and apprenticeship was beginning to break down.[20] The stability, and therefore the reliability, of young men was increasingly uncertain. This was especially true in those markets where seduction fiction was sold—densely settled northern towns and cities.

If writers showed sensitivity to their times, however, their analysis of the problems women faced was limited in scope; these writers insufficiently explored the changing dynamics of nuclear families and the wider community. By concentrating on the character of young men, these writers ignored the decisive trend of the declining influence of the church, courts, and village in sex life and courtship.[21] In the early colonial era, northern communities, especially New England Puritan and Pennsylvania Quaker communities, had closely watched the courtship process of their youth and provided both formal and informal networks of social control over young men and women. When youth erred, punishment was certain. Courts punished illicit sex with fines and whippings, while neighbors admonished and churches demanded penitence.[22] Such patterns changed, however, in the eighteenth century. According to work by Cornelia Hughes Dayton and Richard Godbeer, among others, notions of religious community waned and courts began to relax regulation of illicit sex. The family increasingly privatized, with parents withdrawing family matters from the community stage and youth themselves withdrawing into peer groups apart from parents. Parents did not completely forsake moral stewardship of their children. For a while an interesting compromise developed between children and parents as young suitors bundled, that is, slept fully clothed together, in the parents' home.[23] Still, parents had lost wider supports and young adults were more often on their own, away from parents. As community and family influence declined, young women would ostensibly be left exposed to male sexual predations, vulnerable to seduction and abandonment.

From what we know about the changing rates of illicit sex, such changes in the eighteenth century do seem to have made young women more vulnerable. Premarital pregnancy and bastardy rates reached unprecedented levels in the years during and immediately following the Revolution.[24] Some historians have taken the rise in premarital pregnancy as an indication of a collusion of young couples against their parents. By having an early pregnancy, youth might have forced their elders to accept otherwise unacceptable marriage partners or to push forward the timing of marriage. Undoubtedly at times this is exactly what happened, but the stakes were higher for young women than men. If rising premarital pregnancy meant growing sexual freedom for both sexes, it also meant greater vulnerability for women, especially poorer women whose parents were less able to pressure young men into marriage. In a society where women in most ways remained dependents and where prerogatives for initiating courtship belonged to men, illicit encounters were more likely to be started by men and their costs to be felt more by women.[25] The rising incidence of bastardy in this period seems especially to suggest a compromised position for women. Single motherhood in the late eighteenth century is unlikely to have appeared an attractive option for most women living in a society that offered such limited means of support for single women.

How then to protect young women? Above all, responsibility was placed with the girls themselves. While the authors of seduction tales seem to have had genuine sympathy for the plight of young women, it is also clear that their writings made great demands of female readers, asking them to adopt chastity for their own protection. Seduction fiction writers probably did not conceive of their work as a means to curtail the freedom of women through fear. Those whom we can identify seemed in their other writings and pursuits to be advocates for the causes of women, particularly female education. Susanna Rowson, author of *Charlotte Temple*, established Boston's first female academy for educating girls and young women in 1797.[26] Nevertheless, the seduction tales these authors wrote left a decidedly mixed legacy for women. These tales depicted young women as vulnerable; they most often chose to explain this problem as resulting from exposure to evil men.[27] Thus it appears that seduction tales painted, in terms of gendered personal character, problems that were rooted in larger transformations in the nature of community in early America. By portraying men as lecherous, these stories compounded any threats that may have existed for women. Because they were deemed less naturally moral, men would appear less responsible for their behavior. Young men, in addition to women, were reading these tales, so some real opportunities for influence were squandered.[28] While these writers certainly never endorsed libertinism in men, they were allowing room for its expression by concerning themselves more with cautioning women than reforming men.

A warning to women about the predatory nature of men was not the only message in seduction fiction. There were paths explored, but ultimately not embraced, in these works. Other choices were available in responding to a perceived female vulnerability. One such path was an appeal to male sensitivity. Seduction fiction was rooted in the culture of sensibility.[29] Grounded in Lockean sensation psychology, and most fully articulated by moral-sense philosophers such as David Hume and Adam Smith, ideas about sensibility later infused and operated within a broad range of fields, including religion, science, conduct literature, and fiction. All varieties of sensibility shared some basic similarities, but most importantly a belief in, and a valorization of, the ability of human beings to sympathetically feel the pain of others in distress. Particularly in literature, the "man of feeling" emerged as a central figure. Sensibility had the potential to be a gender-neutral model of sensitivity.

Tales of seduction did sometimes introduce men possessing sensibility into their plots. For example, in Susanna Rowson's *Charlotte Temple*, we see Mr. Temple praise the sentimental emotions felt by Captain Eldridge over the loss of his son and wife. Captain Eldridge appears distraught: "But pardon me. The horrors of that night unman me. I cannot proceed . . . What a mere infant I am! Why, Sir, I never felt thus in the day of battle," to which Temple responds reassuringly, "but the truly brave soul is tremblingly alive to the feelings of humanity." When Eldridge thus reassured offers his own justification for a feeling disposition, Temple replies, "This is true philosophy."[30] Sensibility challenged definitions of masculinity based on stoicism. In *The Power of Sympathy*, William Hill Brown employs one of the situations to which writers about sensibility repeatedly turned to evoke tears in their characters and audience: a confrontation with slavery. The hero Harrington introduces a tale about his own outpourings of sympathy upon meeting a slave by declaring his sentimental nature: "*I* FEEL *that I have a soul*—and every man of sensibility feels it within himself. I will relate a circumstance I met with in my late travels through *Southcarolina*—I was always susceptible of *touches of nature*."[31]

Some writers of seduction tales seem to have hoped to reach young male readers, in addition to the young women to whom they most obviously directed their stories. By depicting regret and doubt in the characters who committed seduction, authors strove to cultivate sensibility in these potential male readers. Hannah Foster, who has been credited with pushing the seduction story furthest as a vehicle for the cause of women's freedom—a subject to which we will return—may have been more atypical in her in-depth depiction of a seducer who was also, at times, a feeling man. In Foster's *The Coquette*, the seducer Sanford first entertains doubts about his plan of seduction and later experiences extreme regret in seeing its ill effects. After committing the crime, Sanford expresses the sentiments usually spoken by the ruined heroines: "Oh, Deighton, I am undone! Misery irremediable is my future lot! She is gone; yes, she is gone for ever! The darling of my soul, the centre of all my wishes and enjoyments is no more!"[32] Susanna Rowson in *Charlotte Temple* also complicates the seducer role by having Montraville express doubts about his seduction schemes and by extending some blame to other characters: Belcour, Montraville's evil sidekick, and the unworthy guardian, Mademoiselle La Rue. Before Belcour helps Montraville discard his nagging doubts, Montraville exclaims: "and should I even succeed in seeing and conversing with her, it can be productive of no good: I must of necessity leave England in a few days, and probably may never return; why then should I endeavour to leave her a prey to a thousand inquietudes?"[33]

In their depictions of regret and doubt, these authors often employed the concept of conscience, sometimes referring to it as an "internal monitor." In using these terms, these authors prefigured language that would become increasingly popular in discussions concerning moral order by the middle of the nineteenth-century.[34] In *The Power of Sympathy*, Mr. Harrington (the hero's father), who had committed seduction earlier in life, tries to locate the source of his regret: "From what innate principle does this arise but from the *God within the mind!*" Mr. Harrington goes on to suggest that there comes a time for all individuals when one's actions must be considered within an "hour of reflection" and one's actions are subsequently judged: "this *internal monitor* sits in judgment upon them and gives her verdict of approbation or dislike."[35] In the words of this same character the ties of the concept of conscience to ideas of sensibility become obvious: "Blessed be that power who has implanted within us that consciousness of reproach, which springs from gentleness and love!—Hail sensibility! Ye eloquent tears of beauty!"[36]

Thus a few authors seem to have allowed their male characters, sometimes even their villain, to display sensibility. But only in these few novels is one likely to find such depictions; periodical stories, which stripped seduction scenarios down to the bare minimum, much less frequently explored such ideas. Moreover, in the novels discussed above, authors spent much more time depicting the evils and dangers of men rather than upholding a sentimental model for them. To the degree that they addressed male readers, seduction fiction writers were more willing to send another type of appeal to potential seducers: a message of fear. Appeals to conscience can be found in the periodicals, but more in the form of a threat rather than an extended hand. For example, in one magazine piece entitled "The Sorrows of Amelia," a direct warning to men is offered: "learn instruction from the fate of Alonzo . . . check the disposition which would prompt you to spread toils for unsuspecting innocence. Guilt will destroy the bliss of the seducer, intrude on his morning pleasure and damp his evening joys."[37] The threat of a guilty conscience could be heightened by depicting its ultimate result as suicide. In a story in *The Gentleman's and Ladies Town and Country Magazine*, which was presented as a letter from the "reformed" rake Edmund to his friend who still practiced the evil arts, the reader learns of the horrible consequences of seduction for the seducer. Edmund relates the story of a young man who felt intense guilt over his seduction of a young woman. This man went to a secluded cabin in the woods; there he worshiped a wax resemblance of the woman he had seduced (and who had died) and ultimately commited suicide.[38]

A heavy burden of guilt was not the only potential cost of seduction for men. Authors also used the threat of damnation. In a story in *The Key*, the reader is informed that the libertine will eventually pay for his crime: "But the thunders of heaven will not sleep; injustice will be visited by vengeance."[39] William Hill Brown in *The Power of Sympathy* dedicates an extended scene to a dream of Mr. Harrington, who visits a Dante-like hell where the worst station is reserved for the seducers:

In their countenances were depicted more anguish, sorrow, and despair—I turned my head immediately from this dreadful sight . . . Quivering with horror, I inquired who they were—"These," answered my guide, with a sigh, "are the miserable race of SEDUCERS—Repentance and shame drive them far from the rest of the accursed. Even the damned look on them with horror, and thank fate their crimes are not of so deep a die."[40]

Melodramatic, perhaps, but the social fear of seduction is quite evident in such threats.

While authors appealed to the anxiety of potential male readers more than their sensibility, both strategies ultimately must have seemed futile if men were truly depraved. A story entitled "A Melancholy Tale of Seduction" that ran in the *Massachusetts Magazine* displays this tension extremely well. Addressed to a libertine, it begins by appealing to his sensibility, asking him to mend his ways: "I hope your mind has not lost all its sensibility, and that there may be a time when this letter shall prove a monitor." It goes on to tell him, in good sentimental fashion, how one of his victims has died of shame (a frequent fate for seduction victims). However, this address gradually seems to give up on any hope of his reform. The author first asks a series of rhetorical questions: "Were there never times when your heart checked you, and obliged you almost to revoke?—Could neither youth; nor beauty, nor innocence, find even a momentary friend in your thoughts? . . . Were your vices only permanent, all your better resolutions transitory?" After asking this final query, the author provides a gloomy response: "They were. To feel for another's wo[e] was a lesson you had never known." At the end of the article, the author warns the seducer that eventually he will be racked with guilt: "Pensive moments will come to make you wretched . . . Be assured, that the burden of misery which awaits yourself, is heavier far than any you have heaped on another."[41] Yet by this point the warning is quite hollow. It seems doubtful whether even the author could believe that this immoral youth, lacking conscience, would ever feel remorse. As manhood was constructed as immoral, it would seem pointless to ask men to mend their ways. Solutions to female vulnerability would have to be found elsewhere.

While early American writers on seduction sometimes sent messages to potential male readers, it was to young women that they most often addressed their advice. These authors sometimes cautioned young women that seduction could be blamed on their own flaws. Warnings against, and depictions of the horrid consequences of, the practice of coquetry were the most frequent forms of such advice. The image of the coquette, a young woman who flirted with men, appears at first glance to complicate any emerging gender dichotomy. In describing coquettes, however, authors rarely portrayed these women as immoral; rather, such women practiced flirtatious behavior out of either naïveté or a misguided fondness for pleasure. Authors told their intended female readers that simply accepting flattery without a blush could be an invitation to a male predator.[42] In a letter in the *Gentlemen and Ladies Town and Country Magazine* addressed to "the unguarded FAIR of this Metropolis," the author warns that one should show no regard for flatterers: "once you acknowledge the slightest tenderness for him, there is but one step further, from the time of such an acknowledgment, between that and seduction."[43] With young men less rooted in local social networks, the stakes were higher for young women when making judgments about men's personal character. Seduction tales erred on the side of caution, emphasizing young men's untrustworthy character.[44] Authors portrayed the path to seduction as a slippery one, easily slid down if one false move was made. Coquetry could begin a train of events that would end in a young woman's own fall.

A fondness for luxury and pleasure was seen as the source of coquetry. These stories warned against an appetite for luxury, supporting Jan Lewis's contention that the seduction tales were a dialogue over republicanism.[45] European aristocratic splendor was weighed against American modesty and virtue in stories condemning coquetry. The choices offered to Eliza Wharton in *The Coquette* are between the modest and respectable minister Boyer and the rakish and aristocratic Sanford. The choice she should have made is made abundantly clear. While we can see an American condemnation of European degeneracy in Foster's depiction of Sanford, we might also appreciate the importance of the characteristic always possessed by seducers such as he: their ability to deceive. Fears of deception were a logical accompaniment to the growing mobility of male youth. Living in a seemingly more anonymous world, parents and community had less opportunity to judge the character of male suitors. In such a precarious situation, great care had to be taken in making choices. This is the import of Hannah Foster's lessons.

While some scholars have highlighted Eliza's explorations of women's freedom in their discussions of *The Coquette*, it is doubtful that Hannah Foster or her contemporaries would recognize such a modern reading.[46] Undoubtedly, Eliza is a sympathetic character; her inner goodness is not in doubt. But the choices she makes are certainly condemned. Trustworthy friends and family all warn her to leave Sanford and accept the hand of Boyer. Perhaps even more importantly, Eliza herself repeatedly renounces her earlier mistakes through much of the second half of the novel.[47] Hannah Foster was sympathetic to the plight of young women—she wrote her novel to warn them of the dangers of men. Most often coquettes erred because their parents or guardians were either missing or incompetent.[48] Thus depictions of coquettes did not really complicate a gender-based polarity of morality; they instead served to emphasize the need for proper parental supervision.

Seduction fiction did explore the option of reconceiving, or at least of restraining, men. And notions of female culpability were experimented with as well. But these were only minor themes. Insisting that young women were innocent and virtuous, seduction fiction repeatedly painted young men as immoral. It always required a series of deceptions on the part of the libertine to accomplish his foul end. The "Story of Philenia" illustrated the wiles of young men: "By a long continued series of the most artful insinuations accompanied by the most solemn protestations of eternal love and friendship he triumphed over the innocence and virtue of the once happy, but now abandoned and disconsolate Philenia."[49] In the seduction of the ever-innocent Charlotte, the machinations of not only Montraville but also Belcour and LaRue were needed to undo her. The struggle between female innocence and male evil was bound to end in the loss of chastity. In one magazine story, "Matilda" lamented what a great loss this was: "where is the perfidious man who has robbed my youth of its peace, my mind of its innocence, my once fair frame of its honor . . . Ah, wretch! he has stolen the deposit, and left the poor cabinet vacant and in ruin!"[50] The most popular metaphor to describe the loss of innocence, as might be expected, was that of deflowering. A line from a *Boston Magazine* story provides a good example: "her innocence was cropped as the flower of the field, by the early ravages of the mower's hand."[51]

The moral purity of women and the morally suspect character of men were asserted so strongly that the one class of women most vulnerable to charges of moral impropriety, prostitutes, emerged as simply victims of male exploits. In "The Dying Prostitute—An elegy," a poem reprinted in at least four different periodicals between 1787 and 1796, the prostitute is seen as a target of male exploits and scorn, as a figure deserving of sympathy:

Weep o'er the mis'ries of a wretched maid
Who sacrific'd to man her health and fame;

Whose love and truth, and trust were all repaid
By want and woe, disease and endless shame.

Curse not the poor lost wretch, who ev'ry ill,
That proud unfeeling man can heap, sustains;

Sure she enough is curst, o'er whom his will,
Inflam'd by brutal passion, boundless reigns

Later in the poem, the prostitute herself most clearly fixes the blame for her fall into prostitution:

Where are my virgin honours, virgin charms?
Oh! whither fled the pride I once maintained?

Or where the youth that woo'd me to their arms?
Or where the triumphs which by beauty gain'd?

Ah! say, insidious Damon! monster! where?
What glory hast thou gain'd by my defeat?[52]

Prostitution was frequently portrayed as an outcome of seduction.[53] Young women who had been abandoned by both the seducer and then society were forced to support themselves on the profits of the sex trade. The connection drawn between seduction and prostitution served to strengthen the gendering of virtue by placing blame for the pursuits of even the most sexually transgressive of women on the exploitive endeavors of men. As the next chapter will demonstrate, the seduction narrative would push at least some reformers to bridge class divisions with benevolence.

Of course, the construction of male immorality was never complete. The tales themselves contain obvious complications. Father figures, for example, are often likable characters (and female readers were told to listen to them).[54] Nonetheless, the drama in these tales revolved around the rake and his victim, not sympathetic males. The overall direction in which the tales were pointing is clear. One gets a fuller sense of the emerging stereotype by considering the broad range of epithets thrown at male seducers throughout these tales: "betrayer," "designing villain," "undoer," "monster," "cruel robber," "base dissembler," "wretch," "faithless youth," "betraying enemy," "fiend," "cruel destroyer," "wanton spoiler," or simply "seducer" are but a sample of the labels employed not only in periodical short stories but in poems and didactic essays as well.[55]

Seduction tales were not the only type of fiction to assert men's immorality. Mildred Doyle, in her comprehensive study of early American periodicals, noted that the second most popular theme, after seduction, was the abuse of wives by cruel husbands.[56] In this theme, as in seduction, virtuous female characters were constructed in opposition to the male figures. The characterization of male figures in the seduction tales had the potential to spill into larger cultural molds of gender that were taking form in American culture as a whole. Although some authors were careful to draw character distinctions between the male figures in their works, collectively their tales convey an image of male depravity. It is not surprising, then, that someone could have penned the lyrics that opened this chapter, which declared "men are all rovers alike." The slightly more circumspect judgment presented in "Almira and Alonzo" perhaps better represents the collective message of seduction fiction to its female readers: "Your spotless bosoms, the seat of honor, unsuspecting of deceit . . . admit too flattering ideas of men . . . Few—few indeed, are deserving the confidence they obtain."[57]

Imagined in this way, young men seemed hopeless. American authors were breaking with an essential component of the British tradition of sensibility by casting off the prospect of male reform. Samuel Richardson, whose mid-eighteenth-century British novels helped inspire American seduction tales, had held out the possibility of male reform in his 1740 novel *Pamela*. Resisting the sexual advances of her master Mr. B, the servant girl Pamela eventually won admiration and an offer of marriage from her pursuer. Richardson himself drew a less rosy picture in a subsequent novel, *Clarissa*, but many British writers on sensibility still continued to believe in cultivating virtue in men. Perhaps most emblematic of the tradition was Henry Mackenzie's 1771 novel *The Man of Feeling*, a tale in which the lead figure meets and assists a range of downtrodden characters. American seduction writers challenged the wisdom of Richardson's *Pamela*, and writings on sensibility more generally, by rejecting the possibility of reforming rakes. Lucy Freeman in *The Coquette* explicitly states what most tales implied in their emphasis on cautioning females rather than reforming males: "'A reformed rake,' you say, 'makes the best husband;' a trite, but a very erroneous maxim, as the fatal experience of thousands of our sex can testify."[58]

It is uncertain how young men might have received such tales. It is certainly plausible that some might have reveled in the exploits of seducers. Correspondence uncovered from the late eighteenth-century does show rakish attitudes among some men engaged in sexual liaisons.[59] Despite the strenuous efforts of authors to stabilize the meaning of their tales, there were in fact opportunities to read seduction tales subversively. For example, as Sanford confided his schemes of ruin to his friend Deighton, young men might have felt part of the circle, cheering Sanford on. Even the condemnations of libertines might have made seduction appear enticing because such warnings made sexual exploits seem dangerous. Perhaps young women too could have gained a vicarious thrill in imagining their literary likenesses pursuing illicit sex. We will see in forthcoming chapters that the seduction plot line in subsequent decades would serve many purposes. Young women would find cover for illicit behavior by claiming victim status. Seduction fiction would also help support a male rake culture. As less moralistic authors entered the literary market in the mid-nineteenth-century, seduction tales became more erotic and voyeuristic. Over the long term, the moral emphasis of seduction fiction proved difficult to sustain.

Nevertheless, we can see a clear moralist course taken by writers in the late eighteenth century. Authors of seduction tales primarily dedicated themselves to warning young women about the depraved nature of men. In their methods of pursuing this purpose, they remained within the tradition of sensibility. Rather than telling tales of seduction because they seemed enticing fare, authors instead hoped to reach young female readers through the principle of sympathy. The tales of seduction that one finds in periodicals in the late eighteenth century and novels such as *Charlotte Temple*, *The Coquette*, and *The Power of Sympathy* are scarcely removed from didactic literature. In the periodicals, many stories have a thin veneer of plot—a few names and places—but they are primarily lectures seeking to impart principles that might prevent seduction. The aim of such fiction was not only to entertain but also to provide readers with real-life lessons. In fact, the line between fact and fiction was often deliberately obfuscated in order to stress the pertinence of the stories. Periodical tales and novels were touted as "founded upon recent facts," or "founded on Fact, veiled only under a fictitious Name." Some stories were presented as publicly published letters between friends.[60] Susanna Rowson frequently intrudes into her story to impart lessons directly to the reader. William Hill Brown and Hannah Foster both have their characters deliver extended lectures to the audience.

These authors believed that the reader could learn lessons from the characters, particularly the unfortunate seduced, because they had the ability to feel the emotions of the characters. Within the body of thought about sensibility, writers such as the Scottish philosopher David Hume had developed an elaborate model of sympathy, explaining the ability of human beings to actively feel the emotions of another, as if their own.[61] The writers of seduction tales sought to use this principle to their advantage, hoping young women would take their lessons more to heart because they could feel the pain produced by seduction. There were competing modes of fiction writing during the eighteenth century. The tales of seduction popular in late eighteenth-century America were clear descendants of the work of Samuel Richardson, not simply because of the shared theme of seduction, but more importantly, because they used fiction to pursue a moral agenda.[62] American writers of seduction fiction avoided the morally risky flights of fancy that often characterized Continental romantic fiction. It is in the context of competing types of fiction that the repeated warnings against novel reading within these novels themselves make sense.[63]

If young men could not be reformed, how else could one react to their treachery? Faced with the treacherous villains of their own construction, seduction writers sometimes cried out for the punishment of seducers. For example, Susanna Rowson wishes for their banishment: "My bosom glows with honest indignation, and I wish for power to extirpate those monsters of seduction from the earth!"[64] The construction of female morality opposed to male immorality has at times provoked an attack on male immorality by women reformers. Decades later, women joining Female Moral Reform Societies would pick up on this potential in seduction narratives, attacking male brothel visitors for their seduction and exploitation of women.[65]

Yet the writers of late eighteenth-century seduction narratives used other means to assist women. Above all else, they resolved the dilemma of male immorality by asking young women to go back to the arms of protective parents.[66] According to these authors, women often suffered the fate of seduction because they lacked parental guidance. Thus Philenia, in a *Massa-*

chusetts Magazine story, had been left an orphan and was thus exposed to the man of her undoing, Fallacio, a false man.[67] Amelia, in a *Baltimore Weekly* story, also lacked parents to guide her: "In her infantine years she was deprived of the tender care of parental affection, and her blossoming beauty was exposed to the all fascinating snares of artful dissimulation."[68] The advice published for the "Unguarded Fair" went so far as to suggest that a young woman in an unprotected state might best be served by not taking the risk of ever entering the marriage market.[69] For women who were not so unlucky as to lack parents, the lesson was clear. Susanna Rowson repeatedly implores her readers to listen to parental advice in addresses such as this: "Oh my dear girls—for such only am I writing—listen not to the voice of love, unless sanctioned by paternal approbation."[70] In *The Coquette*, Eliza, in deciding to seek parental guidance, regrets neglecting this earlier: "had I done this before, I might have escaped this trouble."[71] Readers of "Almira and Alonzo" are reminded that they can escape Almira's fate of seduction and death by not forsaking parental advice: "remember! had the still small voice of age, the gentle whispers of maternal fondness been heard, the much regretted inhabitant of the silent tomb, might have gladdened a parent's heart."[72]

Writers of seduction literature often emphasized the importance of listening to one's parents by showing extreme emotional costs suffered by parents of the seduced young woman (thus again applying the principle of sympathy). Seduction was always depicted as a crime to both the seduced and her family. William Hill Brown depicts the cycle of pain in poetry: "YOU wound—th'electrick pain extends; To fathers, mothers, sisters, friends."[73] Brown illustrates this pain through the father of the seduced and now deranged Fidelia: "Is not the cause of my woe, a melancholy instance of the baleful art of the SEDUCER?"[74] Perhaps fatherhood could belatedly transform men. As daughters approached adulthood, their fathers were exposed to the pain of seduction. Only then could men truly recognize its dangers and appreciate its injuries. The grief of parents could have extreme consequences. A *New York Magazine* article goes so far as to depict a mother's death from grief as the result of a daughter's seduction. To expand the view of parental pain, the reader is told of a dream in which an angel-like creature presents the body of the lost parent: "'View the narrow bed, wherein lie mouldering the cold remains of an unhappy parent—the stroke of death was guided by a much-lov'd child!'" Upon closer inspection, the corpse possesses a deeply wounded heart: "Here, opening her snowy robe, she displayed a bleeding bosom!"[75]

Since one could only evade the male seducer through parental guidance, the ultimate mistake a daughter could make was elopement.[76] Susanna Rowson provides a highly sentimental scene of the pain felt by Charlotte's mother on discovering her daughter's elopement:

"Oh Charlotte! Charlotte! how ill have you requited our tenderness! But, Father of Mercies," continued she, sinking on her knees and raising her streaming eyes and clasped hands to heaven . . . "of thine infinite mercy, make her not a mother, lest she should one day feel what I now suffer."[77]

Rowson wanted readers to feel the costs of Charlotte's mistake, if only as spectators.[78] If young women did not seek parental guidance for their own sake, perhaps they would be moved out of fear of breaking their parents' hearts.

The parental pain depicted in these tales is also open to another reading—while internal addresses within many of the tales directly state that the intended audience for their fiction is young females, the tales also at times seem to be appealing to parents. The extended scenes of parental suffering seem to offer parents an opportunity to indulge their own fears about their daughters' marital prospects. The declining authority of parents in courtship could create fears about events over which they no longer had control. These tales often dwelled upon the pain that might attend the victimization of daughters. For example, one essay printed in the *Lady's Magazine*, during its series of warnings to young women, turns to the topic of the fate of fathers in seduction: "what must be his sensations at losing his beloved, perhaps his only child, by a cursed villain,—her, whom he has so often clasped to his parental bosom with many a tear of heartfelt joy." This article then goes one step further, abandoning the pretense of simply offering warnings to young women, by directly addressing their fathers: "But, wretched man! short lived in thy happiness, see thy fair daughter in all her native charms snatched from thy arms, a fatal victim to the power of SEDUCTION! Can language describe thy misery?"[79] Of course, fathers might have been getting their just deserts. William Hill Brown's guilt-ridden character Mr. Harrington lived to see the fatal effects of his earlier mistakes.

Such explorations of parental pain sometimes considered the problems that would attend old age for a parent without a daughter to provide emotional, physical, or material support. In *The Coquette*, Eliza's friend Lucy considers the fate of Mrs. Wharton in such terms: "But what are our feelings, compared with the pangs which rend a parent's heart? This parent,

I here behold, inhumanly stripped of the best solace of her declining years, by the ensnaring machinations of a profligate debauchee!"[80]

One piece appearing in *Massachusetts Magazine*, entitled "The Duelist and Libertine Reclaimed," takes the exploration of parental loss to its extreme. In this tale, parental concerns supersede a potential lesson for daughters. The story considers the possibility of a father losing both a daughter and a son who are "the pride and comfort of his age." The libertine Antonio seduces and abandons Alicia, the daughter of the old man. Alicia's protective brother is greatly upset by his sister's and father's pain and challenges Antonio to a duel. The story then considers the grave consequences of such a battle: the father might potentially lose both daughter and son. This horrible conclusion is averted by the intervention of an old military officer who instructs the young men about the foolishness of dueling and attempts to reform Antonio by activating his conscience: "Instead of endeavouring to deprive an aged father of a much loved son, and a sister (already made miserable by your artful baseness) of an affectionate brother, you ought, most certainly, to have poured the balm of comfort into their wounds." Unlike most of the tales published in the late eighteenth century, this attempt at reform is successful. Not only do the young men give up their duel, but Antonio marries Alicia, bringing joy to all.[81]

While the seduction tales may have had resonance for parents, they generally did not go very far beyond their primary goals of providing instruction for young women, teaching above all else that young women should be chaste and seek parental protection. Women's ability to seek sexual gratification as independents would be seriously compromised under the gender model the tales offered.[82] The chastity ideal promoted by seduction fiction helped situate women's primary social value in their sexual purity. In the telling words of Hannah Foster's Julia Granby, sexual reputation might transcend life itself in importance: "Not only the life, but what was still dearer, the reputation and virtue of the unfortunate Eliza, have fallen victims at the shrine of *libertinism!*"[83]

What impact did such tales have on courtship patterns in emerging bourgeois circles in America? Was there a reversion to early colonial patterns, whereby parents were given substantial leverage over marriage decisions? This is unlikely. Diaries and correspondence from the early republic reveal that parents continued to grant considerable freedom and privacy to youth in their courting life.[84] Yet we should not conclude that these tales had no impact on courting behavior. Youth and elders found a middle course. Parents did not direct courtship, but children no longer had premarital sex. One historian has described the "invention of petting" as a development of the early nineteenth century. A distinctive new pattern of sexual behavior emerged in which coitus became off limits to young couples seeking affection and marriage. The colonial custom of "bundling" fell out of fashion too. Such practices as bundling and intercourse challenged emerging notions of female chastity. It became women's responsibility to carefully guard men from crossing the line that separated petting from intercourse.[85] Herein lies one role of seduction tales. Their insistence on female purity would help assign women this moral gatekeeping responsibility.

In addition to narrowing women's sexual freedom, the purity ideal had strong implications for other realms of social life. The historian Jeanne Boydston has suggested that women made important gains in economic autonomy during the late eighteenth-century. The seduction tales can be seen as a threat to such gains: the autonomous woman would have little place in narratives that predicted ruin for women who ventured unescorted onto the public stage.[86] The antebellum period would produce a cultural demand for greater male responsibility in sexual encounters, but that resolution lay in the future; nor could it ever be complete in the face of the formative encoding of the sexual double standard the seduction tales accomplished. If Cornelia Hughes Dayton is correct that one can see the emergence of a sexual double standard by the mid-eighteenth-century in the proceedings of local courts in Connecticut (and likely New England courts more generally), this trend gained its fullest and most powerful expression in the seduction tales that were popular in late eighteenth- and early nineteenth-century America.[87] From here on, "chaste" women would have to be on guard against the advances of unrestrainable men.

*   *   *

Ultimately in the American tales of seduction, young men could not be reformed. While these tales employed the devices of sensibility, and on occasion portrayed men as sensitive, they helped push sensibility into sentimentality by gendering empathy.[88] The gender-neutral model of sensitivity possible in eighteenth-century sensibility would yield to the feminized sensitivity of nineteenth-century sentimentalism. Faced with female vulnerability, authors had a range of responses available. By primarily choosing to define men as immoral, rather than asking men to assume responsibility, these writers participated in the construction of gender ideals that would come to dominate Victorian thinking. There was a certain, almost inexorable, logic to their decision. Fiction writers had to render complex social change into personal family dramas. Young men were already accorded more social freedoms than women in eighteenth-century society, so the easiest, and perhaps safest, path was to demand increasing self-control in women. In the emerging American ideology of domesticity, male immorality and female purity would continue to mutually reinforce one another as opposites. That dichotomy had been advanced with particular force in seduction tales. As the nineteenth century unfolded, the male public world appeared more forbidding to women. Writers on the popular bourgeois ideology of domesticity came to insist that women were safest in the home. In the next chapter we shall see that, even before domesticity came to dominate middle-class thinking, reformers in Philadelphia were imagining another, even more restrictive safe house for women.

Victim of Seduction or Vicious Woman? Conceptions of the Prostitute at the Philadelphia Magdalen Society and Beyond

The seduction narrative, initially popularized in late eighteenth-century America, was losing some of its explanatory power as the nineteenth century progressed. By 1833, the iconoclastic advice writer William Alcott could declare: "In nineteen cases out of twenty, of illicit conduct, there is perhaps, no seduction at all; the passion, the absence of virtue, and the crime, being all mutual." As his statement implies, Alcott allowed some room for the possibility of young male rakes committing seduction. Thus he admitted: "But there are such monsters on the earth's surface. There are individuals to be found, who boast of their inhuman depredations on those whom it ought to be their highest happiness to protect and aid, rather than injure." Monsters, however, were not numerous. Alcott insisted that few young women could blame young men for their transgressions: "Let young women, however, be aware; let them be *well* aware, that few, indeed, are the cases in which this apology can possibly avail them."[1] Alcott's comments hint that there may have been some difficulty in applying the seduction motif to the daily world of nineteenth-century America.

Most of Alcott's fellow bourgeois commentators were not as even-handed as he in spreading blame for licentious liaisons. Rather than finding blame "all mutual," bourgeois writers by this era had begun to veer between placing full responsibility on women or wholly blaming men. The seduction narrative did not disappear as the nineteenth century progressed, but it was contested on certain grounds, for certain women.[2] Historians have provided abundant evidence that assumptions about female sexual propriety, cohering about a half-century earlier, retained their force through (and beyond) the antebellum years.[3] If seduction novels like *Char-*

lotte Temple in which female innocence fell to male libertinism could remain tremendously popular, one might ask which women could still be
seen as victims of male predations and which could not. Furthermore, what
was the relationship of bourgeois males to these women of different character? Perhaps the traditional seduction narrative seemed most strained when
bourgeois moralists grappled with the practice of prostitution. The burgeoning sex trade of nineteenth-century America was quite troublesome—
not only because it defied notions of chaste womanhood, but also because it
threatened emerging ideals for sexual propriety in men.[4] Alcott gives some
evidence of this growing valuation of chastity in men. The prescriptive message contained in his castigation of male seducers, that men "ought" to
"protect" rather than "injure" women, suggests that at least some responsibility for preventing illicit sexual encounters had shifted to young men.[5]

While historians have noted the bourgeois hypocrisy of a thriving
prostitution trade coexisting with ideals of male and female chastity, they
have not adequately addressed whether and how the bourgeoisie resolved
this tension between reality and rhetoric. This seeming contradiction might
in part be explained by the increasing predilection of males to bifurcate
women by class status.[6] While men considered sexual propriety important
when interacting with bourgeois women, they may have considered promiscuity more appropriate with women of the lower classes.[7] The seduction
narrative had largely categorized virtue along lines of gender and age, not
class. All young white women, at least, could be seen as virtuous within
its conventions.[8] Deceived by treacherous males, female youth entering the
marriage market were liable to be left seduced and abandoned—forced to
support themselves by the sex trade. Early prostitution reformers in Philadelphia, in fact, seem to have accepted these very lessons from seduction
fiction. The subversion of the seduction narrative, in turn, seems to have
opened the door to harsher assessments of the sexuality of working-class
women.

A case history of the Philadelphia Magdalen Society provides a view of
the difficulties that attended the reductive understanding of illicit sex presented in the conventional seduction narrative. By looking closely at the
progress of the seduction narrative within the small world of the Magdalen
Society, we might better understand how the image of victimized young
womanhood failed when it was applied to wider society. The operators of
the Magdalen Society initially attempted to describe the past of their clients
in terms of the conventional seduction tale. In this, they stood at the forefront of the American reform community. The clash between the founders'

preconceptions and the information presented to them by prostitutes ultimately revealed the limitations of the seduction narrative in dealing with the multiplicity of causes that produced early nineteenth-century prostitution. While the managers initially used the seduction narrative to interpret their subjects, they ultimately found few Magdalens who fit their understanding of prostitution. Facing such difficulties, the leaders of the Society grew increasingly frustrated with the women they managed.

This frustration yielded aggression. The managers began to blame the women themselves rather than the men they had initially held accountable. Over the first half of the nineteenth century, the managers of the Magdalen Society paid increasing attention to the habits and lifestyles of the young women they encountered rather than the seduction schemes of young rakes. The image of the hardened veteran harlot replaced the picture of the innocent young female victim. According to Society leaders at midcentury, the women under their charge had fallen into prostitution because of their participation in the vice-ridden life of the lower classes. Such commentary was not limited to the confines of the Magdalen Society; the dialogue about seduction and vice spilled out into the streets, newspapers, and novels of Philadelphia. In turning against fallen women, Philadelphia reformers anticipated an aggressive new attitude that developed across the Northeast. In locales such as Boston and New York, authors, journalists, and courtroom crowds came to embrace similar dark images of prostitutes. When Female Moral Reform Societies in New York and New England sought to stem the tide of aggression toward prostitutes in the 1830s, their voices often seemed alone in the wilderness.

*   *   *

The Philadelphia Magdalen Society cast its mission in terms defined by the popular fiction of the early American republic. Founded in 1800, the Magdalen Society aimed to address the problem of prostitution. The centerpiece of the institution was an asylum, where, according to its Constitution, the society might "aid in restoring to the paths of virtue,—to be instrumental in recovering to honest rank in life, those unhappy females, who in unguarded hour, have been robbed of their innocence."[9] For those who might have questioned the basic innocence of prostitutes, the founders defended them in *Poulson's American Daily Advertiser* by blaming the arts of seduction for the women's fallen state. They asked: "Is there, I would ask, a village or hamlet in these United States, I might say universe, that has not fostered in its bosom the insidious murderer of female innocence?"[10] The founders of the Magdalen Society were prominent businessmen, doctors, clerics, and reformers within the Philadelphia community, such as Episcopal Bishop William White, Robert Wharton, Edward Garrigues, and Dr. Benjamin Rush. Seduction literature obviously influenced a much broader spectrum of the population than the young female audience with which such fiction is typically associated.[11] The founders of the Magdalen Society blamed male youth, the "insidious murderer[s] of female innocence," who roamed the American countryside, for the presence of prostitution in early national Philadelphia. Gendered notions of virtue undergirded the Magdalen Society's initial understanding of prostitution.

As the organization was founded by wealthy Philadelphians, one might expect there to have been a class agenda behind the Magdalen Society's operations. The historian Clare Lyons has posited such a reading of this society. Lyons argues that the Magdalen Society managers, following the lead of popular writers of the period, used the seduction narrative to stigmatize working-class women as members of a sexually deviant "rabble." Lyons portrays popular fiction as a coercive strategy intended to flatten a vibrant alternative sexual culture extant in late eighteenth-century Philadelphia. In its message to young women to practice chastity for their own protection, the seduction tale undoubtedly worked to constrain women's sexual behavior. Yet popular writers, some of them outspoken advocates for the causes of women, wrote their tales as much out of sympathy for their subjects as out of a desire to enforce sexual propriety. Clearly the seduction tale restricted the sexual freedom of young women, but there were notions of sensibility and benevolence at work within them as well. Initially, the managers of the Magdalen Society exemplified such notions of disinterested benevolence and did not initially see the young women as fundamentally different from themselves in terms of either class or character.

Managers of the Magdalen Society, much like the leaders of Philadelphia's other charitable organizations of this period, saw poverty not as a fixed status, but as a fate that might befall any member of society who did not exercise proper precaution.[12] In early Society notes, Magdalens were sometimes described as having reputable backgrounds.[13] As in the plot lines of contemporary fiction, reformers argued that poverty was the result of the abandonment by friends and family that naturally followed a young woman's seduction. The managers described the usual downward path: "How many might have been saved, who, having made one false step, and finding themselves, though truly penitent, deserted by their friends, outcast of society, and perishing for want of food, have madly rushed into the vortex of most abandoned prostitution."[14]

The founders' blindness to issues of class can be more fully observed by comparing their seduction rhetoric to the language of the Magdalen Hospital in London. Much like the seduction fiction writers who informed their efforts, the founders of the Philadelphia Magdalen Society drew many of their ideas from across the Atlantic. The Society deliberately named and modeled itself on the Magdalen Hospital founded in London in 1758.[15] The borrowing was, however, selective. As suggested above, gendered notions of morality structured the founding vision of the Philadelphia Magdalen Society. In contrast, the London organization seemed to give more room to class in its analysis of prostitution. This difference can be glimpsed in an article published by the founders of the Philadelphia Magdalen Society to announce their organization. The Philadelphia society included portions of a pamphlet from the London institution entitled "An account of the rise, progress, and present state of the MAGDALEN CHARITY, in London." While the Philadelphia founders were largely content to blame "bruttish man" for the seduction of young women, the London operators they excerpted at least gave some notice to the structural disadvantages that many women, lacking property, faced on the marriage market: "What virtue can be proof against such formidable seducers; who offer too commonly and too profusely promise to transport the thoughtless girls, from want, confinement and restraint of passions, to luxury, liberty, gaiety and joy?"[16] Poverty did loom larger in London, but there are clear indications that economic desperation was driving some women into prostitution in Philadelphia.[17] The founders omitted any consideration of the constrained choices brought by poverty in understanding the problems of seduction and prostitution, their records revealing a reliance on the more simplistic narrative of fallen virtue.

After having secured the necessary funds, the Magdalen Society began to admit women regularly to its asylum (Figure 1) in 1807 at the then-rural location of Sassafras and Schuylkill Second (today 21st and Race).[18] Previously, several women had received funds and lodging from "respectable" families, one even lodging with the family of the chairman of the board of managers, John Harris.[19] After the opening of the asylum, all assistance was offered exclusively on site. The Magdalen Society had a long but frustrating history. It lasted for over a century, eventually reborn in the early twentieth century as the White-Williams Foundation, a social service institution for schoolchildren. While in existence, the Magdalen Society's asylum was able to attract only small numbers to its doors, averaging around ten women

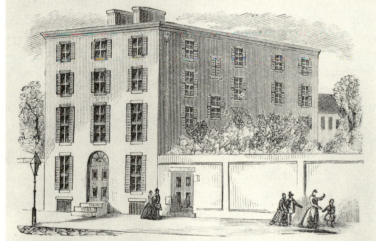

SIXTY-NINTH ANNUAL REPORT

OF THE

BOARD OF MANAGERS

OF THE

Magdalen Society.

An Institution for the Shelter and Reformation of Fallen Women.

FOUNDED, 1801.

To the city the seducer lures his victim. *To the city* women come to hide their shame. *The city* is the great receiver of the fallen who cannot endure to remain in the smaller towns known to everybody. Therefore *the whole country is responsible for the lost in the city;* and every effort to reclaim them should be supported by all Christians. Daily, numbers die; daily, numbers supply their places; and must those who might be rescued, be left unsaved for the want of means to effect it?

PHILADELPHIA:

J. B. CHANDLER, PR., 306 & 308 CHESTNUT STREET.

1870.

Figure 1. Magdalen Society Asylum, ca. 1870. The design was largely preserved from the late 1840s forward, so this engraving from the 1870 annual report depicts the asylum as it appeared at midcentury. The founding date in the engraving is incorrect; the Society was formed in 1800. Courtesy of The Library Company of Philadelphia.

annually in its first decade, fitfully increasing to only about forty a year by midcentury.[20]

In its early years, the Philadelphia Magdalen Society recorded detailed entry notes about each woman taken into care.[21] These firmly demonstrate the deep influence of the popular seduction narrative on the endeavor.[22] To be sure, the tension between the Society founders' preconceptions and the lived experiences of the Magdalens resulted in the managers' mounting frustration against these assisted women. Yet the seduction plot line died neither easily nor completely. The notes reveal an important process of negotiation. At times the women's voices emerge in the construction of the narratives that gained them admission into the asylum. For the women, there were clear costs, as well as benefits, in entering the asylum. While their material needs would be met, they also had to submit to a rigid set of regulations. These codes suggest that the word "asylum" was quite appropriate, for the institution was meant to structure the women's lives, much as the prison of the early republic structured the lives of its inmates.[23] Magdalens were expected to give up communication with those outside its walls. Talk within was limited to "sober chaste conversation." No communication about their "past conditions" was permitted.[24] Additional rules included required attendance at morning and evening scripture readings, application at labor in the intervening hours, and the wearing of uniform clothing.[25] Although such rules discouraged many from seeking the assistance of the Magdalen Society, small numbers of women did make application to the Society.[26]

The entry narratives do not reveal to what degree the life history of each woman was reshaped in order to meet the conventional seduction narrative. Nevertheless, the constant recourse to the language of seduction fiction, often in the face of tremendous countervailing evidence, suggests that the stock figures and plot devices of these tales exerted great influence. An excerpt from one of the first entries, that for "Magdalen No. 7," provides an example:

Nineteen years of age, this young woman a few months past lived in the country, where (as she informs) she was seduced by a young man, who left her and came to this city; to which place she also followed in pursuit of him, but not being able to find him and ashamed after the loss she has sustained to return to her friends, she went into a disorderly House . . .[27]

While terse, these notes contain several of the basic elements of the conventional seduction narrative. The central characters, the seduced young

woman and the mobile young rake, are both portrayed. The geographic setting is also highly conventional. The young man's escape to the anonymous
city displays the oft-expressed fears about the independence granted to
male youth in the early republic. As in seduction fiction, bourgeois standards of female propriety are also invoked here. The young woman feels
too much shame to return to her former abode and thus is driven into a
disorderly house in the city.

How closely this reconstructed story conforms to the particular experiences of this young woman is uncertain. As the parenthetical, "as she informs" betrays, she may have understood the benefits of retelling her story
in a way consistent with the worldview of the Society managers. Subsequent
notes reveal that she had only approached them after having contracted a
disease that compelled her to go to the Alms House for aid. She could only
gain admittance to the Magdalen asylum, a preferable location, after she
had proven "sensible of her transgressions, attentive to religious instruction
and desirous to receive the benefits of our Charity and advice."[28] This
young woman's path to the Magdalen Society may have demonstrated her
savvy recognition of the popular conventions embraced by Philadelphia
charity organizations.[29]

The entry narrative for "Magdalen No. 15" provides another example
of how the managers and their wards produced life histories that relied
heavily on the conventions of seduction fiction. A seventeen-year-old
woman, brought up in New York state, also ended up as the victim of male
artifice:

About 12 mos. ago (as she informs) she left her father's House, with a young man
who had for some time visited in the family, and gained her affections, who having
despoiled her of her chastity (and his proposal of marriage being disapproved of by
her parents), prevailed with her to elope with him under promise of marriage to
Phila., where he took lodgings and remained with her but a few weeks, and then
left her pregnant and diseased; without friends or any means of support . . .[30]

Much like "Magdalen No. 7," this young woman appears to be the victim
of a young man's seductive wiles. The city again provides the proper context for her abandonment. A notable addition here is the role that elopement plays. As in much contemporary seduction fiction, the choice to follow one's heart, without parental consent, ends in disaster. Once again, the
notes suggest the negotiation of the young woman's narrative. One can hear
her attempt to tell her story in a way consistent with the expectations of the
managers. One can almost hear her parroting them when they record that

she "uniformly expressed and evidenced her sorrow for having in an unguarded time, suffered herself to be betrayed and led astray."[31]

Some of the entry narratives even seem to move beyond basic formula and into the plot lines of popular novels such as *Charlotte Temple*. For example, "Magdalen No. 17," a woman of "respectable parents" born in Holland, related a tale with important parallels to that of Charlotte. Like Miss Temple, this young woman found herself transported across the sea by her seducer under an "expectation of being Married." Once in America, the unfortunate seduced woman discovered that this man already had a wife. Thus she was "left in a strange Country, without friends or a sufficiency to support her."[32] In this unfortunate discovery, one hears Charlotte's lament: "do you think he can be such a villain as to marry another woman, and leave me to die with want and misery in a strange land[?]"[33]

Echoes of *Charlotte Temple* also resound in the entry narrative of "Magdalen No. 11." In the tale of this twenty-one-year-old woman, born in Delaware and brought to Philadelphia, one can find a striking resemblance to Rowson's Mademoiselle La Rue. The older woman entrusted with the care of this young female proved, as had La Rue to Charlotte, an unworthy guardian indeed. As La Rue practically prostituted Charlotte to Montraville (receiving five guineas for providing access to her), this woman exposed her younger charge to the dangers posed by a libertine. Keeping company with an immoral man till late at night, the older woman seemingly encouraged the rake to return after she had retired. Much like La Rue, this woman had little sympathy for her young companion, not responding to her calls for help: "she called for assistance but without effect, though verily believes the Woman of the House heard her." Not receiving any response, the young woman was unable to "resist the rude attack," and thus was "compelled to submit to his base designs." The apparent rape of this woman (the managers betrayed some suspicion toward her in their note that the man spent most of the rest of the night "tarrying with her") was dismissed by the older woman.[34] The young woman received "no other redress than being laughed at, and told that a disease was communicated to her."[35] The contemptuous response of the older woman to the plight of the young female is reminiscent of La Rue whom Rowson described as willing to "spare no pains to bring down innocence and beauty to the shocking level with herself." This willful corruption of the innocent, suggested Rowson, proceeded from "that diabolical spirit of envy, which repines at seeing another in the full possession of that respect and esteem which she can no longer hope to enjoy."[36]

The managers of the Society seem to have fully agreed with the author of *Charlotte Temple* about what was best for the seduced young woman. Believing that the rejection by friends and family that followed a seducer's abandonment prevented many young women from returning to a respectable life, Rowson suggested that what such women really needed was an uplifting hand from a friend. "Believe me," she urged, "many an unfortunate female, who has once strayed into the thorny paths of vice, would gladly return to virtue," if only someone would "endeavor to raise and reassure her."[37] The Society's founders stated that this was precisely their intention. In their constitution, they outlined their goal to restore "to the paths of virtue" those seduced young women who were "affected with remorse at the misery of their situation," who were "desirous of returning to a life of rectitude, if they clearly saw an opening thereto."[38]

If the Society managers were prone to understanding their clients' past in terms of the seduction narrative, at times life undoubtedly imitated art. Writers of late eighteenth-century seduction fiction had grounded their tales in real social problems. Yet their didactic intent often drove them to overdramatize the costs of illicit sex. For example, by having friends and family forsake a victimized young woman in their stories, popular writers were probably trying to encourage chastity in young women. Yet the Magdalen Society managers saw ample evidence that abandonment was a quite real problem for some women. Whether families were unwilling to care for their straying daughters because of their offended sense of propriety or because of economic constraints, the record does not show. Whatever the cause for the abandonment of these women, the managers chose to see them as moral outcasts from the society of friends and family. The managers aimed to remove young women from the scorn of uncharitable relatives and acquaintances, hoping that in many cases their help would lead to reconciliation.[39] For example, "Magdalen No. 10," a daughter of "reputable parents" who was "feeling the loss of her relatives," appealed to the managers to "reconcile them to her." When their attempts proved "fruitless" she was admitted into the asylum.[40] In this case, the managers found their belief confirmed that many prostitutes wanted "to reform, repent, and be redeemed from their wicked course; but are discouraged from an apprehension, none who are virtuous will regard or have pity on them."[41] Overall, then, the managers of the Magdalen Society dealt with cases that appeared consistent with the popular seduction narrative that informed their efforts.

But they also faced more challenging cases. One of their earliest entries, that for "Magdalen No. 6," admitted in January of 1808, stands out for its severe judgement of the young woman. The managers wrote: "this poor unhappy young woman by her depraved propensities, and wicked life of debauchery and idleness, was lately reduced to such a state of misery and distress . . . as to afford but little hopes of her recovery." When she applied for admission she "seemed much to lament the wicked life she had lived" and expressed an "earnest desire" to receive their aid. Thus the managers granted her entry. The end of the entry reveals that this woman had already fled the asylum, proving to them that "her heart" was "deceitful and desperately wicked" and that she had been "urged on by the grand tempter to pursue her evil propensities." Most likely, the woman had either obtained what she needed from her stay, or else she grew dissatisfied with the restrictions at the asylum. The managers seemed genuinely surprised that they were misled by her promises of penitence. Thus they also added that her "elopement" may have also stemmed from a "partial derangement of intellect."[42] The harsh tone of the entry is best understood as a reaction to her flight from the asylum.

The clash between the assumptions of the Society managers and the actual lives of the women they admitted was usually more subtle than in the case record for "Magdalen No. 6." In fact, many of the entry narratives contain a strange hybrid of seemingly contradictory material. Instead of finding young seduced women in need of rescue, the managers often found women who had long plied the trade but who now were down on their luck and needed some material aid or a respite from their worldly cares. Historians have shown that in the nineteenth century, especially before the advent of pimps, women might casually enter prostitution for several years and then move on to other occupations. Such behavior defied the conventions of fiction.[43] "Magdalen No. 14" must have perplexed some managers. Relatively old at twenty-six years of age (more than half the women admitted in the early years were under twenty), this Irish born woman had already been married.[44] After losing her husband seven months into their marriage, she moved into a boardinghouse where she subsequently spent six years "abandoning herself to debauchery." Only after she had been taken up "as a Vagrant and Committed to Prison" did she see cause to offer "professions of Penitence" and display a "determination to depart from her evil course of life." Nonetheless, perhaps because she had been conducting herself "with propriety," the managers did not see her move to the "Boarding House" (likely to have been a bawdy house) as an economic choice to enter the profession of prostitution. Instead, she only became a prostitute after "she was seduced" at this residence.[45]

If a young woman spending six years in prostitution seemed to defy the standard seduction story (in light of popular fiction, one would have expected her to have perished in shame or committed suicide by this point), the choice of one woman to practice prostitution while also living with a man must have been even more surprising and disturbing. "Magdalen No. 16" lived as if married with a man for four years. She was twice pregnant, having "miscarried of two Children," and still persisted "in habits of prostitution." If her story contradicted many of their assumptions, the managers still tried to fit it into the conventional narrative, perhaps with the help of this woman, who presently was in "considerable distress," and who, once admitted, "conducted [herself] well." The downfall of this woman, who had "respectable parents," they attributed to her being "seduced at the age of 15 years." Her seducer, with whom she then lived for four years, had, according to her entry narrative, used a frequent tactic of seducers: he "had visited at her fathers House under pretense of Marriage."[46]

If seasoned prostitutes challenged the notions of the Society managers, mistresses must have appeared equally surprising. The checkered past of "Magdalen No. 28" likely encouraged the managers to rethink some of their assumptions. This woman, who had grown up in Mount Holly and later moved to Philadelphia, joined a Spanish man on a journey to Savannah, Georgia, where they lived together until he perished from yellow fever. She then moved back to Philadelphia, where she found a man who supported her until he "became so sensible of the impropriety of his Conduct that he separated from her," leaving her with a "sum of money" and some advice for her to subsequently lead "an orderly Chaste life." After a while, the money dwindled. At this point she "became alarmed" at the prospect of being "reduced to poverty and want." With such "apprehensions" she sought out "one of the Managers for advice and assistance." While this woman couched her appeal in terms consistent with the assumptions of the managers, suggesting that she was afraid that economic need might cause her to "be tempted again to a life of Infamy," the managers knew that she had spent many years in such "Infamy." They probably suspected she was telling them what they wanted to hear. If their doubts were raised, however, they still said they believed "the Sincerity of her professions," and were willing to describe her as having been initially "Seduced by a Spaniard" and then later "again led astray by a person of property."[47]

"Magdalen No. 20" presented similar problems for the standard seduction narrative. She was kept in a boardinghouse by a "person of Considerable note in this City," even bearing him a child. After having lived in ill repute for ten years, she found herself "cast off by the person who had placed her to board" and therefore left in a "destitute situation." Facing poverty, she sought the Society's aid.[48] This woman not only challenged the managers' preconceptions prior to her admission to the asylum; she, like many other women admitted, challenged their views of virtuous woman-hood with her conduct once inside. It took less than a month to discover that she could not be reformed: "Magdalen No. 20 notwithstanding her fair professions at and for some short time after her admission, became so un-governable in her temper, and indecent in her behavior that complaint thereof was made to the Managers visiting." Despite their admonitions to her to be "more circumspect," their efforts proved "unavailing," leading them to expel her from the asylum.[49] Her experience was far from unique. Not only were many women expelled, but others chose to leave without the required prior consultation: so-called elopement from the asylum, a term undoubtedly borrowed from seduction fiction, was a persistent problem for the managers.[50]

If the managers' views were challenged by many of the women who sought their aid, perhaps their preconceptions were even more defied by those who did not. The Society expressed great dismay about how so few young women sought them out. While they never aimed to wipe out prosti-tution entirely, they were genuinely surprised at the indifference of most prostitutes to their venture. Six months after opening their asylum, only four women were willing to enter the institution. The managers responded aggressively to this reluctance: "It is lamentable to observe the Insensibility that generally prevails among these deluded females, and their backward-ness to accept the charitable assistance gratuitously offered to them." The managers believed they had taken "considerable pains" to spread the word about their institution, but that this "wretched class of females" seemed unwilling to part with their "evil habits." While taken aback, they still tried to maintain some hope, suggesting, "it is probable our family will in-crease."[51] While the phrase "wretched class" seems here more a moral judg-ment of prostitutes than a socioeconomic category, in coming years manag-ers would begin to conflate notions of moral character and social class.

Despite their hopes that things would turn around, the Magdalen So-ciety attracted a minute portion of the city's prostitutes to the asylum throughout its years of operation.[52] The historian Marcia Roberta Carlisle has estimated that between 1821 and 1836 the managers admitted only about thirty women a year. With frequent expulsions and flights, involving on av-erage about a third of the population each year, the number living together was considerably smaller, usually about eleven or twelve Magdalens at any one time.[53] While no systematic demography of Philadelphia prostitution for this period is available, New York City is a useful measure. In the 1830s, a period in which New York's metropolitan population was somewhat less than double that of Philadelphia, Timothy Gilfoyle places the number of prostitutes in New York somewhere between 1,850 and 3,700.[54] Contemporary accounts of Philadelphia offer no evidence that the city had any less than half the number of women working in New York.[55] Even if it did, the operators of the Society perceived a great disparity between the total number of prostitutes practicing in Philadelphia and those seeking admission into the asylum. In the decades approaching midcentury, the managers repeatedly expressed regret in terms similar to that of their annual report for 1834: "Yet we cannot but lament and wonder, that of the many unchaste females in a population so great as ours, comparatively so few are found in the only Asylum opened to those who wish to renounce their infamy."[56]

Faced with indifference from without and challenges to their assumptions from within, the Society managers only slowly forsook their understanding of prostitution. Initially, they mostly ignored contrary information. By 1811, the entry narratives were increasingly spare. The women's histories were reduced to a few simple facts: place of birth, length of time since they entered the city, and an indication of when they had been "seduced." Perhaps symbolic of the managers' decision to withdraw their institution further from the difficulties of the outside world was the fence they built around the asylum in that same year.[57] The actual experience of the Magdalens continued to be ignored in the ensuing decades: from 1820 forward, no admission information at all was being included in the minutes; by 1845 the managers could frankly admit that such neglect was regular policy: "the Managers have not deemed it part of their duty to inquire into the history of those who voluntarily embrace this quiet home."[58]

Another manner in which the Society could try to ignore the conflicting information that prostitutes presented was to concentrate more on those women whose demographics and history seemed to fit more closely with the conventional seduction narrative. Specifically, the managers expressed a preference for younger prostitutes who they imagined had more recently been seduced, rather than those veterans whose "hearts have become hardened."[59] Perhaps profiting from the early experience of the Philadelphia Magdalen Society, the House of Refuge established in New York in 1825 aimed at working with young prostitutes rather than those "more advanced in years" who threatened to "exercise a corrupting influence."[60]

Even with such evasions, the challenges that prostitutes presented could never be completely denied. Ejections, elopements, and disorderly behavior were persistent features of life at the Magdalen asylum. For example, in 1817, after a special committee investigation, four women were dismissed from the asylum because they had been secretly leaving at night. A fifth eloped soon after their ejection.[61] Looking ahead, we can see that the hope for reform would be wholly abandoned and the preference for young subjects crystallized in the early twentieth century, when the Magdalen Society became the White-Williams Foundation, an institution performing preventative work with schoolchildren.

While the women's narratives disappeared from the minutes of the Society in the 1820s, the rhetoric of the conventional seduction narrative persisted in its annual reports. Occasionally, an ideal inmate was showcased to help support such rhetoric.[62] The annual report from 1820 demonstrates the persistence of the language of seduction fiction, suggesting young women were "ensnared by artful persons, and robbed of their innocence."[63] Yet this same annual report betrayed some of the growing disillusionment of the Society managers. If some women could blame their downfall on the seduction schemes of base young men, others could only look to their own bad habits. Having an especially poor year in keeping women in the asylum, with nine of twenty-two leaving without permission, the managers blamed "the effects of an attachment to intoxicating liquors," as well as a "general hardness of the heart consequent upon a depraved course of life."[64]

This report was a harbinger of things to come. Over the next three decades, the annual reports became a venue where the managers forged class distinctions. The Society regularly blamed the young women themselves and voiced a growing alienation from the working class. These reformers were on the front lines, discovering how the cultural practices of the poorer sort differed from their own. As members of the bourgeoisie, the managers were in fact contributing to this alienation as they embraced a sober, hard work ethic at odds with the easier convivial style that once had bound those of middling and lower status. Attributing prostitution to women's alcohol use became a conventional feature of these later annual reports.[65] For example, the annual report for 1837 clearly asserts this position: "Perhaps the greatest cause of the unchastity of females in our City is to be found in the profuse use of spirituous liquors."[66]

Comments on other cultural practices also reveal a growing perception of a class-based cultural division separating the reformers from their subjects. The report from 1845 concentrated on urban amusements, suggesting that many women who entered the asylum "have to date their downfall, it is believed, in great measure to that source of crime, the ballroom; where many meet in the pursuit of pleasure, but the end whereof, is pain and sorrow."[67] From the Society's perspective, prostitutes were increasingly enmeshed in a self-reinforcing, class-based web of sin. The reports contain condemnations that closely mirror criticisms made by middle-class reformers of the working class working in a variety of circumstances. The managers not only complained about alcoholism and dance halls but also ostentatious dress, theater attendance, idleness, and neglectful parenting.[68] The asylum into which the women were introduced, they observed, differed in every respect from their former haunts: "when we contrast the scenes of revelry and noisy mirth so recently left, with the order and quiet of their new abode, it must be apparent that the change is very great."[69] Presumably, accustomed to living in quiet homes, the managers had little sympathy for boisterous working-class life.

By drawing class lines between themselves and their charges, the managers could help preserve their ideal of respectable bourgeois womanhood, even while placing more blame on the women under their stewardship. Thus with complete propriety they asked proper ladies to assist in finding candidates. By the 1830s the managers were calling on bourgeois women to enter "the abodes of poverty and wretchedness" to seek out potential Magdalens. The managers recommended that "the virtuous, whose character and standing in society is above suspicion," should "search them out, and tell them of the guilt and wretchedness of their course."[70] Middle-class women might also help correct the depraved propensities of their lower-class sisters by having a "more watchful oversight" over the "humbler members of the household." Thus the annual report for 1849 called on mistresses to offer "kind reproof where vicious inclinations are suspected" in their servants.[71]

The Society's new regulations for the asylum expressed increasing suspicion of the young women held there. The institution came further to resemble the penitentiaries being constructed across the country, most famously, Eastern State Penitentiary, surely visible from the grounds of the asylum, being built on a hill less than half a mile north of the Magdalen asylum. The managers increased restrictions because they feared that unrepentant prostitutes might seduce their charges back into the trade. In 1826, the managers sought to "classify the objects of care" by calling for extra rooms that would allow them to discover "the sincerity of the Magdalens admitted" before they allowed them to enter the "apartments of those who give hopeful evidence of a settled determination to reform." The Society elaborated its reasoning for desiring such an arrangement: "We fear that sometimes a settled and deep design to entice away Magdalens in the house, has excited some abandoned women to enter the asylum."[72] Five years later the Society added another building and carried out its plan of classification.[73] It appears to have continued with these restrictive tendencies; approaching midcentury, the managers sounded increasingly like determined prison reformers, such as those described by the philosopher Michel Foucault. They felt they could compare their institution favorably to *"Penitentiaries, Houses of Correction, and Female Refuges,"* in their efforts at "breaking up vicious habits" through "wholesome restraint and discipline," which would produce "habits of self-denial and obedience in principle."[74] The managers also contemplated a more coercive stance toward those prostitutes who failed to enter the doors of their asylum. In their annual report for 1847, they related that they had appointed a special committee to consider "whether any additional means of filling the Asylum ought to be resorted to." They took only tentative steps in this direction, because they feared that "some sinister purpose" might shape the conduct of forcibly entered Magdalens.[75]

The tendency of growing distrust toward prostitutes probably reached its logical extreme in the assertion that prostitutes could become the seducers of young men. In a complete inversion of the initial discourse of the Society's founders, the managers in their annual report of 1846 justified their work with prostitutes not as a means to save vulnerable young women but young men, whom prostitutes placed at risk. In this report they first noted how prostitutes were a general danger to society: "the evils inflicted upon society in various ways by this class of the community are incalculable." But the managers especially feared damage to vulnerable young men by prostitutes: "How many a young man for whose future portion, usefulness, respectability and the esteem of the good, were reasonably anticipated, has been lured to destruction by her whose 'Feet take hold on death.'"[76]

While in the decades approaching midcentury the Society expressed an increasing hostility toward prostitutes, the seduction motif did not disappear. In fact, it could sometimes assume a heightened pitch when ignited by the flames of religious fervor. Evangelical influences are much in evidence in the Society's annual reports of this period. Evangelicalism encouraged negative judgments on the perceived drinking habits of prostitutes, yet it also encouraged strong condemnations of male seducers. If a decidedly lesser theme in the decades approaching midcentury, the plot line of seduction fiction nonetheless continued to be present, often appearing alongside (and in open contradiction of) rhetoric that attacked prostitutes.[77] The annual report for 1851 contains a rare attempt to resolve the seeming contradictions of these two discourses that had coexisted for many years. It began by condemning the "fell destroyer" who attacked the virtue of the young woman using such strategies as a false "solemn promise of marriage." Once this crime was committed, however, "the unhappy victim of deceit" herself "in turn, becomes the seducer, and tempter of the inexperienced."[78] Framing the life course of the prostitute this way, notions of innocent youth could be played against images of older, depraved women. Hope might still spring for virtuous young women, but if they were raised in working-class homes, their chances were slim.

Thus by midcentury the Magdalen Society was projecting two images of the prostitute: most frequently, that of the seducer, but also occasionally, that of the seduced. In both portrayals, the focus was primarily on the character of the individual, whether innocent victim of seduction or drunken, seductive prostitute. While by midcentury class antagonisms became quite noticeable in the rhetoric of the Society, considerations of economic distress or class exploitation as potential explanations for the presence of prostitution were largely absent.[79] To the managers of the Society, economic status was determined by an individual's habits and way of life. The economic degradation suffered by prostitutes was their own fault.[80]

The evolving discourse of the Magdalen Society, their darkening portrait of women involved in the sex trade, led and informed a larger dialogue surrounding prostitution in mid-nineteenth-century America. Not everyone turned on prostitutes. There were always competing images. The prostitute appeared as both the seduced and the seducer in midcentury fiction, newspaper coverage, and didactic literature.[81] A burst of support for fallen women did appear when the New York Female Moral Reform Society (NYFMRS) began to hunt down male brothel customers and publish their names in the 1830s. However, this better-known reform body was simply one group within a wide range of participants engaged in a dialogue about prostitution.[82] The trajectory of the Philadelphia Magdalen Society in fact seems to better reflect that of American popular culture than does the stance of this reform group. While the culture of sensibility had encouraged many to sympathize with prostitutes in the late eighteenth century, by the mid-nineteenth century a considerably less benevolent view of these women had emerged in America.

While some historians, including Carroll Smith-Rosenberg, have portrayed the NYFMRS as breaking new rhetorical ground by concentrating blame on male seducers rather than female prostitutes, it should be clear by now that the NYFMRS was airing well-worn complaints in their weekly journal *The Advocate of Moral Reform*. The motif of the fall from seduction into prostitution had been explored in American publications for nearly a half-century before *The Advocate* took up this topic. Furthermore, in terms of prosecution, a trend toward blaming women took hold in these years; Barbara Meil Hobson has shown that early nineteenth-century Boston police and courts increasingly saw prostitution as a female offense.[83] In addition, as shown below, popular debates in novels and newspapers exhibited growing skepticism toward prostitutes. Thus the New York Female Moral Reform Society seems to have been fighting an embattled position, not staking new ground, in their rhetoric.

Perhaps the most heated contest over seduction in Jacksonian America was the Helen Jewett case in New York. The historian Patricia Cline Cohen has scrutinized coverage surrounding this prostitute's murder in 1836. When the fashionable young clerk Richard Robinson was accused of murdering Jewett, Cohen finds, Robinson's ensuing trial produced sharply conflicting images of Jewett.[84] It appears that the emergent picture of the vicious woman, being generated in Philadelphia, was also developing in New York. In the debate surrounding Jewett's death, and in popular representations more generally, the fallen woman often emerged as the potential seducer of young men. Joseph Holt Ingraham's 1843 book based on the Jewett case, *Frank Rivers*, echoed the judgments of many of his contemporaries. He suggested that prostitutes, and not young men, were the real danger: "she was the seducer, not he . . . Her beauty was her power, and she triumphed in it. She felt a sort of revenge against the other sex, and used every art to tempt and ruin young men."[85] New York was not alone in hosting contentious debates about prostitutes. Boston newspapers would fight a similar battle a decade later when prostitute Maria Bickford was murdered. Daniel A. Cohen has found that some journalists joined the defense counsel in trying to smear Bickford's character, one writer calling her "a woman of the vilest passions." Undoubtedly inspired by such views, the courtroom crowd lustily cheered when the verdict for Bickford's murderer—not guilty—was announced.[86]

Philadelphia had its own sensational trial that triggered heated commentary about seduction. The 1843 trial of Singleton Mercer revealed that class resentments ran in both directions in antebellum Philadelphia. As bourgeois reformers were expressing growing aggression toward impoverished prostitutes, working-class Philadelphians began to voice frustration with the sexual liberties granted to wealthy young men at the expense of working class girls. The Mercer trial, which inspired George Lippard's subversive novel *The Quaker City*, opened a forum for working-class protest in the courtroom and in the penny daily that covered the trial, the *Public Ledger*.[87] When Singleton Mercer murdered the wealthy rake Hutchinson Heberton for seducing his sister, Sarah Mercer, he became a popular hero. Crowds thronged the courtroom for the trial and celebrated his acquittal. Mercer's murder of Heberton was given further validation by state legislators. Responding to popular petitions, legislators drafted and passed an anti-seduction law only days following the conclusion of the Mercer trial.[88] Confirming what one scholar has termed the phenomenon of "rape without women," the popular reaction to Mercer's trial was as much about status concerns among jostling classes of men as it was about fears for women.[89] Mercer's ability to protect his sister's body determined his independence as a man.

A number of months after its conclusion, the editors of the *Public Ledger* reflected on the lessons of the Mercer trial, as well as two new cases involving seduction in Philadelphia and New York at the time. Condemning the culture of libertinism that permitted wealthy rakes like Heberton to prey on young women, the *Ledger* protested: "the majority of men in what are called the 'respectable ranks,' each one believes that he is justifiable in proceeding to any extremity which women will permit. *He* is under no obligation to restrain his own passions. This obligation devolves on woman alone." The *Ledger* called on women to recognize the bonds that should unite their sex across class lines. Regrettably, the "rich merchant's wife" often "failed to close her doors to the scoundrel who has seduced the daughter of a poor mechanic!" Women were to close ranks by refusing company to such "villains." In doing this they would force more males into being "*marrying men*." In seeming dialogue with the managers of the Magdalen Society, the paper rejected the opinion of those who would portray a victimized young woman as a "monster of wickedness." Instead, they believed blame rested with the segment of fashionable society that encouraged the seducer to "yield to his own passions" and "even congratulate[d] him upon indulging them to her ruin."[90] Here was a strong working-class counterpoint to the views emerging among bourgeois reformers.

George Lippard, a nineteenth-century labor activist, expressed similar sentiments in *The Quaker City*. Published in 1845, after having been serialized a year prior, the novel sold 60,000 copies within a year and 10,000 copies annually during the next decade; it went through twenty-seven American printings in four years.[91] Like the commentary of the *Public Ledger*, *The Quaker City* revealed sentiments much at odds with those in middle-class reform circles.

Lippard handled the Mercer case somewhat differently than did the penny daily. While the *Public Ledger* was content to make casual reference to the wrongs done to Sarah Mercer and then launch into an indictment of bourgeois society's acquiescence in the seduction of poor women, Lippard delves more deeply into the Mercer case in order to more fully explore the class variables at stake in seduction. He concocts two parallel plots of seduction, one where the victim is poor and the other involving a daughter of wealthy parents. He questions why seduction is seen as a crime only when committed at the expense of a well-to-do family.

Lippard does not portray the character representing Sarah Mercer, Mary Arlington, as coming from a family living under hard circumstances. Indeed, the Mercers appear to have been of middling status and on their way up. While Sarah's father was a "mechanic" who had retired on only a "modest competency," he was an elder in his Southwark Presbyterian church. His son, Singleton Mercer, was a clerk with the mercantile firm of Carson and Newbold in Philadelphia.[92] Singleton had secured entry into the expanding white-collar world of the middle class and saw the insult of seduction as a threat to his family's rising social capital. It was reported in the trial that Singleton responded to the news of his sister's "seduction" (testimony reveals in fact a rape) by saying "we are ruined, *everyone of us.*" Interestingly, Singleton had initially threatened to murder his sister, not Heberton, for the shame she brought on the family name.[93]

In *The Quaker City* Lippard pushes the Mercers into the upper class and constructs a second seduction plot involving a working-class victim in order to highlight the class assumptions surrounding seduction. Lippard presents the Singleton Mercer character, Byrnewood Arlington, as a seducer himself. In implicit dialogue with Mercer, who regarded seduction as a crime calibrated by a family's social capital, Lippard insists that the pain of seduction is felt equally by victims of any social class. By the novel's end Byrnewood comes to the realization that the seduction he committed against his family's servant was as grave a sin as that committed against his sister.

We can learn something about Lippard's intentions as a novelist by considering the justifications he offered for his effort. He defended himself in a new preface for his controversial novel in 1849, claiming that his original intent had been to help raise money to protect his poor orphan sister in the case of his own death. While this melodramatic plea is not wholly convincing, the problems he imagines his sister facing do open themselves to interpretation. He feared for her, he stated, because he "knew too well that law of society which makes a virtue of the dishonor of a poor girl, while it justly holds the seduction of a rich man's child as an infamous crime." Lippard said that he decided to write a book "founded upon" the idea "*That the seduction of a poor and innocent girl, is a deed altogether as criminal as deliberate murder.*" Lippard was in no way denying the injury done to Sarah Mercer or any daughter of privilege. He validated Singleton Mercer's murder of Hutchinson Heberton by suggesting that the "*assasin of chastity and maidenhood*" was "*worthy of death by the hands of any man, and in any place.*"[94]

While this novel covers far more than seduction, Lippard fulfills his promise to stand up for injured women, while also validating male working-class protectors whose manhood was at stake. Within his sprawling indictment of Philadelphia's ruling class and his experiments in seedy sensationalism, Lippard explores the injustices done by male rakes. While his seduction plots are in some measure highly conventional, they also include class analysis.

It is important to note that Lippard's book recapitulated many conventions of seduction fiction. His treatment of seduction has all of the sympathy, as well as many of the limitations, of turn-of-the-century seduction novels such as *Charlotte Temple*. Lippard expresses sorrow for victimized women. Yet he also upholds notions of chastity that constrained female youth. Mary Arlington is to be pitied, not condemned. She is about as close as one can get to a pure victim in a seduction novel. It takes an elaborate plot, including a sham marriage to her seducer Gus Lorrimer, to achieve the seduction. In fact, it is not clear that a seduction per se occurs: Mary's seduction scene is quite murky and comes across more like a rape, complete with shrieks for mercy, than a willful surrender of chastity.[95] Although Lippard condemns the double standard that saddles women with the consequences of men's sins, he usually fails to strike at the root of assumptions surrounding the ideal of chastity that helped uphold it. Characteristically, he notes of Mary, "The guilt was not hers, but the Ruin blasted her purity forever."[96] While the "Ruin" is lamented, it is not denied. Lippard repeatedly plays into the notion that a woman who has lost her virginity has lost all her social worth. As Mary's father comments, "Better death than dishonor!"[97] His honor had been irreparably harmed too. The descent into prostitution after seduction was inevitable. Lippard's portrayal of Bess, a once-seduced prostitute who turns from evil to good, does hint at the possibility of a ruined woman being redeemed. Nevertheless, Lippard repeatedly has sympathetic characters, including Mary herself, accept the fate of life-long shame for lost chastity.[98]

Where Lippard is more unconventional, as noted above, is in his concern with a growing class code surrounding seduction. Lippard insists that the seduction of a poor young woman is equal to that of a rich one. Consistent with the Heberton and Mercer case, Lippard has the rake Gus Lorrimer pay for his crime of seducing the well-to-do Mary Arlington by dying at the hands of Byrnewood Arlington. It is in the second plot involving Byrne-wood's seduction of the family servant, Annie, that Lippard works his class angle most fully. While Byrnewood has heroic dimensions and ultimately is likable, he has much to learn over the course of the novel. Lippard's portrayal of Byrnewood as a seducer most likely provoked Singleton Mercer's attempt to have the play based on *The Quaker City* shut down before it opened for production in Philadelphia.[99] When Byrnewood Arlington discovers that Gus Lorrimer has set up Byrnewood's own sister for seduction and demands that Lorrimer withdraw, Lorrimer confronts Byrnewood with his own past: "'Devilish odd, ain't it? That little affair of yours with *Annie*? Wonder if she has any *brother*? Keen cut *that*." Lippard ultimately has Byrnewood realize that in "crushing the honor of an unprotected girl," he had accepted the class conventions "which the Lady and Gentleman of Christian Society recognize with tacit reverence": "Seduce a rich maiden? Wrong the daughter of a *good* family? Oh, this is horrible; . . . But a poor girl, a *servant*, a domestic? Oh no! These are fair game for the gentleman of fashionable society." Not only did young rakes encourage such behavior, noted Lippard, but "upon the wrongs of such as these the fine lady looks with a light laugh and supercilious smile."[100] Lippard turned the tables on the bourgeoisie. For him, reformers' criticisms of fallen women were little more than self-serving hypocrisy.

The Singleton Mercer trial, especially as handled by George Lippard in *The Quaker City* offers a glimpse into a substratum of opinion at odds with that of the managers of the Philadelphia Magdalen Society. While bourgeois society was becoming more inclined to suspect sexual deviancy among the lower social orders, Lippard cast aspersion on the rules of the bourgeois parlor that extended protection only to women who moved in respectable high society. Sides in this antebellum American debate certainly did not divide completely along class lines. Timothy Gilfoyle, for one, has suggested

that many young working-class men joined their bourgeois peers in participating in a sporting culture surrounding prostitution.[101] Many of the evangelical crusaders in Female Moral Reform Societies who espoused sympathy
for prostitutes stood solidly within the emergent middle class.[102] Still, considering the growing aggressiveness of the bourgeoisie toward prostitutes,
it's not surprising that some of the more vocal supporters of women's
honor began to be working class radicals like George Lippard.

* * *

Clearly, not only in the records of the Philadelphia Magdalen Society, but
also in a broader popular culture context, two opposing dialogues about
seduction coexisted by midcentury. The prostitute figured prominently in
such discourses, alternatively imagined as either the innocent victim or seductive temptress. If the experience of the Magdalen Society is representative, the emergent picture of the prostitute as villain may have resulted from
a growing sense of frustration among the bourgeoisie with a class of women
who seemed increasingly culturally distant and distinct.[103] Rapid urban
growth, booming immigration, and increasing class segregation were certainly key elements in this estrangement. Yet equally important were the
unrealistic expectations of the bourgeoisie. Considering the preconceptions
of both the Magdalen Society and the American reading public, whose
image of the prostitute was highly informed by seduction fiction, their frustration is hardly surprising. Expecting to find victimized young innocents,
they instead often found worldly women who seemed indifferent to reformers' standards of bourgeois propriety. Writers veered fitfully between the
two images of the prostitute, neither proving fully satisfying. Ultimately,
few seemed able to transcend descriptions of gendered character, one class-
specific (the prostitute as depraved lower-class harlot), the other age-
specific (the prostitute as innocent young victim of male depravity), in explaining the presence of prostitution in the antebellum city.[104] A discourse
born of anxieties about female youth on the marriage market had become
a prerogative of class. In middle-class circles, only bourgeois women could
still be imagined as pure victims.

Having explored the fate of the seduction narrative in antebellum
America through the window of the Magdalen Society, we may now tentatively answer the question posed at the beginning of this chapter: along
which lines was the seduction narrative reconfigured? If the seduction narrative less often explained prostitution, it nonetheless resonated with many

midcentury bourgeois Americans. To the degree that it made sense to them, one of its primary functions must have been to uphold the image of the fundamental purity of bourgeois womanhood. Yet the image of the depraved male encoded in the traditional seduction narrative had also been rejected in some measure. As Chapter 6 will demonstrate more fully, by midcentury, bourgeois males were being urged to respect women by adopting a standard of chastity. As William Alcott had urged his readers, men were to "protect and aid," not "injure," the innocence of women. But many bourgeois males were participating in the thriving practice of urban prostitution of this period. To the degree that they resolved the tension between these conflicting codes (whether on an individual or collective level), the line of class may have appeared a useful dividing point. If working-class women were immersed in a vice-ridden world, the rules of the bourgeois home need not apply to them. While bourgeois reformers certainly never recommended the visitation of prostitutes, one can imagine that their writings may have influenced their class peers in just such a direction. By portraying prostitutes as depraved and beyond hope, moral reformers may have encouraged their class peers to question whether such women truly deserved the respect demanded for proper ladies. The prostitute was simultaneously alien and available to midcentury bourgeois men.

Chapter 3

"The Most Powerful Instrument of College Discipline": The University of Pennsylvania and the Advent of Meritocracy in the Early Republic

For those who tried to guide the young, eighteenth-century ideals did not fare well in the early American republic. Theories of sensibility were forsaken as writers imagined the dangers of young men on the marriage market. Reformers abandoned notions of female innocence as they carried on work with prostitutes. Similarly, notions of civic virtue would fail in the realm of education. At the dawn of the nineteenth century, however, many still held out hope for the operation of virtue in public. Prominent American founders believed that the male youth who undertook the noble venture of higher education would inspire others to serve the public weal in their occupations and public office. According to these thinkers, colleges could serve as an engine of reform. This vision cut across emerging political boundaries forming between the Federalists and Jeffersonian Republicans. Politicians on both sides seemed to value higher education, agreeing that America's most promising youth should complete their training in citizenship in colleges.[1]

The optimism of this republican vision for American schooling was perhaps best articulated in the prize-winning essay of Samuel Harrison Smith, a University of Pennsylvania graduate and Jeffersonian newspaper editor. In his anonymous 1797 essay for the American Philosophical Society, Smith identified the benefits of education for both the individual and society. According to his essay, the citizen would learn to protect liberty for himself and others: "[He] will be a free man in its truest sense. He will know his rights, and he will understand the rights of others." If Americans collectively could concentrate on the science of government, they might even achieve its perfection: "No circumstance could so rapidly promote the growth of this science as a universal illumination of mind. The minds of millions centering in one point could not fail to produce the sublimest discoveries." In its perfected state, America would truly serve as a city upon a hill: "She would soon become a model for the nations of the earth."[2]

According to this shared discourse, Americans could simultaneously address their private and public interests. Many believed that a more utilitarian focus would help popularize higher education for the common man. Dr. Benjamin Rush was perhaps the most persistent advocate for education reform in early America. Known for his increasing elitism as he aged, Rush nonetheless shared with many of his contemporaries a preference for instruction in the "American language," rather than traditional instruction in the classics. In presenting his vision of education for a Pennsylvania audience, Rush suggested that it was obvious that those who wished to pursue "the professions of law, physic, or divinity" would benefit from "a perfect knowledge of our language," but he also wanted to highlight the benefits of such an education for occupations such as clerk or merchant: "in a state which boasts of the first commercial city in America, I wish to see it cultivated by young men, who are intended for the compting house, for many such, I hope, will be educated in our colleges."[3]

Both Benjamin Rush and Samuel Harrison Smith believed that the capstone of the American collegiate system would be a national university where America's future leaders would receive their postgraduate training. Many American political leaders agreed. Their plan for a national university represented the high-water mark of the vision of republican education. To the disappointment of its supporters, a national university—proposals for which were first debated in the Constitutional Convention and subsequently advocated by the first six American presidents—was never established.[4] If many of the founders were disappointed by their inability to realize this pinnacle of their vision of American education, this would only be the start of their frustrations. Not only would forming a link between government and college at the federal level prove unattainable; even at the state level, only the weakest of relationships were established between colleges and their home states. The same emergent forces that had doomed the attempt to form a federal university worked against close government-school cooperation at the state level: Americans were increasingly heterogeneous as the frontier, religious sectarianism, and local loyalties pulled them apart.[5] The republican hopes for colleges did not wholly rest on formal linkages between colleges and governing institutions. Yet there were further grounds to believe that colleges were becoming a poor training ground for American citizenship. The efforts of those who wished to make the college curriculum more utilitarian had been widely resisted. Classes appeared increasingly irrelevant to American life. In what the historian Richard Hofstader once called the "great retrogression" of colleges in the early nineteenth century, schools adopted or maintained curricula dominated by the classics and religion. Perhaps most discouraging of all were the students who populated these colleges—or the lack thereof. Early American colleges seemed to languish with paltry numbers of students who were too young, undereducated, and incredibly disorderly.[6]

One of the final projects in the life of Thomas Jefferson can illuminate the essential challenge faced by college leaders in this period. An exemplar of the optimism of the republican vision of education, Jefferson would also embody its disappointment. Jefferson spent many of his later years struggling to realize his vision of a university for Virginia. In finally bringing his plans to fruition, he knew that one of the greatest challenges he would face in achieving the success of his institution would be preventing student disorder. In writing to the Harvard educator George Ticknor, who was facing some similar difficulties himself, Jefferson claimed that "the rock which I most dread is the discipline of the institution." Jefferson was keenly aware of the need for new methods of creating order within American colleges. While regretting that American parents cultivated "premature ideas of independence," Jefferson nonetheless believed that colleges should not resort to the "degrading motive of *fear*": "Hardening [students] to disgrace, to corporal punishments, and servile humiliations cannot be the best process for producing erect character."[7] In these attitudes Jefferson was reflecting the changed climate of American opinion about the exercise of authority over youth.

It is fitting that the unfashionable John Adams was one of the only prominent leaders to question this new wisdom. Even fellow Federalist Harrison Gray Otis could only marvel at Adams when the former president suggested the revival of flogging at Harvard, following a riot in 1818:

Old Mr. Adams mistakes the genius of the age to tell of whipping and to practice scolding. The principles of Government in States and Families are changed. The understanding and the heart must be addressed by persuasion and reason, and the bayonet and rod reserved for the last emergency. A boy of 18 for all the purposes of Government, is as much a man as he will ever be.[8]

Jefferson took such notions to their logical extreme. Rather than simply trying to soften the rule of college authorities over students, he sought to dispense with such rule entirely. Reenacting his early political career, Jefferson rejected a family model for grounding authority and endorsed in its place a contract among the governed. Eschewing the traditional notion that college leaders should act as parents (in loco parentis) Jefferson called instead for student self-government. Students would regulate their own behavior through a judicial body of their peers named the Board of Censors.

Despite Jefferson's best efforts, his experiment failed less than a year after it commenced. In 1825, at the end of a year that had been rife with disorders, Jefferson summoned a group of students who seemed unwilling to police themselves. Forced to choose between a faculty that was threatening collectively to resign and his design for student self-governance, Jefferson called on the students to account for their actions. A violent confrontation had broken out between fourteen students and two professors. Rather than admonishing the perpetrators, sixty-five students (more than half the student body) presented a joint resolution to the faculty in which they attested their allegiance to one another, refusing to testify against each other in any prospective investigation. The students were asked to appear before the board of visitors, who were meeting at Monticello. Sitting with Jefferson were fellow ex-presidents of the United States James Madison and James Monroe. When one of the board members asked that the fourteen students responsible for the violence step forward, Jefferson was astonished to find his own nephew among them. A professor in attendance recorded Jefferson's reaction. He noted that Jefferson expressed outrage when he discovered that "the efforts of the last ten years of his life had been foiled by one of his family." Jefferson attacked the students with the "language of indignation and reproach." In constructing a new disciplinary code that dissolved student government, Jefferson informed the students: "coercion must be resorted to where confidence has been disappointed."[9] Two and a half decades into the nineteenth century, few of the founding generation could have doubted the deplorable state of American colleges.[10]

Rather than promoting virtue, colleges of the early republic were besieged with student riots and disorder.[11] Frustrated college authorities struggled to resolve the behavioral problems that afflicted their schools. This chapter will consider the nature of the problems they faced and the solutions they ultimately enforced. Colleges were beset with student disorder because college leaders were in too weak a position to govern their schools. The great number of American colleges, most of them eagerly founded in the wake of the Revolution, struggled to find students. With students in great demand, coercive government appeared too great a risk.

In addition, the very shape of the old college order was now in question. The revolutionary era shattered the patterns of hierarchy that had structured the colonial college. In the wake of a Lockean "revolution against patriarchal authority," the in loco parentis patriarchal ideal was badly outdated.[12] Students could no longer be treated as submissive subjects to the patriarchal authority of college faculty. Nor did class rankings based on parental prestige seem appropriate in a democracy.

Many colleges eventually resorted to harsher discipline and massive expulsions. More important and enduring, however, was their turn to a new strategy of meritocracy. College leaders believed that student disorder was nurtured in students' propensity to form horizontal bonds of sympathy and loyalty. If old forms of enforcing ranks on students seemed outmoded, perhaps a new hierarchy based on merit might prove more workable. Over the first half of the nineteenth century, college authorities began to create a system of classifying students that can be understood as a meritocracy. By employing either individualized rankings within each class or assigning letter or number grades to students' performance and behavior, college teachers tried to discourage student combinations by making students compete with one another for class positions. Such a disciplinary system would resonate in America, for the bourgeois ideology of the self-made man insisted that status was earned by disciplined striving. A close look at one school's struggle to combat student disorder can reveal the halting steps taken toward this new system of college governance. A consideration of the experience of the University of Pennsylvania will also reveal that at the heart of the new meritocracy was parental authority reborn.

*   *   *

The University of Pennsylvania (Figure 2) did not witness the type of disruptive and violent riots that plagued many colleges of the early republic, riots of a severity that distinguished this collegiate era from the eras that both preceded and followed it.[13] Yet authorities at the University of Pennsylvania did suffer, in exaggerated terms, some of the other problems associated with colleges during this period. The school attracted small numbers of students, most of whom were young and undereducated. Not only were admission standards low, so too were degree requirements. A student who entered at the lowest class would graduate in three years.[14] Even though the school did not suffer major riots, college authorities seemed obsessed with issues of discipline. They were well aware of the problems that existed else-

Figure 2. President's House. Watercolor by William Strickland, n.d. Built as a residence for the United States president in 1790, this building served as the Penn campus between 1802 and 1828. The more prosperous medical school sits to the left of the college. From the Collections of the University of Pennsylvania Archives.

where and feared their appearance at their school. Anxious to protect a reputation already stained by a small enrollment and low standards, the university's leaders feared that such disturbances would further injure the school.

To a worried board of trustees in 1824, the University of Pennsylvania appeared on the brink of collapse. There were only fifty-seven students enrolled in the college. Furthermore, the few students who did attend were proving difficult to govern. The board expressed their dismay in a published report. In this address, they emphasized the school's disciplinary problems: "That a deficiency exists either in the system, or the administration of the college discipline, is too obvious to be denied or doubted." They were certain that such disorder deeply hurt their school. High expectations had been frustrated. The trustees expressed regret that an institution that was "munificently endowed" and set in the midst of "an intelligent population anxiously desirous to discover opportunities for educating its youth without seeking them abroad" could not establish a better reputation or attract more students: "[It] languishes without a name, and gives instruction to a number of pupils so limited, as scarcely to exceed that of an ordinary grammar school." In seeking to assign blame for the low state of the college, the board looked toward the professors. The board believed that to "redeem the credit of the college," its professors would have to start showing "an ardent and exclusive devotion" to "fearlessly and faithfully" perform the "duties of their honourable trusts." The duty they felt the professors had been performing most terribly was the governance of the students. While the board might give guidelines for governing the students, the professors on their own would have to cultivate their ability to inspire respect. According to the board, the professors needed to start displaying a "dignity of deportment and extensive learning," which would inspire "affectionate deference" and "obedience."[15]

This published attack by the board on the school's professors marked the beginning of the end for the Provost Frederic Beasley (Figure 3) and his colleagues. Dr. Beasley, an accomplished Episcopal priest trained in moral philosophy and theology at Princeton under Samuel Stanhope Smith, had been hired in 1813 to revitalize the struggling college department at the University of Pennsylvania. He apparently had failed to gain the sought results. Four years after the trustees published their accusatory report, in June of 1828, Provost Beasley, Professor J. G. Thomson, and Tutor Gather Van Gelder were dismissed from their positions. Professor Robert Patterson left at the same time, having accepted a post at the University of Virginia. Thus only one instructor in the College of Arts remained, Dr. Robert Adrain, who had been hired the previous year as part of a new regime the board envisioned.[16] It is altogether clear that by the time the board's report on the "existing state of abuses" in the university appeared, most confidence in Dr. Beasley had been lost. His fellow instructors seemed more the victims of circumstance. The board of trustees wanted to start their institution anew.

If Dr. Beasley lost, in the sense that he was fired from his post, he won in the sense that his vision of college governance ultimately prevailed. He had not been working alone; college leaders across the young nation were embroiled in similar battles. Dr. Beasley had struggled to order the school in two primary ways. First, he believed that as provost, he and his fellow professors would have to gain greater authority over the students. While the board believed that Beasley had failed to command respect, Beasley blamed the board for undermining his authority. By frequently intervening in matters of daily governance and by allowing students too easily to appeal to them in disciplinary matters, Beasley insisted, the board had subverted his authority with the students. Second, Beasley wished to govern the students through a system of meritocracy. By granting students frequent marks of distinction vis-à-vis one another, Beasley sought to entice the students to behave properly. Both of these means of establishing college governance were not achieved by Dr. Beasley, but his successor, Provost William De-Lancey, would insist upon these reforms as conditions for the acceptance

Figure 3. Frederic Beasley. Artist unknown, n.d. As provost, Beasley led the troubled University of Pennsylvania between 1813 and 1828. Courtesy of the University of Pennsylvania Art Collection, Philadelphia, Pennsylvania.

of his appointment. Dr. Beasley could not be the man to oversee the new system; his character had suffered too greatly in the struggle. His early efforts, nonetheless, deserve to be revisited.

Upon assuming the position of provost in 1813, Dr. Beasley outlined a broad program for the reform of the University of Pennsylvania. Beasley sought to improve both the college's standards and discipline. In fact, he saw the two issues as inextricably intertwined. In a lengthy inaugural report to the board of trustees, Beasley both identified the problems he saw afflicting the university and offered solutions to these perceived difficulties. Beasley began this report by suggesting that the students admitted were either too young or too unprepared for college studies. He saw this difficulty as the "great and radical evil of the Institution," noting also that that this "observation applies in some degree, to all our Colleges in this Country." From our current perspective, the students were quite young: when Beasley arrived, students were entering at an average age of about fifteen and a half years old and graduating at about eighteen and a half.[17] Beasley's estimate about the immaturity of students at all American colleges also appears to be corroborated by the statistical record. Except for some New England schools, where declining economic prospects sometimes drove older students to join younger classmates, American colleges had a rather young population.[18] Beasley's point of reference here was likely Germany, since American educators were becoming enamored with German universities in the early nineteenth century. As educators were well aware at the time, in Germany the gymnasium acted as a brake on college admissions, delaying the entry of students into universities by about three years compared to American colleges.[19]

Beasley believed that the combination of student immaturity and inexperience gravely hurt the school. He said this potent mixture "vitiates the whole system of instruction and discipline." Not only were students admitted in an unready state, he noted, but they also passed through the school without ever learning much: "they are hurried thro[ugh] the course of studies prescribed in the College with little or no understanding." Beasley believed that this lack of attention to standards created a vicious cycle that discouraged prospective students of quality. He insisted that the school's "prostitution of its honors upon unripe and unqualified Candidates" was sapping "the confidence which the publick should repose in it," a confidence that was utterly necessary to the school's "growth and prosperity."[20]

The problems that Beasley identified were rooted in the weak bargaining position of American colleges in relation to their prospective student bodies. With colleges being founded at a rapid rate in the early republic, schools had to compete with one another to attract students.[21] Revisionist work on colleges in the early republic has shown that their proliferation did cause net gains in enrollment across the country, but what this work has largely missed is the great strain caused by the competition of multiplying schools. Even the most prestigious schools could not attract more than a couple hundred students into their programs. Incentives for college attendance were few; schools had little more to offer students than the polish of learning.[22] Young men could make it on their own without college degrees, for cities were offering expanding business opportunities and the nascent professions had few educational requirements.

Under pressure to find students, schools often had to compromise their programs to attract them. Maintaining low admission standards was one way to enroll more students. With a dearth of secondary schools in America during this period, colleges tried to boost enrollments by admitting younger students. Cutting school costs, especially professors' salaries, was another way schools tried to attract more students. Some colleges, the University of Pennsylvania included, offered programs for less than the standard four years, while others allowed many students to enter their programs with advanced standing.[23] Perhaps the most extreme example of the negotiating power of students in this respect was the successful class boycott by students at Dickinson College, where students forced college authorities to allow them to complete their college course work in the span of a single year.[24] Finally, colleges were forced into compromising school discipline. Reverend John Todd, a popular advice writer, was quite right to observe in 1835 that in a country where "colleges are so numerous," each institution would have to be "circumspect" in its behavioral demands in order to gain "its share of students."[25]

Beasley aimed to stem this tide. To improve standards, he wished to extend the program to four years, even for currently enrolled students. He felt that such an extension for these students would have to be carried out tactfully, suggesting that if he did not gain the senior class's "consent and concurrence," there might be a revolt of some sort: "Serious evils and convulsions might be occasioned to the College by an attempt to force such a measure upon them against their inclinations and without having, in due time, apprized them of our intentions." Even if the program was not extended for those enrolled, Beasley believed, standards could easily be improved within a few years by raising the bar for admission and by requiring an extended program for new entries.

Beasley also suggested some methods to improve the schools' disciplinary system in his inaugural report. Beasley's major life work was an attempt to rescue John Locke's *Essay Concerning Human Understanding* from the taint of David Hume's skepticism; it is hardly surprising that Beasley demonstrated a clear understanding of the educational principles of Locke and his followers—ideas that many of his less schooled contemporaries shared.[26] Observing a critical Lockean distinction between childhood and youth, Beasley felt that the methods of controlling students employed in a college could not be the same as those used in a grammar school: "it is certainly not expedient to establish the same species of government in the one as in the other." While Beasley does not state what the distinction in the species of government might be, his audience certainly understood what he meant. According to commonplace Lockean wisdom, coercive techniques such as corporal punishment might be used with children but were inappropriate for managing youth.[27] The university had already stipulated in its laws for 1801 that corporal punishment could only be used for students in its grammar school under the age of fourteen.[28] If the Lockean revolution against patriarchal authority precluded coercion, however, it also proffered new methods of instilling discipline.

Beasley suggested several Lockean means to create order. One set of suggestions invoked seemingly traditional methods of inspiring obedience, but these proposals were dressed in the distinctive clothing of Lockean sensational psychology.[29] Beasley argued that the school would have to use more pomp and circumstance to awe its students into respecting authority. As a close student of Locke, Beasley believed that spectacles could deeply influence the impressionable minds of youth. He told the board that attention to "exterior form and formalities" was central to upholding authority, suggesting that "no Institution, human or divine," could long survive "among creatures as much under the dominion of their senses as men" unless some attention was paid to displays that were "calculated to strike and captivate those senses." Beasley further suggested that colleges were particularly well positioned to take advantage of this principle of sensational psychology: "youth, more especially, are the slaves of those impressions made upon their minds by outward objects—All shew and ceremony have a powerful influence upon them." With these principles in mind, Beasley called for a chapel room in which to hold daily service. That chapel would also be a perfect site to hold various ceremonies during the college year. These ceremonies could include such solemnities as having an officer exhort students to "yield all due submission," while students themselves might on such occasions offer formal promises of obedience. In addition, on such occasions, participants would be draped in proper regalia, with professors wearing "gowns suited to their rank" and students dressed in lesser robes.[30]

Even more important than this management of sensation impression through "exterior form," would be a reworking of the school's "inward structure and organization." Specifically, what Beasley had in mind was the creation of hierarchy among the students. School authorities during the early nineteenth century had no doubt about the cause of student disorders: students honored loyalty to one another above loyalty to their superiors. Within such horizontally bound groups, the values of college government were spurned. The term most often employed by school authorities to describe student peer groupings was "combinations." This term was also used at this time to condemn emerging labor unions. Just as the middle class would stand against working men's groups, so would college leaders stand against student combinations. The term most likely entered the parlance of college leaders in 1802, when Princeton explicitly outlawed combinations in its revised college laws. Notably, Beasley's mentor and lifelong friend Samuel Stanhope Smith was directing Princeton at the time. A famous trial against cordwainers who had organized a labor union in Philadelphia in 1806 helped spread the expression.[31] Whether applied to students or working men, it evoked a sense of internal loyalty and aggression to outside authority.

To better appreciate Beasley's plan to create student hierarchy, we should more fully explore the rhetoric about student combinations. An understanding of student disorder is well displayed in a two-part article published in 1823 in the *New England Palladium* in response to student disorders at Harvard, entitled "Advice to the Young Gentlemen Under-Graduates." This article was an unsubtle satiric attack on the student values the writer believed responsible for Harvard's disorders. It was signed "Swift," invoking the famed author of *Gulliver's Travels* to ensure that no one missed the satiric intent. The author's identity is unknown, but there is no doubting this writer's sympathy for college authorities. The author begins by disingenuously urging young men to discard any silly notions about using college as an opportunity for improvement; instead they should aim for the "higher purpose of obtaining a reputation with their classmates." To accomplish this goal, a student must disobey college authorities: "The first and most decisive step to be taken towards this great and important end, as every scholar in College knows, is to oppose the government."

Leaders for these worthwhile endeavors can be found among those who "in other respects" are "the most worthless of the class," those young men who had no chance of being "distinguished as scholars": "These are the very persons whose genius points them out as your leaders . . . whatever they propose you must subscribe to, otherways you will be *unpopular*, and very likely be put down on the *black list*." The author assures the imagined student reader that even if he faces the "disgrace" of being ejected from the college, he can take pride in having displayed loyalty to his friends, even though "they will, very probably, never waste a thought upon you after you are gone."[32]

The author elaborates further on the means by which the students could collectively oppose college government, revealing most clearly the perceived principles uniting student peer groups: "Above all, combinations must not be forgotten. This is the great machine, and may be likened to the power of the lever in mechanics, it can effect any thing and every thing (except perhaps your own good and individual advantage)." Combinations were to be employed to protect students from college authorities. If one student were attacked, his peers would collectively stand by his side. This principle was never to be compromised: "however wrong he may be, and however unjustifiable or disreputable his offence, still you must be his advocates; for not to stand by a classmate or fellow student, right or wrong, would be tantamount to betraying him." Ultimately, "Swift" describes a code of blind and misguided loyalty to one's peers that demanded reflexive opposition to college authorities. Through satire he pleads with the students to strive to gain the approbation of their professors, rather than that of their classmates.[33]

Whether or not one accepts the author's derogatory estimation of student combinations, there are useful lessons about the nature of student disorder in the early republic in this commentary. Joseph Kett and Steven Novak have been quite right to argue that students' propensity to express horizontal rather than vertical allegiances was a defining feature of student disorder in this period.[34] Students do not seem to have been attracted to political issues from the larger society, but there was a political cast to their riots and disorders. Students collectively contested the right of college professors and trustees to punish their peers. Whether one is more inclined to respect these students' claim for "manly independence" or the college leaders' derisive dismissal of these "rights-of-boys politicians," it is clear that students felt some right to collectively defend perceived infringements on their liberties.[35] Horizontal loyalty was an underlying feature of student disorders, and college authorities readily understood this. Their challenge was to find some means to forge competing vertical loyalties.

Provost Beasley had a scheme to encourage just such sympathies. Students might more willingly strive to please their professors if the professors had some ready means to express their approval. In seeking to order the students, Beasley suggested that some plan needed to be devised that would "render scholarship and good moral conduct honorable and their opposites dishonorable." Beasley thought such values might be encouraged by having professors nominally mark students at the end of examinations, as well as at commencement: "discriminations will be made among them and honors conferred exactly in proportion to their respective degrees of merit." By seeking to use students' "sense of shame" or, more positively, "their principles of emulation and honor" to their advantage, professors might motivate students into both good scholarship and good behavior. Here was a clear application of the Lockean devices of parental esteem and disgrace. Here too we see that Lockean philosophy was tied up with what Michel Foucault has described as a technique of disciplinary power, the use of incentives to direct behavior.[36] Students would behave and work hard in order to gain the reward of their professor's approval. Beasley insisted that his model of government was a "parental one" and his proposals confirm this contention.[37] Unlike Jefferson, Beasley did not wish to reject in loco parentis. Rather, he sought to update that model to fit current thinking about parenting and pedagogy. Just as his contemporary Joseph Lancaster was doing in his popular monitorial schools, Beasley, as good Lockean parent, was stressing rewards over coercion, the carrot over the stick, to shape student behavior.[38]

Ironically, in the context of the classroom, such a "parental" tack tapped deeply into the emerging market values of competition that were transforming Philadelphia and American society. Beasley was quite willing to indulge such passions to his advantage. According to Beasley, if one were interested in "furnishing young gentlemen with motives which shall constrain them to industry and application," one would have to touch "every spring of ambition, emulation, and honor within them." To most fully realize this proposal, then, Beasley asked the board to order "Medals and premiums of different kinds" that professors would use to "distinguish" students for their scholarship and behavior.[39] Situated as he was in the middle of a rapidly expanding entrepôt, Beasley would have known well the workings of ambition. As many aspiring youth were chasing commercial wealth just outside the walls of his college, so could youth within his institution be motivated to win college rewards.

Beasley was insistent that his proposals for a meritocracy would simultaneously promote order and high standards. He saw students' scholarship and behavior as highly interdependent. When the board expressed "doubts concerning the expediency of bestowing any Medals," Beasley most directly articulated this perceived connection. In his response to the board, he first expressed his conviction that his meritocratic scheme was his most important proposed innovation: "I can say that I am as fully convinced as I can be of any moral truth whatever, that the distribution of these Medals and honors, is the vital spring of the Institution." Beasley then explained that his plan was the only means by which he could act upon students' sense of pride to promote his desired ends of high scholarship and improved discipline: "It is, at this moment, to the pupils the most animating motive to study and to us the most powerful instrument of College discipline."[40] Overall, then, Beasley's vision for enforcing student discipline and promoting high academic standards drew deeply on the popular Lockean educational principles of the day. Students would respect authority because it would be cloaked in ritual and symbols that would influence their impressionable minds. More importantly, students would work hard and behave properly so that they might gain the favor of professors who would bestow meritocratic distinctions for their efforts.

The idea of honoring student performance was not entirely new. Seventeenth-century Harvard may have for a time used something akin to merit rankings.[41] Closer in time, in eighteenth-century colleges, students at graduation had often been assigned "parts," orations in the branch of scholarship in which they were skilled. Yet such honors hardly anticipated the regular and systematized structure that grading would become for colleges in the mid-nineteenth century. In fact, other principles entirely had been used to order students. Ranking students based on parental prestige had been one means employed until the revolutionary period. As described by the historian James Axtell, once such rank was fixed, it was expressed in a wide range of ways: "As he was placed in his class, so a student would recite before the faculty, seat and serve himself at meals, sit in chapel, march in academic processions, (etc.)"[42] Another manner by which students had been ranked in colonial schools was by their year. As a student moved from freshman to senior, he would accrue more privileges. Students participated in the enforcement of such class distinctions, the most popular expression of which was known as "fagging," whereby underclassmen would be forced to serve upperclassmen. Most fundamentally, as discussed above, students had been ranked as inferiors in relation to their patriarchal professors, whom they owed their primary loyalties. By the late eighteenth-century, all these methods of ordering students had fallen out of favor at American colleges in response to growing democratic sentiments.[43] The vision of merit ranking that Beasley proposed represented a model of hierarchy that might order students anew.

Beasley was by no means alone in turning to distinctions of merit to order his students. As he was quick to point out to a resistant board, other early nineteenth century American college authorities were beginning to devise various schemes of marking student behavior and performance.[44] Similar thinking about merit rankings seems to have been developing in England as well, though it is unclear whether Americans were taking note of this.[45] The eventual product of such collective efforts would today be recognized as grading. Across the young republic, number or letter grades began to be used to designate student rank. The first known use of this type of marking system was at Yale in 1783, where Ezra Stiles created four named categories to organize students by merit. Yale also appears to have been the first school to use numbers or letters to mark student performance. In 1813, Yale developed the now familiar four-point scale. By midcentury, grading or the use of individualized rankings had become commonplace in colleges and was taken up by common-school reformers like Horace Mann. As grading entered common schools, it became a broadly shared experience for bourgeois Americans. Beasley's fully reasoned advocacy of the awarding of nominal distinctions and medals, if awkward in comparison to number or letter scales, still seems to fit into a larger pattern. Beasley, like his peers, was seeking to order students on a new hierarchy of merit.

Little is known of the origin and exact progression of ranking and grading schemes. In fact, it appears that many schemes developed independently. The English reformer Joseph Lancaster, whose monitorial schools enjoyed a brief fashion in Philadelphia and New York, emphasized merit groupings, so perhaps some responsibility lies there.[46] Heretofore, scholars have not been able to adequately explain the rationale behind these grading schemes. Finding few written explanations for such changes, the author of the closest study of these developments wished that she might be able to "know the minds" of the men who initiated "this business of evaluating individual attainment."[47] Provost Beasley's writings seem to offer a view into such a mind. And this was a mind fully grounded in the dominant educational philosophies of the day.

Beasley's writings suggest that the turn to meritocracy might be understood as a turn toward a market-oriented Lockean parenting style with the intent to restore school order. David Allmendinger's contention that colleges were absolving themselves of parental duties during this period, then, is not fully convincing. In loco parentis was changing, not disappearing.[48] There is clear evidence that Beasley's peers shared his conviction that student performance and student behavior could be addressed simultaneously. As new merit scales were developed in early nineteenth-century colleges, schools employed "demerits," loss of merit points, for disorderly behavior.[49] For Beasley and his peers, a system of meritocracy promised improved standards and orderly students.

Much to his regret, Beasley failed to gain board assent for many of his plans for reforming the school. While he did get a chapel room, students and professors did not have enough gowns to wear for special events within it.[50] While he persistently pressed for an extension of the school's program from three to four years, and for higher entrance standards, he did not see these reforms fully enacted until his tenure as provost was already doomed.[51] Beasley's plan for distributing medals also was resisted and ultimately defeated by the board.[52] The board not only resisted measures that Beasley pressed for upon assumption of his post; it also failed to respond favorably to proposals he offered during his residence.

While it is difficult to explain board refusals on many of Beasley's individual plans, the general state of contentiousness between Beasley and the board can be easily understood. Personality conflicts may have played some role, but the great sense of alarm for the school's survival shared by both parties was ultimately responsible for the troubled relationship. Beasley constantly struggled with the board to gain more autonomy in running the school. As an outsider to Philadelphia, born in North Carolina, Beasley had little leverage with a board composed of local elite. Although an accomplished scholar and priest, Beasley was no match for a group of eminent Philadelphians who viewed service on the board as a privilege of status and who were well accustomed to closely controlling the institution entrusted to them. In a period when the position of college president was generally weak, the leading position of provost at the University of Pennsylvania was even weaker.[53] The fact that many of Beasley's students were drawn from the same set of elite Philadelphia families that dominated the board of trustees likely further compromised an already weak position.[54] The three-way struggle between the board, Beasley, and the students would ultimately sink Beasley's provostship.

Unable to enact many of his plans to cultivate student discipline, Beasley still aimed to command obedience. He believed that "interference in the internal regulations of schools" by the board would have a "pernicious" influence and would prevent students from holding "respect and reverence for their Teachers."[55] His analysis seemed to be informed by his experience. Especially as the board lost confidence in Beasley, it began to closely regulate his operation of the school, repeatedly instituting special committee investigations. The correspondence regarding these investigations reveals his loss of authority.

In 1823 Beasley was asked, among many other things, to justify his granting of "holidays" to students. In response, Beasley explained that he used holidays much in the way that he had aimed to use merit distinctions—as a reward. Beasley frankly admitted that students had considerable negotiating power. Collectively, they were going to take days off; it would be best if the professors at least gained some steering power. He reminded the board that it was "no uncommon thing" when he had first assumed his position for students to "absent themselves in whole classes." He argued that a collective penalty might have been disastrous to the college: "To subject whole classes . . . to punishment, was thought a measure of some delicacy, and likely to be followed by serious if not dangerous consequences." Rather than risking a potential riot, Beasley thought the professors should "assume to themselves the power of determining the degree of extraordinary indulgence" the students should receive. Adopting this tack, the professors achieved favorable results, finding that "an occasional act of this nature," had disposed students to "a more cheerful acquiescence under their authority."[56]

While Beasley's confrontation with the board over holidays suggests that he was more willing than they to be lenient with the students, the opposite generally held true. The board was preoccupied with maintaining and increasing the school's student population. Accordingly, they were unwilling to eject students or to harshly discipline students who might then want to leave. Also, the board maintained lax admission standards. When colleges across the country finally accepted the risk of depleted enrollments by collectively creating blacklists of students who had been ejected from their schools, the University of Pennsylvania trustees stood alone in deciding that their school would be willing to admit such ejected students.[57] Once admitted, disorderly students seemed to find an ally in the board. For example, while colleges elsewhere had begun attempts to break combinations by making students individually account for themselves, the board refused this measure to Beasley.

A more detailed look at this specific confrontation over combination breaking reveals clearly how Beasley's authority was undermined by both student disorder and board resistance. In a published proposal to the board, Beasley asked for special measures to deal with a series of student problems. This proposal reveals various seemingly petty offenses that were being committed by the students. Students were surreptitiously interrupting recitations by making noises and engaging in other types of disruptive "unseemly levity." Classroom order also was being disrupted by students putting "offensive substances" on the "Stoves or Grates" in the back of the room. Students also were committing vandalism, such as "breaking windows" and "destroying the woodwork." In all these instances, detecting the offender was difficult. Bound by loyalty, students would not inform on one another. Beasley, who seems to have possessed an overly serious demeanor, did not want to suffer any such signs of disrespect. He wanted to put an end to these pranks by calling "on every member of the class, individually, to declare whether he was or was not guilty of such misconduct." If students refused to offer an answer to such queries, they would be assumed responsible and suffer the consequences of the offense.[58]

The board's response to this proposal was their report on the school's "existing state of abuses" in which they blamed the professors for the problems afflicting their school. They did not disagree that the offenses students were committing were serious. Such offenses threatened to further weaken the school's public reputation. But the measures Beasley proposed were unacceptable. The board refused to believe that "extraordinary powers were required to enable the insulted professor to detect the individuals who committed the offence." They argued that "the mode of detection" suggested by Beasley, an obvious affront to students' bonds of loyalty, would "produce such serious evils that no emergency could justify its use."[59] Lurking in their response was a fear of provoking a riot that might sink their institution.

The emerging struggle between Beasley and the board over student discipline came to a head when Beasley attempted to expel a student who had been involved in the classroom disorders. His battle with this student, ironically named Joseph Peace, fully exposed the weakness of Beasley's authority. Several months after the board had refused Beasley his proposed means of exposing the students responsible for disorder, Beasley asked the board to dismiss Peace from the school. According to Beasley, Peace had been a "Ringleader in all those irregularities and disturbances which took place during the last Session" that had "greatly interrupted the course of study" and had "reflected disgrace upon the Institution." Beasley presented Peace for dismissal now because a few days earlier he had "made an attempt to revive those disorders in the Classroom" that had "proved so fatal to the improvement of the pupils during the last Session." This time Beasley had managed to gain a confession from Peace, so the provost did not want to waste this opportunity to expel him.[60]

Doubting Beasley's judgment, the board demanded a fuller account of Peace's offenses. By retelling the many particular offenses committed by Peace, Beasley must have lost much of any remaining dignity he had in the eyes of the board. Beasley understood this would be the probable result. His loss, however, is the historian's gain, because Beasley offers the modern reader a detailed view of the problems faced by the college faculty. Beasley opened his account by protesting the degrading nature of the enterprise. He stated that at every college with which he was acquainted, the power to dismiss students was "left entirely in the hands of the Faculty." If the trustees were going to retain this power, they should at least trust the "discretion and justice of the officer of the College"; they shouldn't find it necessary to make a deep inquiry into the grounds for which this penalty had been recommended. However, since they had asked for such an account, Beasley would oblige.[61]

Peace was the type of leader against whom "Swift" had warned. According to Beasley, "Mr. Peace" was one of that "class of young men" that one could find "in all our Seminaries," who stood foremost in disrupting the order of such institutions. Beasley began his account of Peace's offenses by detailing his involvement in the disruption of a public exhibition by the Philomathean Society (Figure 4). At the annual exhibition of this student educational society, Peace and a number of other students "evidently combined together with a view to disturb the performance, disconcert the Speakers, & perpetrate every other indecency & outrage in their power." None of the speakers could be heard over the noises that these students made "at a part of the room most remote from the view of the Professor." Especially at the end of each oration, these students made "such loud, continued & indecent tumult" that there was "the appearance of a complete riot." They had abandoned all decorum. All appeals to the decency and honor of the students were in vain.[62] While these disruptions were going on, some of these same students were mocking the professors by "displaying to the Assembly, indecent placards, exhibiting grotesque figures of the provost

Figure 4. *Mr. Sharswood delivering an Oration*. Artist unknown. From *The Journal in Four Numbers, Edited By a Senior*, 1826. A member of the society drew this depiction of a Philomathean Society exhibition. Courtesy of the Philomathean Society, University of Pennsylvania.

and Professor Thomson," thereby "endeavouring to expose them to ridicule and contempt." Beasley knew of Peace's involvement because the janitor saw him engaged in these activities, but Peace managed to escape punishment by "a subterfuge."

After the events at the Philomathean exhibition, Peace's conduct had been characterized by "a continued series of improprieties" and "gross outrages." Beasley became embroiled in a deep personal conflict with Peace. When Beasley asked Peace to account for the incidents at the exhibition, the student showed not only a great "contempt for the authority of the College" but more particularly "the most rooted antipathy" to Beasley. Beasley felt that Peace had a deliberate strategy in mind. Peace had "derided his hostility against a single Member of the Faculty," even though all the faculty were "equally concerned against him." He did this, "no doubt, from motives of policy, in order to give some colour of excuse for his conduct, & make it appear that he had peculiar grounds for his resentment." Apparently, Beasley was rising to the challenge.

Peace proceeded to mock Beasley in a variety of other ways. Whenever the provost crossed paths with Peace, this youth not only failed to offer the usual "marks of respect" but, along with his peers, brazenly chose to "display audible & visible signs of disrespect": "I could not pass thro[ugh] them upon the steps or within the building, without hearing from some, as soon as my back was turned, every derisory sound that their organs of utterance could emit." One time, when Beasley turned around, after passing a group of students, he saw Peace "scraping, bowing & waving his hat in derision" at him. After discussing a number of other subversive acts committed by Peace, Beasley ended his letter to the board by relating a final incident, one for which he now hoped he could finally "rid the College of this turbulent & injurious Member." The incident occurred at a time that threw the disreputable condition of the college into full relief. Beasley had been hoping the students would be inspired to proper behavior because "mutual goodwill & patriotick enthusiasm" had been awakened within the "citizens of this Metropolis" by the "appearance among them of one of their Revolutionary Leaders." At the very time that the Marquis de Lafayette was visiting their city, Peace disrupted class by rolling gunshot from his elevated seat in the recitation room down to the floor below. His intention, of course, was to "awake the merriment of the Class, & thereby interrupt its orderly recitation & renew that scene of confusion which during the last session was so injurious." The disappointed hopes of republican dreams was painfully apparent.

Having related this final incident, Beasley reiterated his general estimation of Peace: "he is a youth not to be subjected to rule, regardless of all authority, & therefore, dangerous in an Institution of learning." The real danger of a student like Peace was that he pulled in others to his disruptive designs: "The young caught the spirit of insubordination & disorder from so bold a leader." It was now up to the board to make "a wholesome example" of Peace by expelling him from the school.[63] The board gave Beasley a less than supportive response. They agreed to allow the faculty to expel Peace, but they gave Peace the opportunity for readmission if he apologized and made assurances regarding future behavior (an opportunity he seized). To a certain extent, Beasley had gotten his way, but his character must have been greatly tarnished in the board's eyes.[64] Joseph Peace had made a fool of him.

After this struggle over Joseph Peace, relations between the board and Beasley continued to sour. The board intervened even more frequently in college governance. In the next three years, two more special committees were formed to investigate the state of the college. The board demanded regular detailed reports from the faculty on the operation of the college, asking, for example, for accurate rolls of attendance so that they might monitor it.[65] Several months after the struggle over Joseph Peace, Beasley almost completely ceased corresponding with the board. Primary responsibility for board communication fell to Professor Patterson, who was forced to act as an intermediary between the warring board and Beasley.

By the end of 1827, the board took decisive steps to oust Beasley. A committee on the "State of the University" definitively recommended his dismissal. It began its report with a familiar refrain about the poor state of the college, suggesting additionally that further decline might result in the school's complete failure: "[it] seems to languish in feebleness and obscurity, and apparently to approach an absolute extinction." In seeking to explain the condition of the college, this report even more fully blamed the professors and provost than had the board in its report of 1824. Primary responsibility fell to Dr. Beasley. The committee reported that "the main and leading cause of the distressing condition" of the school was "an incurable want of confidence in the Capacity of the provost for the government of such an institution." The committee recommended that the board act quickly to address this problem. If it did not, the committee urged, "at no distant period, there will be nothing left of the University of Pennsylvania, but its board of trustees."[66] Six months later, Provost Beasley was dismissed.

When William DeLancey assumed the provostship of the University of Pennsylvania, he expressed a vision for the school that must have struck a familiar chord with anyone who had been connected with the school fifteen years prior. Whether DeLancey drew his ideas from Frederic Beasley is uncertain, but there is no doubting the similarity of their visions. Drafted from the ranks of the board itself, DeLancey, while not a native Philadelphian (he hailed from an eminent New York family), was better positioned to be effective in dealing with the board.[67] Like Beasley before him, DeLancey saw the discipline of the institution as a vital matter. He concluded that student disorder stemmed from a misguided sense of rights and responsibilities: "the youth of our charge, while they strenuously assert the claim to be treated as men, are apt very often to conduct themselves like boys." They would have to be treated accordingly: "The cords of discipline are to be tightened. A close adherence to the rules of the college in respect to diligence, attention, and deportment, will be exacted of every individual." Students were to abandon "all combinations to resist [the school's] authority."[68]

While DeLancey wanted to enhance discipline, he did not call for new measures. Rather, he wished to use the tools that Beasley had fought for but had failed to achieve. DeLancey gained more power for the faculty: "The board of trustees have placed in our hands a larger amount of authority in the discipline of the College, than has hitherto been entrusted to the Faculty."[69] DeLancey gained for the faculty the right to independently dismiss and suspend students—a power they proved quick to exercise.[70] Like Beasley, DeLancey believed that merit ranking could be a useful tool of discipline. He realized that even as he was tightening college discipline he could not turn back the clock to the colonial college. The use of physical discipline was unreasonable. Reporting on his new regimen, he explained that "the means employed by us" are "merely moral," meaning applying only to the mind. Nevertheless, such "moral" measures could be quite effective. The faculty made "appeals to the principles of shame and honour" of the students "by ranking them among their class-mates in an order of merit." Such distinctions emphasized the "honours of successful application" and the "disgrace and infamy of idleness or voluntary ignorance." For DeLancey, like other college leaders, student behavior was a vital component in determining merit: "The principles on which we settle the question of comparative merit are, their scholarship, their punctual attention to their duties in the class-rooms, and their general deportment as students."[71] He created a system of merit rolls that were determined after recitations and examinations, read aloud to classes, and sent home to parents or guardians at the midpoint and end of each school term.[72] Beasley's plans had finally been realized.

Although Beasley's scheme of merit ranking had been instituted at the University of Pennsylvania and was developing elsewhere around the country, one should not assume that this was immediately a triumphant strategy for ordering students. There were initially significant limitations with meritocratic schemes. Grades, ranks, and honors could only be effective if students, parents, and the public at large invested some meaning in them. Provost DeLancey soon learned this lesson. Although initially he had assumed he had parental support, two years into his administration he was condemning parents who "mar our efforts" by exhibiting "indifference" to "college honours and distinctions."[73]

If some parents did not immediately embrace meritocratic measures, neither did their children. Student disorder attended attempts to develop grading and examination systems.[74] For example, student resistance was crucial in defeating what was perhaps the most radical meritocratic scheme attempted at an early nineteenth-century school, Harvard's Law 61 of 1825.[75] Professor George Ticknor's plan to grade student performance and then reorganize classes according to student proficiency, a plan adopted into Harvard's revised code of laws for 1825, was met with much student anger. Less than a week after Harvard's classes had been reorganized into merit groupings, President Kirkland was reporting to the committee of the overseers that "great violence" had been done to both the recitation rooms and the rooms of college officers.[76] Students expressed dissatisfaction by breaking windows with stones and wooden billets. Professor Levi Hedge reported to the committee that students continued to have mutual sympathies for one another, despite the merit-based divisions. The fourth division of the class, by being "taken from their alphabetical places and kept by themselves," developed a "mortifying sense of their inferiority." Yet the other students did not look down on them. Instead, the fourth division gained the "sympathies of the other students," who engaged in "disorders and oppositions" on their behalf.[77] The power of sensibility proved dangerous when serving to bond students.

Even if some students and parents did come to value merit distinctions, they might question a professor's ability to make such judgments fairly or accurately. In fact, problems surrounding the authority to evaluate seem to have had something to do with Frederic Beasley's failed plans of medal distribution. This is suggested in an 1820 letter to the board complaining about the distribution of commencement awards. A parent, who felt his son had been slighted, first admitted the intrinsic value of distinctions that stimulated competition: "I am fully aware that distinctions, properly made, are great excitements to emulation." But if they were done unfairly, the school would suffer: "But when it becomes the practice of the provost to distribute honours for the purpose of gratifying private personal dislike, or of distinguishing favourites, the spirit of emulation will be checked." He reminded the board that Beasley's judgment in this respect had been questioned before: "I am not the first from whom you have had complaints," asking them to recall "the exceptionable manner in which the Medals were distributed in your examination of the Junior Class last winter."[78] It was soon after these exams that the board, who already had been resistant to the medal distribution plan, finally voted to end it for good.[79]

*   *   *

While grading and evaluation systems of various sorts proliferated across the American college scene over the first half of the nineteenth century, they could not prove truly effective until the advent of professionalism in American life in the second half of the century.[80] Until college teachers had gained a clear level of professional autonomy, their ability to judge students fairly or accurately was vulnerable to doubt. Until a college degree became a necessary credential for admittance into the practice of various occupations, students had little to lose in spurning the judgment and rules of college authorities.

The marginal position of colleges in the early American republic made them vulnerable to student revolt. Not only did students seem to have little to lose in disrupting the college order, the very nature of that order itself was largely in question. Assuming their independence from patriarchal authority, and having few distinguishing ranks among one another, students developed strong peer loyalties that obstructed college governance. Certainly such loyalties developed in other eras, but the absence of student hierarchy and the crisis of in loco parentis encouraged their heightened expression during this era. In addition, the precarious position of colleges exaggerated the importance of student disorder. Even at schools untouched by major riots, such as the University of Pennsylvania, where student disorder seemed to never transcend youthful pranks, school authorities became preoccupied with maintaining college order, fearing for their very existence. America's founding fathers had hoped for more for their colleges. Yet the colleges of the early republic would offer something back to American society, a new model of hierarchy. As with the development of the ideals of chastity, fears of youth released from patriarchal authority once again played a central role in the development of bourgeois values. The meritocratic ideals developed in early nineteenth-century colleges would directly touch only a small number of the aspiring bourgeoisie during these years. Colleges were neglected in preference to direct engagement with the market. The meritocratic principles inspired by youthful disorders would later await the middle class when it increasingly patronized colleges, as higher education credentials became a gateway to white-collar and professional occupations. Yet, as we will see in Chapter 5 in exploring notions of the self-made man, the values developed in colleges also had resonance in their own time. As wealth became more unevenly distributed across the American landscape, a justifying ideology was needed for such a seemingly undemocratic phenomenon. Americans could tell themselves that the meritorious deserved to stand atop their society. The self-made man, they insisted, had earned his place.

Harvesting Youth: The Competition for Souls in Early Nineteenth-Century Philadelphia and Beyond

Princeton Seminary professor Archibald Alexander recognized the need for action. If moderate and more conservative Presbyterians were going to hold any sway over the future generation, they were going to have to devise a strategy to beat the disruptive revivalists who catered to the passions of the young and uneducated. Resistant to the fiery preaching style that revivalists used to win converts, ministers of a more orthodox bent needed another way to fill their churches. According to Alexander, Sunday schools could be used to bring youth into their churches. Previously "unknown and uncustomary," the Sunday school system was a new "piece of moral machinery" provided by God to advance his kingdom.[1] As educational institutions, Sunday schools were amenable to training the mind rather than inflaming the passions. Yet ministers could not count on this usage. Alexander urged his orthodox brethren not to remain "indifferent spectator[s] of this powerful system." It would "go forward whether you lend your assistance or not." Alexander insisted that it was ministers' "incumbent duty" to give the Sunday school system their "direction." Established preachers needed to oversee the operation of Sunday schools to ensure "that nothing is inculcated which is contrary to sound doctrine." Sunday schools, as much as camp meetings, were liable to the "spirit of wild fanaticism" that could be "introduced by ignorant zealots."[2]

Alexander was articulating a vision for Sunday schools in 1829 that was already beginning to take hold across the nation. The American Sunday School Union (ASSU), organized in 1824 and centered at the seat of Presbyterian orthodoxy, Philadelphia, was steadily enlisting conservative ministers to its rapidly expanding cause. Youth were given a central place in Sunday schools—not so much as students but as teachers of younger children. By spiritually empowering youth as teachers of the gospel, the managers and ministers supporting the ASSU were making important concessions to a developing religious marketplace that was increasingly oriented to youth.[3] As with college professors who had to struggle against one another for students, conservative ministers were locked in a competition for the attention of youth. In making concessions to youth, they hoped to stave off the more serious disruptions of age hierarchy being encouraged by zealots. According to Alexander, under the careful guidance of pastors, "our intelligent young people" teaching in Sunday schools could actually become "accurate Bible theologians." These "young men and women" would not disrupt pastoral authority. Instead, they would grow into being "useful and respectable members of the church."[4] Such a vision for the role of youth in the church was a relief to those alarmed at how youth had been emboldened by Methodist and New School Presbyterian preachers who were encouraging young adults to preach disruptively in the streets and criticize their seemingly impious elders.

Alexander knew there were those in the emerging Old School party who resisted relinquishing any pastoral prerogatives to lay persons, especially the young. In the eyes of such critics, to take religious instruction out of the hands of ministers, "those to whom, according to the economy of Christ's house it had been regularly committed," was to usurp clerical authority and prestige. While Alexander was quick to concede that the "faithful preaching of the gospel" was the "GREAT MEANS" to spread religious knowledge, he urged his brethren to read the "signs of the times" and support the cause of the American Sunday School Union. Sunday schools were a "wide field for a noble, a holy competition."[5]

Philadelphia has been mostly ignored in narratives of the developing religious culture of the early republic. If lacking in the drama of the revival activity of the Burnt-Over District, it, like other major East Coast cities, may in fact have been considerably more representative of, and its institutions more influential in, the developing religious culture of bourgeois America.[6] While never wholly swept up in revivalism, Philadelphia certainly had its share of revival activity. Not only did Charles Grandison Finney stage a successful year-long campaign in Philadelphia, but the city also had its own homegrown revivalists who had been vigorously at work long before Finney arrived and continued in their labors after he was gone. The emerging Old School Presbyterian party in Philadelphia, which in 1837, along with their allies across the nation, rent their church in two, were intimately aware of the dangers revivalism posed to age hierarchy. Most noticeable was the Reverend James Patterson (Figure 5) who centered his activities

REV^D JAMES PATTERSON, PASTOR

Figure 5. James Patterson. Engraving of 1837 painting by Bass Otis. The energetic Patterson inspired youth with fiery sermons in early nineteenth-century Philadelphia. Courtesy of the Presbyterian Historical Society, Presbyterian Church (U.S.A.) (Philadelphia).

in the Northern Liberties district of Philadelphia. Largely forgotten by historians today, the labors of James Patterson were hard to ignore during his own time. For many years Patterson had been successfully promoting religious revival in his church, across the city, and even further abroad. One of Patterson's greatest preoccupations was the enlistment of youth to his cause of spreading religious enthusiasm. Patterson was quick to invest young adults with spiritual authority, even at the expense of disrupting families. Many a youth was reborn under his persuasive sermons. By spiritually empowering youth, Patterson was mirroring the efforts of preachers within revival-oriented denominations such as the Methodists, as well as those ministers most sympathetic to revivalism within the Presbyterian fold.

Opponents of religious enthusiasm were forced to develop a counter-offensive. Wishing to protect Calvinist orthodoxy, which discountenanced too heavy a reliance on human agency in promoting revivals, but also fearing the depletion of their churches, moderate and conservative Presbyterians, as well as like-minded allies in other denominations, devised strategies to save their churches. Over the course of the 1820s and early 1830s, they embraced Sunday schools. In such institutions they recognized a means to gradually nurture children into future church members, while giving youth a significant role in advancing their cause. The activities of both camps ensured that the rising generation would be a Christian one, whether respectful of their elders or not.

*   *   *

As Charles Finney and his allies in upstate New York were scorching Oneida County with their revivals, conservative and moderate Presbyterian and Congregational ministers along the eastern seaboard listened to incoming reports nervously. Orthodox Philadelphia Presbyterians saw much to dislike in the vigorous means, the so-called New Measures, that Finney and others were using to encourage immediate conversions. Rather than waiting more patiently for God's dispensation of grace, these revivalists were placing potential converts in a spiritual pressure cooker with repeated and highly emotional prayer meetings and services that forced each person to make an immediate choice about the future of his or her soul. Sitting at the seat of Presbyterian hyper-orthodoxy, many Philadelphia ministers and their congregants were disturbed by Finney's theological laxity. The published standard-bearer for Philadelphia Presbyterian orthodoxy was Ashbel Green's *The Christian Advocate*.[7] In reporting on the activities of Finney and

Figure 6. Ashbel Green. Engraving of ca. 1813 painting by Charles Willson Peale. Green was a stalwart opponent of the revivalist New School Presbyterians. Courtesy of the Presbyterian Historical Society, Presbyterian Church (U.S.A.) (Philadelphia).

his allies, Green found a "peculiarly seasonable" indictment of their revivalism in a pastoral letter written by a group of Oneida ministers who opposed the excesses of religious enthusiasm in their midst.[8] Ashbel Green (Figure 6), like his fellow orthodox brethren, was not entirely an enemy to revivals. In fact, Green himself had quite famously used a religious revival to battle student disorder and infidelity at Princeton College while he was president there in the second decade of the nineteenth century.[9] Yet Green had specific ideas about what a proper revival looked like. It did not resemble the extravagant enthusiasms he was hearing about in northern New York.

Green roundly endorsed the pastoral letter of the ministers of the "Oneida Association," finding the "whole letter" to be "excellent." Green said he and his spiritual brethren had been planning soon to make a statement on the recent developments in the Presbyterian Church and found in this letter "nearly all that we wished to say." He decided to publish the lengthy piece in its entirety in two installments, finding it difficult to make choices about excision, with each part appearing "as good as another."[10] Much of this pastoral address was concerned with the extravagances the revivalists had encouraged in youth.

According to these ministers, Finney and his allies had handled youth unwisely by not cooling their religious ardor following conversion. There was "great danger" in failing to calm their passions. Spiritually reborn youth seemed to adopt a stance of righteousness, failing to yet discover their "ignorance and imperfections." Filled with a "high conceit of themselves," these converts were apt to "shut their minds against the cautions and counsels of their fathers." Revivalist preachers only worsened this problem by actually encouraging youth in their spiritual self-confidence by telling them "how *well* they appear" and by making "comparisons between them and old Christians to the disadvantage of the latter." Even more disturbingly, revivalists encouraged disrespectful language by "young men and boys" toward ministers and parents. The Oneida pastors listed examples of some of the taunts they heard from zealous youth: "'You old, grey headed sinner, you deserved to have been in hell long ago,'" "'this old hypocrite,'" "'that old apostate,'" and "'that old veteran servant of the devil.'" These ministers wanted newly converted youth to be "humble" and "teachable," not disposed to "despise the admonitions of age and experience."[11] This directive to calm the passions of youth was consistent with a larger orthodox philosophy that emphasized education over enthusiasm. These ministers regarded it as a "dark sign" when converts think "they *know enough*, and have no need to be taught." In their view the church was at risk when "*feeling* is substituted for *thought*."[12]

The indulgence of youthful pride was manifested in a number of specific religious practices deployed by the revivalists. Most disturbing to the Oneida pastors was the way revivalists encouraged both young men and women to come forward and assume a "prominent place" in the prayer meetings used to promote revivals. In "promiscuous meetings" newly converted male and female youth, as well as women of older ages, were being given the opportunity to give spiritual testimony of their conversions and to lead in prayer. The "pillars of the church" were thrown into the background while the young assumed center stage. While certainly the young "should be trained to activity and usefulness," they needed to remain in a position of "subordination to superiors." These pastors thought it "safest" if a pastor, or in his absence, church elders, take direction of all such meetings. They alone should determine who could "speak and pray" before others.[13] The improperly guided meetings had been liable to extravagances of all sorts. At group prayer meetings and church services participants had indulged in such extravagances as *"Loud groaning, speaking out, or falling down."* In failing to be more careful in discriminating between *"true religion and false,"* revivalists had allowed "animal passions" and "selfish affection" to be "excited." The potential long-term costs to the church were great in the pastors' view. Those who were attracted to the revival meetings of itinerant preachers would no longer take their own local pastors seriously: "We think there is danger of despising those means of grace which we have at home." In addition, respectable folk would be turned off from religion entirely by witnessing the disorderly scenes of enthusiasm. "True religion" would be cast into "contempt." Potential church members would "throw away the good with the bad."[14]

Ashbel Green was no stranger to the scenes the Oneida pastors were describing. Philadelphia Presbyterians had witnessed the disruptions of revivalism in the activities of their own James Patterson.[15] Since 1814 Patterson had been busy building his church in the Northern Liberties district of Philadelphia. His tremendous success was hard to deny. Starting with 53 original communicants in 1814, by the time Green had published the "Pastoral Letter" in 1827, Patterson's church was by far the largest church in Philadelphia and one of the largest churches in all of America, claiming about 1,000 communicants.[16]

Members of the Philadelphia Presbytery probably supposed that James Patterson had solid orthodox credentials when he originally arrived in the city. He had spent two years in theological training at Princeton under Samuel Stanhope Smith. In his first settled position as a pastor in Bound Brook, New Jersey, Patterson reportedly had a more traditional approach to preaching. He grew dissatisfied, however, with the infrequency of conversions in his church. Patterson was filled with the ardor of one who had been dramatically converted to his faith, not slowly nurtured within the church. Following his conversion as a youth, he prophetically disobeyed the wishes of his father by choosing to train for the ministry, rather than taking over the family's modest farm in Bucks County, Pennsylvania. Now in his first pastorate, Patterson was not content preaching pleasing sermons to a self-satisfied congregation. He turned to more "simplicity and directness" in his pulpit addresses.[17] While offending some of his pastorate, with whom he soon had a falling out, his adopted approach may have recommended him as an appropriate preacher for the newly created church in Northern Liberties. This district contained a large portion of working-class citizens. Using the "simplest, strongest, most sinewy, most thoroughly Saxon forms of speech," Patterson was likely to be well understood by the audiences he would draw there.[18]

In his new pastorate Patterson became renowned for his passionate and fiery preaching style. One memorialist likened him to "an old prophet of Israel risen from the dead" who had come "to warn the wicked to flee the wrath to come." Eschewing the Presbyterian custom of preparing written sermons, Patterson often preached spontaneously, using skeletal outlines at most.[19] Reflecting on his time with Patterson, Charles Finney recalled that the Northern Liberties pastor would "preach with the tears rolling down his cheeks, and with an earnestness and pathos that was very striking." He was also known to inspire the same emotions in his audience. Reverend Daniel Carroll recalled that Patterson sometimes inspired all his listeners to be "melted into tears," a result he supposed owing to Patterson's adeptness at "*adapting* his instructions to the *character* and *capacities* of his hearers."[20]

Patterson also took the gospel out of his church and into the streets and fields. Early in his ministry Patterson discovered that some of the most impoverished citizens in his district would not come into his church on Sundays. Many of them spent the day relaxing in open fields nearby. In the summer of 1816 Patterson initiated the practice of preaching sermons in the fields to reach the unchurched. He would continue to do this in subsequent summers. He also tirelessly traveled door to door, making home visitations in neighborhoods in and around Northern Liberties. In addition, the pastor traveled farther afield to reach new audiences. Patterson made frequent distant trips to spread the gospel, being called to numerous "protracted meetings" in locations like Washington, D.C., traveling into the purportedly heathenish German counties of Pennsylvania, and even once taking a trip through the West along the Mississippi River. Apparently for a while Patterson contemplated a career like Finney as an itinerant, but after considering the needs of his family, decided to remain with his congregation.[21]

Amid his congregation Patterson worked continuously to fan revival flames. He asked the congregation to fast and pray for revivals. Once such seasons began he held daily services, one time holding meetings for almost ninety days straight. Patterson encouraged his congregation to follow his example. He stressed to them the "importance of being up and doing." Patterson sent his congregants into the streets to warn the "careless" of the "danger" of neglecting worship. In general, Patterson wanted his congregants to "cooperate" with him "in the conversion of sinners, and in advancing the cause of truth." This use of "lay preaching," as it came to be known, rankled many Presbyterian ministers in the city. They considered it a "trespass upon the rights of the clergy."[22] Patterson became a focus of the emerging Old School party's resentment, but he was not an easy target. Unlike Albert Barnes, whose 1830 Philadelphia trial for heresy would be a key event in the schism of the Presbyterian church, Patterson was uninterested in articulating a theological philosophy to support his vigorous Christian activism.[23]

Nonetheless, Patterson did become loose with his Calvinism, and his embrace of religious enthusiasm and promotion of lay activity brought vigorous criticism down upon him. After growing frustrated with heated presbytery meetings, Patterson and his allies Reverends J. P. Wilson and Thomas Skinner, petitioned the Philadelphia Presbytery for a formation of a new presbytery in 1826. In his personal journal Patterson noted that their aim was to "promote peace" by gathering in seclusion those members who were not "suspicious of revivals of religion, and of the men who endevour to promote them."[24] Peace would not be theirs. Although Patterson and the rest of the developing New School party in Philadelphia eventually got their own presbytery in 1832, strife continued to rivet the denomination as a whole.

Assuredly irksome to the Old School party was Patterson's vigorous enlistment of youth to his brand of Christian enthusiasm. Both in his revivals and in his encouragement of lay preaching, Patterson concentrated his greatest energies on the young. The fullest surviving record of Patterson's embrace of youth is Robert Adair's *Memoir of Reverend James Patterson.* Because any discussion of Patterson's ministry must rely heavily upon this book, it is important to analyze it critically. Started soon after Patterson's death at age fifty-eight in 1837, but interrupted by the death of its first author, the *Memoir* when it appeared in 1840 was written in the spirit of a defense of the New School, formally organized as a denomination two years prior. Dying shortly after the Old School had moved to divide the denomination by abrogating the Plan of Union at the General Assembly of 1837, Patterson seemed almost a martyr to the New School cause.[25] Mostly a biography written by Adair, interspersed with frequent passages from a journal kept by Patterson, the *Memoir* is also filled with numerous testimonials. Adair and the other contributors to the *Memoir* had an interest in defending Patterson's theology and in downplaying any extravagances that might have pertained to his ministry. The emerging bourgeois constituency of the New School gave additional incentive to portray Patterson's revivals as exhibiting proper decorum.[26] Yet these men also believed Patterson had died for a noble cause. Thus there was a counterbalancing interest in demonstrating the fervency of Patterson's piety and his commitment to revivalism. Such strong faith would prove itself in overcoming opposition. Emerging throughout the *Memoir* is a picture of a man intent on rousing youth against those that might oppose them in their desire to serve God.

James Patterson's revivals had a special hold on the young. Adair notes that in Patterson's first major revival in 1816, youth were the bulk of those reborn. On one particular evening when seventy new members were admitted into the church, most of the new communicants were between the ages of thirteen and twenty. Only four of the seventy were above the age of thirty. This pattern characterized this revival season as a whole. Patterson wrote in his journal that he knew of only one "old person awakened in all this revival." This season of grace lasted for seven months and added 180 new members to Patterson's church, as well as swelling church membership across the city.[27] Patterson's success was conspicuous, especially so because of the scenes of enthusiasm associated with the services.

In ushering young men and women into his congregation, Patterson caused familial strife. A Miss "C. W.," a woman who had cried out "in great distress, and swooned away" at a service, was soon after paid a visit by Reverend Patterson. He notes in his journal that she complained to him about being "persecuted by her parents." She also confided to him that she was "tempted sometimes to leave her father's house, not caring what may become of her." The specific advice Patterson gave in this instance is lost, but the woman related to him two nights later that after spending a "night in prayer" she had become "enabled to bear reproach and suffering for Christ."[28] While Patterson does not appear to have encouraged this woman to leave her parents, neither does he seem to have been willing to tell her to forsake Christ in deference to their wishes. Evidently, her turn to fervent Christianity was causing dissension in the household.

The familial tensions Patterson encouraged are even clearer in other journal entries. In one instance the "daughter of a Unitarian" came to his church out of "curiosity" so that she might "see for herself the things she had heard of by rumour." Patterson writes that, once she was there, it "pleased the Holy Spirit to convince her of the sinfulness of her heart." This young woman's mother noticed her daughter's "anguish" and called on a Unitarian preacher to give her "needful counsel." Patterson records that the mother soon after "forbade" her daughter from "coming to our meeting," but such was the young woman's "anxiety on the subject of religion, that she disregarded this prohibition." Robert Adair especially relished this instance of Patterson encouraging youthful rebellion because it came at a loss to the Unitarians, an important victory that no Old School critic could deny. He took the opportunity of this case to make the "painful reflection" that there are "parents, and even those who profess to be ministers of Christ" who would "stand in the way of sinners" and "attempt to prevent them from entering the kingdom of heaven."[29]

The rebellious behavior Patterson was encouraging was not necessarily a call to the young to stake a claim for freedom. Rather, youth were being told to place duty to Christ over duty to familial authority. The result, however, was often the same when parents belonged to churches other than Patterson's or no church at all. Adair unconvincingly downplays the revivalist's subversive potential in reference to a case of an "interesting young lady" recorded by Patterson. The pastor noted in his journal that "father and mother united to keep their daughter from the meetings." The daughter defiantly informed her mother that she "'must forsake all for Christ.'" Even though facing "chastisement from her father" and threats of "being cast out of his house," the young woman "after prayer and reflection" decided to "unite with the church, leaving the consequences with God." This woman's angry father then "decided to put his threat into execution," but luckily a "pious relation" was "providentially" at their home and managed to restrain "his wrath." Commenting on this incident, Adair draws a moral for the reader, suggesting it was the performance of duty for which this young woman was rewarded: "The path of duty is always the path of safety. Though the portentous cloud may, at times terrify the obedient disciple, God will be his sun and shield." If, in fact, this was simply an instance of a young woman doing her spiritual duty, it still came at the cost of defying her parents' wishes.[30]

Patterson was willing to castigate the old in front of youthful audiences. In a journal entry relating to a field service in the summer of 1828, Patterson relates that in "affectionately" addressing the youth gathered there, he "told them that it seemed as though nothing could be done with the aged, and that the only hope was the young." Patterson boldly delivered this message in the midst of older folk who "then stood around me, hardened in sin and ripening for wo[e]."[31] Perhaps his aim here was to shame the elders into following the pious example set for them by the young. This approach likely only steeled the resistance of the aged.

Patterson's ministry disturbed workplace hierarchies, as well as those at home. At least one employer had the youth under his charge emboldened by the pastor. In a journal entry from June of 1818, Patterson recorded that "R. M., an apprentice, about fourteen years of age" had been attending his religious meetings and had fallen under "deep conviction." This male youth informed Patterson that his master, a baker, had forbidden him to leave his workplace on Sunday. In addition, the youth was "threatened with punishment" if he tried to remain up at night to "read and pray." This master also "forbade" the boy to "read the New Testament," telling him that 'it will fill your head with foolish freaks.'" Patterson in response subversively instructed the youth to "be much engaged in prayer, and in reading the scriptures" and to "commit his case to God." The challenge Patterson was encouraging was all the greater; taking a shot at the leading lights of the city, Robert Adair noted: "It will scarcely be credited, but so it is, this master was a prominent member in one of the churches in this city!"[32]

Patterson not only encouraged youth to perform private devotion and attend public service, but also called on the "young convert" to be "*actively* engaged in the cause of the Redeemer." The pastor vigorously pressed youth to engage in "lay preaching" of various forms. Adair suggests that prior to Patterson's arrival in Philadelphia, ministers considered it "injudicious to introduce the young man" into promoting religion no matter "how pious and humble" because the "modesty becoming a young Christian would dictate that he take no part in these services." While Adair might have exaggerated former restrictions on the young in the Presbyterian Church, it is nonetheless clear that the pastor took things too far for the comfort of his Presbyterian brethren. As discussed above, Patterson found himself in the midst of a controversy surrounding his employment of "lay preaching."[33]

In addition to calling on the young to lead in prayer, Patterson sent young converts to make home visits and engage in acts of Christian benevolence. Ironically, one of the schemes of benevolence Patterson encouraged was the institution of Sunday schools. In 1815 Patterson urged a group of young women to establish the first evangelical Sunday school in the city: the Union Sabbath School Association of Northern Liberties. By 1819 there were already five such schools being directed by 55 teachers, instructing over 650 students.[34] Prior to this, there had been Sunday schools, but they were not based on an evangelical model. The first Sunday school society to appear in Philadelphia had been the First Day Society. Organized by Benjamin Rush and others in 1791, its schools differed markedly from the much more popular evangelical Sunday schools that would rapidly spread across Philadelphia and the rest of the country in the early decades of the nineteenth century. Evangelical schools differed in at least two important respects: they were taught by lay volunteers, not paid teachers, and their instructions concentrated more on inculcating religion and producing conversion, and less on basic reading and writing skills.[35] While moderate and conservative Presbyterians would soon warm to the new Sunday school scheme, recognizing its potential for battling the revivalists, for Patterson and other revival-friendly ministers, Sunday schools were simply one weapon in a wider arsenal for evangelizing the city.

In calling on young women, in particular, to lead Sunday school instruction in his district, Patterson was anticipating a wider trend that would characterize evangelical religion in Philadelphia and beyond. Bruce Dorsey has shown that women were more numerous and active than men in evangelical benevolent organizations in antebellum Philadelphia. This greater participation owed something to the fact that women predominated in the membership rolls of Philadelphia's revival-oriented churches.[36] There is not much information available about how Patterson may have treated male and female youth differently. Because communicant lists do not survive from after the start of Patterson's ministry, we cannot know if he was more successful in converting young females than young men. Anecdotally, at least, it seems that way. Religious choice may have resonated more with young women because they were cut off from some of the expanding opportunities enjoyed by young men. Patterson did notice the feminizing trend in revival religion and acted to redress it. In one large citywide revival in which the pastor participated in 1831, he took particular notice that women were overcrowding his church, leaving little room for "impenitent males." Patterson and the other ministers involved decided to hold a special service for male youth. In newspapers and in handbills they advertised that "a sermon would be preached with special reference to young men, *not professors of religion*; and that the lower part of the church would be reserved for them." Patterson happily reported that the idea was a great success, with the bottom of the church "filled to overflowing, aisles and every part of it, with young men, apparently in the very vigour of life." Nearly one thousand young men packed into the church for the service.[37]

A summary view of James Patterson's ministry suggests that his brand of religious revivalism had important implications for age hierarchy in Philadelphia. Patterson encouraged the young to embrace revival religion, even when it violated the wishes of their elders and disrupted their families. In addition, the pastor urged young converts to evangelize the city through prayer meetings, home visits, and benevolent activity. Patterson faced heated criticism from more conservative quarters in the Philadelphia Presbytery for his evangelical endeavors. When refused his petition to form a separate presbytery in 1826, Patterson searched for more allies to strengthen his cause. There was one obvious candidate, who was gaining notoriety in northern New York.[38]

In April of 1827 James Patterson began to call on Charles Grandison Finney to come to Philadelphia, a call Finney answered in January of 1828. Patterson had missed an earlier opportunity to meet with Finney in July of 1827. Patterson had been invited to the now-famous conference in New Lebanon where Finney squared off against Lyman Beecher. Patterson and his Philadelphia revivalist ally Thomas Skinner both declined the invitations proffered to them, perhaps to avoid further inflaming recently heated tempers.[39] While the memory of this convention now centers around Lyman Beecher's threat to crush Finney and his extravagances, observers at the time would have recognized that nearly everyone involved was more sympathetic to revivalism and too liberal in their theology for the comfort of the Old School party in Philadelphia.[40] Getting Finney to come to town, however, was one way Patterson could circumvent Old School ministers by appealing directly to the people who would flock to see him.

When Charles Finney arrived in Philadelphia the conservative faction fell strangely silent. Both Finney and Patterson were confused by this. Finney noted in his *Memoirs* that he found it a "remarkable thing" that his "orthodoxy" was "not called in question by any of the ministers" in town. He noted as well that "Brother Patterson was himself, I believe, greatly surprized that I met with no open opposition."[41] The silence must have been especially surprising because Ashbel Green had already taken shots at Finney. In addition to reprinting and heartily endorsing the sharply critical "Pastoral Letter" from the Oneida ministers six months before Finney arrived in Philadelphia, Green had attacked Finney a second time in his journal just a month before Finney landed. While Finney was preaching nearby in Wilmington, Delaware, Green rebuked Finney for his theology and for the "extravagances" of his revivals, which Green likened to the enthusiasms of Cane Ridge. Green's critique fronted a republication of Asahel Nettleton's negative review of Finney and his "New Measures."[42] Following this multipronged attack on Finney, however, the Old School muted their voices.

The silence of the Old School party upon Finney's arrival in January might in part be explained by the fact that Finney was beginning to temper his revivalism, cultivating more of a bourgeois constituency, and was therefore less likely to offend.[43] Yet their reticence was most likely a deliberate strategy. There was growing cause for silence. The conservative faction was beginning to realize that the charge of cold formalism they had been suffering would stick all the more to them if they continued to openly criticize revival activity.[44] There is some evidence of a deliberate decision to withhold criticism in correspondence written by Lyman Beecher while in Philadelphia at the General Assembly meeting in May of 1828. When Finney arrived in Philadelphia, his enemy Reverend Asahel Nettleton of Connecticut positioned himself in New York and began to publish criticisms of Finney and send them into Philadelphia. In May of 1828 Lyman Beecher wrote to Nettleton asking him to forestall such publications, saying that he had discovered when conferring with other ministers that "the opinion of everyone is to forbear farther [sic] publication, if possible." There was growing sentiment that by keeping such controversy before the "public mind" the cause of religion would be hurt to the detriment of all parties.[45] Beecher negotiated a formal cease-fire with Finney. While no Philadelphia ministers signed this published agreement between Beecher and his Eastern allies and Finney and his upstate New York revivalist friends, they did seem to see the merit in observing it.[46] Controversy would soon resume in the Presbyterian church, but future antirevivalist attacks moved more squarely onto the grounds of theology, perhaps an arena perceived as less likely to pique public interest.

Charles Finney seemed to enjoy considerable success in Philadelphia, although not the type of sweeping success he would have in places like Rochester.[47] Finney would later comment in reference to his Philadelphia labors that in a "great city," unlike a smaller town, one "cannot estimate the greatness of the revival" even if "converts may be greatly multiplied" because one cannot be "acquainted with all the inhabitants."[48] Nonetheless, Finney preached to packed churches throughout his visit and was pleased with his success. Finney first preached for a few months in Patterson's church. He then spent most of the remainder of his time preaching in the German Reformed Church on Race Street, the church reported to have the greatest seating capacity in the city.[49] Patterson's church rolls swelled by 119 during the time Finney was with him. While Finney was at the centrally located Race Street church, the pastor there claimed to witness "some hundreds" converted to religion, swelling churches in various denominations across the city.[50]

Finney extended patterns well established by Patterson by cultivating a following among youth and encouraging youth rebellion. Importantly, he won an audience with Sunday school teachers in particular. Finney noted in his *Memoirs* that Sunday school teachers flocked to his Philadelphia meetings. Confirming this impression is a letter received by Finney from a Philadelphia correspondent who informed Finney that he was certain "that the great body of the pious youth, comprehending Sabbath School teachers, are pleased with your labors: and with that kind of preaching which is called *revival* preaching." The teachers were inspired to hold large prayer meetings together. Shortly before Finney left Philadelphia, they gathered for a concert of prayer, which was reported to have had between 700 and 800 in attendance. A few weeks later an estimated 1000 teachers participated in a "Teacher's Fast Day" meeting.[51] Finney, like Patterson, encouraged youth to challenge their elders. In his *Memoirs* he records two different instances of encouraging religious boldness in female youth. Finney recalls his conversion of "the daughter of a Baptist minister of the Old School stamp." In his successful effort to convert this young woman, Finney worked to show her how "the instructions of her father" had been "entirely wrong." Finney convinced another "young lady" of the sinfulness of her finery. This young woman then felt compelled to approach a "very richly dressed lady" in the street in order to convince her of her vanity. Finney highly praised this young woman for her courage.[52]

While Ashbel Green and his Old School allies saw fit to take Presbyterian controversy indoors in the form of heresy trials and to concentrate their rebukes of Finney and New School men on theological grounds, Green did indirectly criticize Presbyterian revival activity again not long after Finney left Philadelphia. It is worth considering this attack, for it helps us to understand the problems Old School men and moderates would try to solve with Sunday schools. This attack was a letter in six installments in *The Christian Advocate* entitled "Practical Methodism," published in 1830 and 1831.[53] Like the "Pastoral Letter" earlier, this publication noted the disruptions to age relations caused by revivalism. Purportedly written by a New England correspondent, this series of letters did have much to say about American Methodism and its practitioners. The writer criticized Methodists' Arminian theology, and even more so their enthusiastic and confrontational worship style. Methodist revival activity had flowed from the West back East during the early nineteenth century, taking the form of camp meetings not far outside Philadelphia. Revivalism was also beginning to take hold in Philadelphia's Methodist churches.[54] The excesses of the

Methodists were certainly cause for alarm for Green and the Old School party. Just as importantly, this series was intended to be a critique of New School revivalists who seemed to copy the Methodists in their own activities. Green did not fail to explicitly draw this connection.

Historians have shown that Methodists developed a religious style that empowered youth. Encouraging early conversions, freedom to speak at religious gatherings, and a quick promotion into the ministry, the Methodists readily involved the young in their religious practices.[55] Recognizing these tendencies, Green's anonymous correspondent condemned Methodists for catering to youth. By relying on camp meeting revivals, he insisted, Methodists admitted youth into the church without true religion. To make matters worse, they boldly conscripted members raised in other denominations. Green's correspondent related a tale of a circuit rider that heard of religious stirrings among the youth of a town and rode in to gather them to the Methodist fold. This he did, even though "they were, nearly to an individual, the children of parents attached to other denominations." He bemoaned the fact that Methodists found "*little value*" in "*Christian instruction*," regretting the passing of a time when "the labouring oar of ministerial duty was the instruction of the rising generation." In those days "none were admitted to the church, without a knowledge of its doctrines and duties." In its place had arisen a system in which "a person professes conversion to-day, and is admitted to the communion to-morrow."[56] Faced with such disregard for Christian teaching, the need for Sunday schools directed by credible ministers was manifest.

Most disturbing about the spread of Methodism was the influence it was having on ministers of other denominations who were pressured into copying it. Green's correspondent noted how the Methodists' "example" was "exerting a deleterious influence on other portions of the church." Ministers in "other denominations" in order to "prevent their adherents from becoming Methodists, 'where they can get religion so easy,'" admit persons to membership "before the consent of enlightened piety and judgment would pronounce them qualified." If Presbyterians were pressured into copying the Methodists, Green had no sympathy for those who would capitulate. To imagined New School readers, he wished to state "explicitly" that "if any of the means for making proselytes" employed by Methodists were "used or countenanced in any part of the Presbyterian church," he "denounces them as unchristian." In fact, such an approach by a Presbyterian was "even more censurable," because it differed so sharply from the "doctrines, and order, and usages of the Presbyterian church."[57]

The criticisms Green aired in *The Christian Advocate* were not Old School Presbyterian sentiments alone. Conservative factions in a number of denominations shared in his antipathy toward religious enthusiasm. Especially close allies for Old School Presbyterians in Philadelphia, despite important theological differences, were the High Church Episcopalians. The bishop of the Episcopalian Church in Pennsylvania, William White, preached ideas strikingly consonant with those of Ashbel Green. Not surprisingly, he was also a supporter of Sunday schools, serving for many years as head of the traditional First Day Society in Philadelphia. In 1832, following a year in which James Patterson and revivalists across denominational lines promoted a city-wide revival, White delivered a charge to the Diocese of Pennsylvania on the topic of revivals. Mirroring the commentary of conservative Presbyterians, White delivered a High Church condemnation of Low Church empowerment of the young.

Bishop White held the prioritizing of emotion over studied piety to be a dangerous form of pandering to youthful passions. In describing the effects of revival seasons, White concentrated on the dangers of letting loose "the power of sympathy." In religious gatherings, under revival influence, participants experienced "extreme excitements of mind" and "violent agitations" of the body. The "nervous part of the system" was roused into dangerous action. Revivalists mistakenly read a state of aroused "animal sensibility" as a "test of grace." No longer the mark of a feeling soul, sensibility here is a dangerous propensity to guard against. White insisted that the "influence of the Holy Spirit" could only be read in a "settled habit of the affections."[58] According to White, religious devotion was to be steadily nurtured, not violently excited. He insisted that passions could move in unforeseen directions. The unpredictability of the emotions explained why "so many young persons" after experiencing "enthusiastic fervours" underwent "sudden transitions, not always stopping short of deviation from morality." He was alluding here to the charge of sexual transgression that had been attached to revival religion since at least the First Great Awakening. In the early nineteenth century, unguided camp meetings, in particular, were feared as sites of seduction.[59]

White believed that the most regrettable feeling generated in youth by revivals was a spirit of righteousness. He found it a telltale sign of the disorderly nature of recent revivals that "young persons" under their influence "arrogate to themselves a degree of authority scarcely due to their seniors." Prideful youth had the "desire of being thought teachers" when they had hardly had time to "establish the character of learners." According to

White, a "truly Scriptural Revival" would be characterized by the "humility of the persons visited by it." Lay preaching was one form of such arrogation of religious authority. White censured prayer gatherings in which converts disclosed "their spiritual states" and narrated experiences that "should remain in secret." To White, giving spiritual testimony at prayer gatherings was simply "another form of the fault of praying at the corners of streets." Both revealed "self-exaltation" and "ambition."[60] Thus, for White, as for the more conservative ministers in the Presbyterian Church, revivals were dangerous because they were liable to disrupt hierarchies, particularly those of age and learning.

*   *   *

Facing the baleful influences of revivalists who swelled their churches with young converts, moderate and conservative religionists searched for some means to fill their churches without endangering their orthodoxy. Initially bristling at Sunday schools because they were dominated by laymen, moderate and conservative ministers began to see the potential benefits of this evangelical institution. Conservative and moderate preachers were actually in some measure predisposed to the Sunday school scheme because they valued religious teaching over enthusiasm. This would become truer as they embraced the notion of nurturing young children in religion. Especially when facing the disruptions of dramatic conversions, these conservative spokesmen stressed religious nurture as an alternative means to enter the church.

The warming of religious conservatives to Sunday school nurturance is revealed in some comments of Ashbel Green in *The Christian Advocate*. When Green published Asahel Nettleton's critique of Finney, he prefaced Nettleton's review with a discussion of the various paths to conversion. Green recommended gradual religious nurture most highly. He treated quick renovations of an individual's heart with caution, while he viewed mass revival seasons with skepticism. After making the necessary prefatory remarks about the Holy Spirit being the sole agent of rebirth, Green stressed the role of parents in nurturing conversion. According to Green, when children of "pious parents" are baptized into the church and then "from the first openings of their intellectual and moral powers" are "carefully, tenderly, prudently, prayerfully, and perseveringly brought under the influence of sacred truth and Christian discipline," the effect would be a "*sound conversion.*" Such conversions could happen at a "very early age" and ordinarily "take place without any great convulsion of the soul." In fact, the conversion is "so silent and seemingly gradual, that its date cannot be accurately ascertained." Reflecting how far the Old School itself had drifted from the Calvinist tradition of the past, Green suggested that such growth into regeneration was not at all dubious but rather the most trustworthy of conversions. From "conversions of this kind" had been produced "some of the brightest examples of unquestionable Christian piety that have ever adorned the church."[61]

If not explicitly a refutation of Calvinist orthodoxy like the "New Measures" and Arminian theology of Finney, Green's emphasis on nurture did subtly challenge the traditional Calvinist view of children as unregenerate.[62] Green was in essence recommending Lockean nurture over evangelical breaking of the child's will. He was not simply reflecting larger transformations in views of children prevalent within American society; in some measure he had been forced into this view. How had an Old School die-hard like Ashbel Green come to recommend nurturance into conversion so strongly? This becomes most clear in another article he published. Revealingly, this piece immediately followed the first installment of the Oneida "Pastoral Letter" that detailed the disruptions in age hierarchy attending revival seasons.

In "The Christian Education of Children" Green's writer advises parents to guard "against severity on the one hand, and indulgence on the other." The emphasis of the article was its caution against the former, not the latter. The goal was to ensure that children would grow up to be "practical Christians," that is, adults who would feel Christianity as a set of habits and as an inclination in their hearts. In warning against severity, the writer explicitly outlined its costs. The "natural" outcome would be to "excite" in the minds of children "such anger, indignation and bitterness as are not only sinful, but very apt to break out at last into acts of resentment and rebellion against the parents themselves." In fact, if children are corrected "in anger," they might be inclined to view themselves as more morally upright than their parents. Harsh treatment could become the "means of giving them, ultimately, an ascendancy over the erring parent." In place of hard usage, the writer recommended that the parent "unite familiarity with dignity." Parents were to be "free" with their children. Parents were to win the "confidence and affection" of their children, to make them "companions." Overall, "much indulgence, tenderness, and forgiveness" were to be "mingled with the discipline of children," if parents wished to "not provoke them to wrath."[63] To see a conservative periodical like *The Christian Advo-*

cate offer advice like this suggests that Lockean pedagogy had made serious headway in American culture. This article also reveals a palpable concern about the power of youth. Green's writer was advocating that parents stave off rebellion in youth by winning children's affection when they were still young.

Sunday schools came to be seen as a critical support for both parents and ministers in raising respectful children. While Sunday schools were initially conceived as a means to reach children of unfit parents, they were quickly repackaged as a helpful support for the godly.[64] Old School theologian Archibald Alexander explained how Sunday schools could be of assistance to even the most faithful of parents. Alexander pointed out that children were likely to be "more attentive to lessons of morality and religion coming from others, than to those which they learn from their own parents." From parents, children necessarily would from time to time receive "advice and reproof" and were therefore likely to "contract a habit of heedlessness when admonished by them." But when instruction came from one "who claims no authority but that which is founded on kindness," children would be "mute with attention" and would be "tenderly affected" by "what they hear from their beloved Sunday-school teachers."[65] The tensions and emotional strains that would arise between parents and children could prove to be an obstacle to bringing children into the church. Teachers could help circumvent this. To avoid family strife, parents could look to the support of Sunday schools.

If Sunday schools could help parents in raising respectful and pious children, they were potentially of even greater benefit to ministers. Pastors, like parents, could win the affection of children before they became rebellious youth. Reverend Isaac Ferris, speaking on behalf of the American Sunday School Union at their annual gathering in 1834, pointed out to his intended audience of ministers how they could lay "the foundation for usefulness" in youth by "securing early their affection and confidence." If ministers became involved in Sunday schools, they would not have to approach the young from an "awful distance." Instead, every passing year would witness an increase in feeling. Youth would learn that "their minister loves them, and is their best friend." Ferris said that by forming a bond with children one could avert the dangers of youth. When "they cease to think of themselves as children, and are passing into manhood and womanhood," the minister could rest assured that they would be "saved from the vortex ready to swallow them" because he had achieved such "a hold on their affections." Thus Sunday schools represented an important strategy of prevention. Youth would not fall to temptation or rebel against their elders if properly nurtured in Sunday schools.[66]

Prevention, however, was not the only means by which Sunday schools could address problems presented by youth. As spokespeople and leaders in the Sunday school movement began to articulate a vision for the developing far-flung network of schools, youth assumed an ever more central position in their vision. As teachers, youth in Sunday schools became simultaneously instructors of the gospel and the subjects of ministerial guidance. Youth were vital because they represented the future of the church.[67] By giving youth an important, if supervised, role in their churches, religious moderates and conservatives could avert the depletion of their churches while also preventing the serious disruptions to age hierarchy encouraged by enthusiastic revivalists.

Philadelphia was both the organizational center of the American Sunday School Union and one of the sites of its greatest popularity. The ASSU had been built on a groundswell of support for Sunday schools in Philadelphia and across the country. In 1824 the Philadelphia Sunday and Adult School Union renamed and officially reorganized into the national society it had already started to become. The Sunday school movement in Philadelphia continued to grow under the auspices of the ASSU. By 1832 almost 12,000 Philadelphia children, close to 30 percent of all school-age children, were enrolled in ASSU-affiliated Sunday schools. While the national rates never reached the dramatic heights of Philadelphia, the rapid expansion of ASSU schools was nonetheless impressive. With only 1.4 percent of eligible children in ASSU schools in 1824, by 1832 the national percentage had grown to about 8 percent.[68]

Support for Sunday schools was strongest of all within Philadelphia's Presbyterian churches.[69] The solutions that the Sunday school movement offered to problems with age and authority that plagued ministers in Philadelphia and across the country undoubtedly proved part of its attraction. The appeal was not for conservative ministers alone. In fact, many New School Presbyterians were nearly as uncomfortable with the extravagances of religious enthusiasm as men in the Old School camp. Perhaps even a majority of Philadelphia ASSU members sided with the New School when the church split.[70] These were not New School men of the Patterson stamp. Cultivating a bourgeois audience and promoting only respectable revivals, moderate New School preachers also sought orderly means for bringing youth into service for their churches.[71] These religious moderates, along with numerous conservative spokesmen, re-envisioned Sunday schools in a manner that had a broad appeal.

Sunday schools proved to be an arena where the New and Old School could achieve more agreement than within their own church polity. In an effort to win more orthodox brethren to the Sunday school cause, advocates of the American Sunday School Union stressed the circumscribed nature of youth's authority in the operation of Sunday schools. In published annual sermons, in topical addresses, and in periodicals and annual reports, advocates of the ASSU sketched a picture of Sunday schools as appendages to denominational churches. This emergent vision for Sunday schools, taking hold in the 1820s and '30s, departed from the spirit of the earliest evangelical Sunday schools encouraged by men like Patterson. Sunday schools were less often conceived as evangelizing outposts to stir revival seasons, and more often as supports for keeping children of the godly within the church fold. Only for areas decidedly in the hands of particularly suspect denominations, such as the Methodist stronghold of the Mississippi Valley, were Sunday schools seen as appropriate for proselytizing efforts.

According to Sunday school advocates, ministers could ensure that their churches would be filled and their authority respected by offering support to Sunday schools in their district. Lay leaders in the ASSU made strong efforts to enlist the support of ministers in their venture. The ASSU held its annual convention in Philadelphia concurrently with the General Assembly meeting of the Presbyterian Church. Ministers were invited to play both substantive and ceremonial roles in the ASSU's annual meeting. Few Presbyterian ministers could have missed the import of Old School stalwarts Ashbel Green and Ezra Stiles Ely offering their labors and blessings to the ASSU with their participation in the third annual meeting in 1827. Green was asked to offer the benediction, while Ely wrote and delivered the society's annual report.[72]

Lay and clerical supporters of the Sunday school cause outlined important roles for ministers to play in the weekly operations of local Sunday schools. While, officially, Sunday schools were run by teachers with the oversight of lay managers, advocates depicted a hierarchy with local clergy sitting atop the schools. In an ASSU publication entitled *Plans and Motives for the Extension of Sabbath Schools*, the writer stressed how ministers would ultimately direct Sunday schools. If arranged properly Sunday schools would appear like a "*high school*" with the minister being the "principal," while lay managers would act as "master(s) under him," with teachers as "monitors under them." Not surprisingly, Joseph Lancaster's monitorial model enjoyed great popularity with Sunday school proponents.[73] Ministers would be the ultimate source of biblical truth in the schools. Turning to an organic analogy, the pamphlet writer suggested that "as the heart at every pulse throws abroad the blood, first into the larger and thence into the minuter vessels of the body, so will the minister diffuse weekly the life-giving truth of heaven." Teachers would ultimately be accountable to ministers for their knowledge. This writer suggests that ministers treat the teachers as his students. Ministers were to "excite the teachers themselves to diligence, by subjecting them to the same kind of examination in the presence of their pupils." A weekly "Teachers' Meeting" would give the minister the opportunity to instruct teachers in their assigned weekly lessons.[74]

Such meetings in fact did become prevalent in Sunday school operations, generally denominated "Bible classes."[75] Bible classes were specifically targeted at youth. In some places they were held exclusively for teachers, while in others they were instituted for youth more generally. The second annual report of the ASSU noted how Bible classes had been instituted at some schools and were "worthy of general imitation." By the means of such classes, youth who had "become too old willingly to submit to the usual exercises of the school" might still "receive the benefit and be subject to the restraints of religious instruction." A clergyman contributor to this same report articulated the place of Bible classes in ordering youth. He explained how in his congregation he had "endeavoured to encourage the general attendance of children and *young persons*." By placing youth in Bible classes, the entire Sunday school system could become an "organized system of mutual co-operation." The church could be become a "disciplined army, where every one *knows* his place, and where every one has a place and a duty, in the grand onset against sin."[76]

Yet for all this rhetoric of order and hierarchy, youth were still being granted more authority than was customary within most established denominations in past times. While some advocates of the ASSU called for more elders to get involved in Sunday school instruction, most recognized that such responsibilities would largely fall to youth. An Episcopal rector in Baltimore, J. P. K. Henshaw, in his 1833 sermon for the ASSU correctly noted how "youth of former generations" had little role in the "operations of pious charity." Sunday schools, however, had "thrown open a wide field of benevolent effort, affording ample scope for the exercise of the ardor, enthusiasm, and activity of youth." This activity, however, was to be "under the guiding influence of the wisdom and judgment of age."[77]

The first teacher's manual written exclusively for the ASSU tried to achieve a similar balance between giving vent to youth's zealous energy and keeping youth accountable to their elders. The title of the volume, *The Teacher Taught*, captured the spirit of its message. Its readers were instructed that "every truly pious and intelligent Sabbath-school teacher" would desire to be "under the inspection" of the "ministers in whose congregation he labors." Yet the book's author was also careful in his preface to bow to his readers: "We hope our title will be without offence." He insisted that "the desire to dictate is far from us." Instead, he was offering needful, friendly counsel. Youth would be given an appropriate share of authority that ministers were obligated to respect. According to the author, there was adequate room for teachers to be "efficiently employed for the building up of the Redeemer's kingdom" without having to fear that they would be rebuked for "encroaching" on "the rights or province of his appointed ministers."[78]

The Sunday school teacher's position as both the subject and agent of Christian instruction was also revealed in frequent discussions of the reformative potential of Sunday school employment. According to such commentaries, Sunday schools could help youth keep steady habits and avoid temptations. A Philadelphia Baptist preacher, James B. Taylor, sounded a familiar alarm: "thousands of our youth are already lured into the paths of the destroyer." The "contagion to which they are exposed on every hand," included "theatres," "gaming tables and lottery offices," and "intemperance and lewdness." Sunday schools offered an "asylum" from all such dangers.[79] J. P. K. Henshaw similarly, if less dramatically, noted that a "multitude of our precious youth" had been saved from "thoughtless folly—the sparkling and airy nothings of fashionable life—having no end but pleasure" by becoming employed as teachers in Sunday schools.[80]

The ultimate reward for Sunday school teachers was to experience a sound conversion. Sunday school periodicals and annual reports became preoccupied with counting the conversion of Sunday school teachers.[81] Archibald Alexander captured the prevalent sentiments on this important matter. The seminary professor noted that the benefits of Sunday school teaching were not limited to "mere improvement in sacred knowledge." In many cases the result of such labors had been the "conversion of the heart to God." According to Alexander, there could be no doubt that a "larger proportion of Sunday-school teachers, have become truly pious, within a few years than of persons of any other class or description."[82] J. P. K. Henshaw helped explain this occurrence, suggesting that while youth were in the process of "inculcating the principles of Christian belief" they would necessarily "find their own faith confirmed and strengthened." While urging children to "repent," they would be diligent to "make their own calling and election sure." Many teachers would find that "while attempting to instruct others," the "light of salvation" had "dawned upon [their] own souls."[83]

Because youth would acquire sound biblical knowledge as teachers in Sunday schools, these were conversions that could be trusted. Old School theologian Charles Hodge, in an annual sermon before the ASSU, noted: "It is from the class of scripturally educated youth that the church receives her largest and most valuable accessions."[84] Sunday schools would perform their ultimate service to the church by providing future ministers and missionaries. ASSU advocates were quick to point to their schools as the logical training ground for youth who would enter seminaries, the ministry, and missionary labors.[85] Overall, Sunday school teachers would gain sound scriptural training and perhaps even saving grace through ministerial guidance and their efforts to instruct the children beneath them.

Beyond conscripting youth to service as teachers in Sunday schools, agents of the American Sunday School Union tried to influence youth through an aggressive publication program. Producing books for both children and youth, the ASSU sought to battle the corrupting publications emanating from American and foreign presses. The president of Brown, Francis Wayland, in his 1830 sermon before the ASSU outlined clearly the potential created by rapid advances in printing technology in the early American republic. According to Wayland, the "press" was "enabling every man to exert his whole moral and intellectual power upon the thoughts and opinions of mankind." While Wayland hoped the power of the press would be used to effect the "universal diffusion" of Christianity, he saw the potential for either good or ill in its application. Improvements in technology would result in either the rapid spread of religion or in "the establishment of a more firmly rivetted system of slavery, than the world hath yet beheld."[86] Managers of the ASSU had been quick to recognize the potential of the press and acted to capitalize upon it. By its third year of operation, the board of the ASSU was announcing an extensive new program to "place before youth none but fair examples, and to put into their hands only those books which will store the mind with useful knowledge, and convey to it religious truth." In the annual report for 1826, they boldly announced their intention to "create and meet a demand for books adapted to improve the heart of the young." The managers of the ASSU had "observed with regret that improper books are too generally placed in the hands of youth—books abounding with foolishness, vulgarity, and falsehood." In response, the board would aim to publish books until they had become "so abundant as to force out of circulation those which tend to mislead the mind."[87]

The ASSU in fact had certain market advantages not available to private authors and publishers who aimed to influence youth. As a charity organization, it was not selling its books for profit. In addition, the ASSU used an extensive voluntarily administered book depository system to distribute its works. Additional techniques to lower costs included the sale of collections of books, called libraries, rather than the sale of individual volumes. Offering both carefully pruned versions of previously published works and newly produced books, the ASSU soon published a tremendous number of volumes, approximately six million by 1830. Along with the other prominent "united front" evangelical organizations such as the American Bible Society and the American Tract Society, the ASSU helped provide, according to the historian Lawrence Cremin, the "preponderant body of reading material" for Americans in the early national era.[88]

Yet for the extensiveness of its publishing program, the ASSU could never ensure that its books alone would be read outside its schools. As the emerging penny press catered ever more to the popular reading public, dangerous literature abounded. In 1836 Reverend James B. Taylor could still complain that "the volumes of the American Sunday-school Union ought to receive a much wider circulation." He recommended the ASSU's works because, "unlike the ephemeral and in many instances licentious publications which are daily issuing from the press, they leave behind them impression of the purest kind."[89] But purity was not so certain. The ASSU had to compete with other publishers, so they had to print books that to some degree catered to their intended audience.

Archibald Alexander discussed this dilemma at some length. The professor noted that in the past few Americans had availed themselves of church-operated libraries, because works in them were "not suited to the taste, nor level to the capacity of common people." The "experiment" tried by the ASSU had proven that "small books, written in a lively style, and rendered interesting by pleasant narratives" were "the kind of reading which is adapted to the taste of a large part of our adult as well as youthful population." If winning more readers, however, this publishing program also garnered orthodox critics. Alexander noted that the "principal objection" raised against ASSU publications was that they were too "light and fictitious" in character. Alexander conceded, in fact, that too much light fiction had been issued, which tended to "vitiate the taste of the rising generation" who would lose their "appetite for solid, instructive reading."

Nonetheless, Alexander insisted that fiction needed to be used to advance moral purposes. It would be "impossible to suppress all fictitious writings, or to restrain young people from reading them." Therefore, it was wise to offer alternatives that were both "innocent and instructive."[90] Once again, the ASSU was making concessions to win youth to its message and cause.

While measuring the success of the ASSU in shaping the minds and hearts of the rising generation of Americans in the early nineteenth century is nearly impossible, one cannot but marvel at the scope of its activities. In addition to becoming one of the largest publishing houses in America, the ASSU could claim a staggering number of schools connected with its organization. Across the country by 1832 over 8,000 schools led by over 40,000 teachers, enrolling over 300,000 students, were affiliated with the organization.[91] While the actual control that the ASSU exerted over schools was limited, especially for auxiliaries farthest from the urban East, Sunday schools did develop in ways consistent with the vision of its conservative advocates. Initially acting more as proselytizing agencies reaching unchurched groups such as frontier dwellers and the urban poor, Sunday schools increasingly ministered to the children of church members. In addition, Sunday schools became more aligned with individual congregations, thus alleviating much of the threat to a pastor's authority that an evangelical school might present.[92] In such schools there was no longer danger of some zealous youth stealing future congregants for a different church or denomination. The preoccupation with stabilizing local authority seemed to negate the utility of belonging to a national society, so it is not surprising that this organization declined in the mid-nineteenth century.[93] But the number of Sunday schools continued to grow; by 1875 there were almost 70,000 such schools across the country.[94] Gone was much of the original evangelical mission that had inspired the earliest schools. But the emergent vision of the ASSU continued to prosper through the nineteenth century and beyond, with Sunday schools gradually nurturing children into the churches of their parents.

*   *   *

The religious enthusiasms of the Second Great Awakening produced considerable threats to age hierarchy. Preachers like James Patterson empowered youth to spread the gospel and to overcome the resistance of impious elders. Preferring emotionally intense revival gatherings to the staid services of settled pastors, youth seemed to endanger the very future of established churches. Facing such challenges, orthodox ministers searched for some means to preserve order while replenishing their churches. Youth could not simply be forsaken. As Isaac Ferris preached to an already converted Philadelphia ASSU audience, youth represented the "germ of the church"; they were "all the materials for sustaining and promoting the interests of religion, as the fathers pass away."[95] The solution embraced by Ferris and Reformed pastors and congregations across the country was the Sunday school. In such an institution, children and youth could be gradually attached to the churches of their elders. Yet winning the rising generation did not come without concessions. Pastors had to hand over some of their prerogatives in Christian instruction to the youth within their churches. In addition, Calvinist orthodoxy was eroded in at least two major ways. The philosophy of nurturance adopted in Sunday schools encouraged a view of children as innocent, not unregenerate. Also, the sentimental literature of the ASSU gnawed away at the scholarly rigor of the Reformed tradition. As bourgeois America was fully Christianized, Protestant religion became less a consuming devotion and more a badge of respectability. Yet this was not a total loss. After all, it was certainly decorous to show respect for one's elders. And the pews and coffers were all filled.

Chapter 5
"The Young Man's Friend":
Advice Manuals and the Dangerous
Journey to Self-Made Manhood

In the Jacksonian era, urban opportunities beckoned the young. Northern cities, as centers of religious revival, schooling, and publishing, were potentially places of great moral nourishment. But the expanding urban marketplace also offered brothels, taverns, gambling houses, oyster cellars, and theaters. With so many dangerous choices available, it was easy for the young to be led astray. To make matters worse, young men were receiving less and less guidance in the workplace. As male youth headed off to seek new fortunes, they forsook traditional occupational rites of passage such as apprenticeship. One might suppose that youth, seeking upward mobility, turned to colleges to help secure social status. But as we have seen, higher education was not such an obvious path to respectability in the Jacksonian era. More importantly, higher education seemed irrelevant to the expanding capitalist world. Finding the staid environment of the recitation hall ill suited to their utilitarian ends, most aspiring young Americans pursued education on their own. As a British visitor, Thomas Hamilton, noted in 1833, Americans seemed most interested in finding education that yielded "an immediate marketable value." Rather than relying on the uncertain benefits of the arcane knowledge of the classical curricula, they preferred the "actual observation" that was "directly available in the ordinary avocations of life."[1]

While colleges were notoriously slow in changing their curriculum, some college leaders did begin to recognize their need to adapt to the market. Because such men were perceptive observers of their changing social world, it is worth briefly revisiting the college campus before we move out into the streets of Jacksonian America. The most famous spokesman for college reform during the early nineteenth century, Francis Wayland, noted that in a society in which "every man among us is the architect of his own fortune," colleges would have to concentrate more on providing "useful" education.[2] Introducing the elective principle into college education, that is, permitting students to choose between courses, was one way that schools began to allow students to shape their course of studies in ways that would better fit their vocational goals. Such bending to the popular will, however, was not without its costs for educators. If students had the ability to choose between their instructors, then instructors had less moral authority over their charges. Provost William DeLancey, Frederic Beasley's successor at the University of Pennsylvania, saw these implications clearly. DeLancey condemned the error of turning the "*taught* into a tribunal to decide upon the character, qualifications, and aptitude of the teacher." The provost was convinced that instructors were "fast sinking" into "mere competitors for popular favour."[3] Delancey's observations certainly had even greater applicability to developments beyond the college: How was one to morally govern youth who had the freedom to choose their own instructors?

The education of male youth had changed dramatically since the eighteenth century. In the colonial era most male youth who were not college-bound received an education that closely interwove work, moral precepts, and practical lessons. Apprenticeships and indentures, whether formally or informally contracted, bound young men to employers in relationships of paternalism. As surrogate parents, employers were expected to shape the habits and behavior of their dependents. Apprentices generally lived under their master's roof. They were expected to give obedience and labor in exchange for instruction. In the piecemeal transition to wage labor, the employer's educational responsibilities were gradually shorn from their contracts with laborers. Historians have generally narrated the transition to wage labor from the perspective of the increasingly unskilled wage laborer.[4] From this perspective, the emerging wage-labor force gradually lost any claim to the education and skills necessary to reach master status. Status in the workplace, previously structured more by age, was now structured more by class, as many adult men found themselves permanently lodged in subservient positions. Yet this narrative does not account for the work lives of many youth, especially those middling young Americans who managed to reach bourgeois status during the transition to a market economy. As youth became less fixed in long-term dependent relationships, they could more easily leave unsatisfactory employment situations behind. The ideal of the self-made man began to replace expectations of prolonged obedience and paternalistic instruction. Youth would gather knowledge and experience whenever and wherever they could. This is not to suggest that the strength of the bargaining position lay totally in the hands of these aspiring youth. Nonetheless, employers did have to worry about holding on to their young workers, particularly those workers who had an eye fixed on their own rapid advancement in the storefronts, offices, or workshops of commercial America.

The bourgeois dream of the self-made man relied upon an abiding faith in the pursuit of self-interest in the marketplace. At least since Max Weber famously explored the problem of the Protestant work ethic, scholars have been intrigued by America's fascination with upward social mobility. If Puritans took comfort in the evidence of grace that riches conferred, there was still something bolder about the ambition that Americans demonstrated in the Jacksonian era. According to historian Joyce Appleby, Weber's initial challenge to scholars to find the legitimating mores that drove the transition to a market economy still needs to be met. The role of youth in this, she notes, is quite important: "The elaboration of a national market depended on many, many young men leaving the place of their birth and trying their hand at new careers." This mobilization of "entrepreneurial talents" demanded that youth be willing to uproot in order to "take on novel economic undertakings," to "take risks with one's resources—above all the resource of one's youth."[5]

This chapter will not fully or directly address the problem of how the values of market capitalism were formed. What it will do is lay witness to the gradual embrace of self-interest as a motivational tool displayed within popular advice books marketed to male youth during the Jacksonian era. This literature was in part an attempt to facilitate self-advancement through self-education. Within these texts one can observe diffuse debates about moral philosophy (what today we would call psychology) concerning the motivation of human behavior. In searching for the best means to motivate youth, the advice writers ultimately turned to the promise of material success. Such a strategy, however, was adopted ambivalently. These advice writers saw many risks in indulging selfish desires. From their perspective, the newly independent male youth was ill equipped to withstand urban temptations. Brothels, taverns, and gambling houses were around every corner. Jacksonian advice writers experimented with emergent notions of self-control, particularly the concept of conscience, to guard against these dangers. For all their fears, however, these writers still knew they had to win an audience with the young. Pushing the bourgeoisie more fully toward laissez-faire principles, these advisors catered to and encouraged the profit motive in the young.

* * *

As political liberalism translated into economic liberalism, the Market Revolution pushed the revolution against patriarchal authority into the economy.[6] During the 1830s and 1840s, an almost wholly new genre of literature emerged to address concerns about youth embarking into the world of the market economy.[7] Certainly young men had been addressed as an audience before, typically in texts such as etiquette manuals or religious lectures, but this new literature bore distinguishing marks. One of the central and distinct themes of the emergent advice manual was the danger faced by youth as they left the parental home and entered the city. Expressing deep fears about the disruptions of capitalist society, these texts can in many ways be understood as an expression of antebellum reform. Their authors sought to contain the dangerous expansion of market freedoms available to male youth. Simultaneously, however, these works also served as guides to helping the young man make it on his own. Highly ambivalent, these guidebooks both embraced and rejected notions of the self-made man.

If books for young men expressed reservations about male youth heading off on their own, their authors nonetheless considered young men's ventures to be legitimate. The same could not be said about the reaction to migrating young women in these years. Female youth, like young men, were streaming into cities looking for wage-earning opportunities. There were two fundamental reactions to this development: denial or deep suspicion. Many moralists simply ignored the reality of women's participation in the market. While many working-class women were obtaining jobs in manufacturing, outwork, and domestic service, the ideology of domesticity created by middle-class moralists posited an imaginary world where women were safely ensconced in the home away from public dangers and competition. Some women, however, could not be so easily ignored. This was especially true of those who entered the white-collar world by working in storefronts. Instead of being overlooked, women who ventured into conspicuous sales work were associated with prostitution. These public women were presumed to be sexually available, their bodies seen as one of the attractive wares used to lure buyers. Thus, to put economic advice books for young men in larger perspective, we should recognize as we proceed that young men were rhetorically recognized in ways that young women never were.[8]

The guidebooks for young men appeared at a time of tremendous urban growth and market expansion. The 1830s and '40s witnessed the maturation of what historians have come to call the Market Revolution. This rapid expansion of American capitalism was underwritten by a series of transportation innovations that promoted expanded internal trade and greater regional specialization. Canals, steamboats, and railroads began to stretch across the country. In labor-rich cities, entrepreneurs created manufacturing establishments to take advantage of low costs of production and distribution. Meanwhile, profit-oriented farming boomed in the fertile lands beyond the Appalachians. Abandoning the exhausted farmsteads of their parents, youth migrated west for fresh soil. Cities proved an even greater magnet, with droves of young adults flocking there to find work.[9] These urban areas became immense, confusing, anonymous places where older notions of moral oversight became irrelevant. Witness the growth of the largest metropolises: in 1790 Philadelphia and its suburbs contained about 42,000 residents; by 1830 it had almost reached 190,000. Within two more decades the population more than doubled, mushrooming to about 409,000. New York and its neighboring boroughs in 1790 numbered a little over 33,000; by 1830 it had boomed to 390,000; by 1850 it stood at almost 700,000.[10] Simultaneously, cities were becoming more geographically divided. Shopping and manufacturing districts split away from residential areas, as neighborhoods and residential streets themselves became more segregated by class, race, and ethnicity. Young working men and aspiring clerks increasingly lived in boardinghouses beyond the oversight of their employers.[11]

The advice books written for young men entering the city were themselves made possible by the economic forces producing massive urban growth and change. The publishing industry had been reinvented through innovations in labor, technology, and distribution. Starting in the late eighteenth century, owners of printing houses began to break down traditional work routines, dividing, among other things, the task of type composition from the work of pressing book sheets. The introduction of stereotyped printing plates in 1811 and steam-powered printing presses in the late 1820s, further deskilled labor routines and exponentially boosted production. The advent of railroads completed the revolution, expanding distribution range, while concentrating the production processes in Boston, Philadelphia, and New York. The secretary of the New York Publishers Association could proudly boast that between 1842 and 1853 the range of books printed had multiplied at ten times the rate of the American population itself. As noted in the previous chapter, religious-affiliated societies, especially the American Sunday School Union, had been at the forefront of the publishing boom, the ASSU having published about six million books for its Sunday school students by 1830.[12]

Yet with all this expansion, the publishing industry still faced some important market constraints. The prices of most titles were still out of reach of the working-class and immigrant population. In addition, books were much harder to acquire in rural locations than in the major Northeastern urban centers, even into the 1850s.[13] It was mostly the urban middle-class that was stocking its homes and libraries with the millions of books pouring from American presses. Not surprisingly, the advice manuals for youth, which entered the marketplace in the 1830s and '40s, were targeted at young middling men migrating to the cities, and not to immigrants, working men, or rural residents.

Historians who have studied the advice guides for young men have generally chosen to emphasize one or the other side of the mixed message of these texts. Some authors have seen them as largely efforts of social control; others have emphasized the economic liberalism propagated in these texts.[14] Rather than trying to choose a side in this debate, we might more fruitfully problematize the ambivalence of these texts directly. If authors were in fact trying to contain young men, might there have been inherent limitations against achieving such goals in books that were to be popularly marketed? In the midst of a competitive market for the attention of youth, these writers were pressured into pandering to the economic desire of their readers. They needed to sell youth on the benefits of buying their books. These writers did try their hands at social control, experimenting with notions of religious duty, sentimental emotions, and the conscience. Ultimately, however, they would turn to promises of economic success to win over their readers.

We can learn something of the character of these works by sketching a broad portrait of their authors. These writers shared a penchant for preaching. This tendency would have come quite naturally, for many of these men (and they were all men) belonged to the ministry. George Burnap, A. B. Muzzey, Joel Hawes, Daniel Wise, John Todd, and Daniel Eddy all balanced time in the pulpit with time at the writing desk.[15] John Angell James was a famed minister in England who saw his timely advice book, *The Young Man From Home*, reprinted and warmly received into American circles.[16] Not surprisingly, a number of these authors lent energy to the Sunday school cause. Wise, for example, served the Methodist church, as it moved into respectability, as corresponding secretary and editor of publications for the denomination's Sunday School Union.[17] John Todd and A. B.

Muzzey both penned Sunday school works, *The Sabbath School Teacher* and *The Sabbath School Service and Hymn Book*, respectively. Even those writers who did not belong to the ministry made careers out of delivering moralizing messages. T. S. Arthur, a professional author who wrote dozens of advice books and didactic tales, received his greatest fame in writing a temperance novel, *Ten Nights in a Bar-room*. William Alcott, probably the most successful of advisors for youth, also pursued a moral reform agenda throughout his life. Alcott's greatest personal passion was medical reform. No conventional doctor, Alcott practiced medicine infused with religion. The historian Robert Abzug has described how Alcott was visited with a vision atop a hilltop in Connecticut and created "neo-Mosaic law" for pure living. Alcott titled his autobiography *Forty Years in the Wilderness of Powders and Pills*, imagining himself as a modern Moses.[18] All these advisors, then, were men who viewed the advance of mammon with trepidation.

Let us now turn directly to the books they wrote. Advice manuals addressed to male youth appeared in droves in the 1830s and '40s.[19] Advice writers corroborated the testimony of novelists, foreign travelers, and domestic commentators, all of whom noticed youth striking out at younger ages.[20] These authors insisted that the young enjoyed earlier independence in relation to both parents and prospective employers than in former times.[21] How did they explain this development? A. B. Muzzey, for one, linked the early independence of youth to the "passion for Gain" that typified the American public. Even the "very school-boy" had learned the values of capitalism, willing to part "with almost his needful apparel," simply for the "sake of a good bargain." The result of the spread of such values was a dangerously early start in the business world: "Our young men are fired with a thirst to commence business prematurely, that they may enter those paths which lead to the boundless accumulation of property."[22] This early independence was troubling to advisors. Reverend John Todd expressed concern about the dangers that awaited youth: "Our very boys have to buffet those waves of temptations which men can hardly resist. Long before they are grown up, they leave the homes of their childhood—they must go abroad and play the part of men."[23]

Advisor George Burnap offered an extended and rather impressive analysis of the precocity of youth. Early independence, he concluded, was a particularly American phenomenon. Many "foreigners" recognized that the young in America assumed a "preposterous precociousness" and "an insubordination to superiors." Agreeing with their sentiment, Burnap noted that youth were leaving home at younger and younger ages, some now leaving as early as fourteen years of age. Even the young man who stayed at home insisted on following "his own pursuits, his own hours, his own company, his own opinion." Putting on airs, he "mounts his cane and his segar, and commences a gentleman of pretty importance." This "premature independence," Burnap claimed, found its "cause, but not its excuse, in the peculiarities of our condition and institutions." The expanding market economy, driven by steamboats and railways, was opening new resources to the young.[24] In the "old world" the young still were forced to long remain "under the parental roof" because the "population was dense and disproportioned to employment." In America, however, "the state of things" was "reversed," because the "resources of nature" were not "half exhausted by the population." Enjoying higher wages, American youth did not have to remain "dependent on parents for support" and therefore were not "subjected to their authority." In addition to economic advantages, Burnap noted, American youth lived under a "Republican government, which is an attempt to live as far as possible without any government whatever." The result was that a "Republican feeling" had "extended itself down to the very children." The "family circle" had "become revolutionized from a monarchy down to a little democracy, leveling age, sex, and condition." While not denying the benefits of republicanism, Burnap did regret "the early abandonment of the young to follow the bent of their own inclinations."[25] Democracy and capitalism had taken their toll on patriarchy.

In criticizing such precocity, these advisors faced stiff competition. William Alcott recognized that above all he had to counter the powerful example of Benjamin Franklin. Alcott was aware that the young printer was "often triumphantly referred to" by those who desired early independence, so he made sure to tell his readers that for each successful case like Franklin's there were "hundreds of contrary character."[26] Franklin's decision to abscond from apprenticeship in his brother's Boston printing shop at age seventeen and seek out broader horizons in Philadelphia was a tempting model for young men to emulate. His story had been widely popularized. Franklin's early life had been chronicled in various versions of his *Autobiography*, while the maxims underlying his rise in the world were promulgated in his *The Way to Wealth*.[27] Beyond the real-life example of Franklin, fiction writers were beginning to generate a wide array of characters who boldly pursued their self-interest in the marketplace. Early to mid-nineteenth-century American popular culture was filled with characters like Davy Crockett and Natty Bumppo, single men who lived outside traditional family boundaries. In popular literature, young men would often violate the trust of others to get ahead in the world. While portrayals of these liminal figures were sometimes negative or ambivalent, many novels and periodicals valorized mobile men who sought to make good on the gullibility of others.[28] Collectively, these figures confirmed the sentiments of John Jones Hooper's Simon Suggs who declared: *"It is good to be shifty in a new country."*[29] Known as confidence men, for their penchant for playing on the credulity of others, these dubious figures were the literary expression of a rapidly expanding market economy where the pursuit of economic self-interest stood preeminent.

The authors of advice guides aimed to combat the roaming disposition encouraged by popular novels and the example of Franklin. Youth leaving home too early was only part of the problem. Advisors also noticed that the young seldom stayed in any job for long. John Angell James noted that a "liability" for the young man leaving home was his likelihood to develop an "unsettled, roving, and romantic disposition." If this occurs, then even once a "useful and honourable employment" is found, the youth is quick to remove to "another situation." Not content there, he again "removes somewhere else."[30] Clergyman Daniel Eddy offered similar commentary, telling his readers that "whatever" they chose as an occupation, they had to "*persevere in it.*" "Do not be a mechanic to-day, and a trader to-morrow" or a "school-master now, and a physician soon," he intoned.[31] Youth's eagerness for economic mobility could have disastrous results. William Alcott rhetorically wondered whether repeated business failures were due to "the fact the young rush into business too early."[32]

Protecting youth from the dangers that attended their independence was, in fact, the very pretext for the publication of these advice guides. As the young man was leaving home, he would need a portable counsel to guide him on his way. Exposed to the temptations of the market, especially in its urban context, youth needed to be warned of the treachery they would have to avoid.[33] Much like the writers of anti-masturbation texts published during these same years, authors of guides for young men prefigured notions of adolescence by imagining youth to be a time full of danger and temptation. According to these self-help manuals, many dangers lay waiting for youth as they arrived in the city. Prostitution, not surprisingly, was one. George Burnap characteristically described the slippery slope that could lead a youth to the brothel. Starting merely by looking at "obscene books," a young man would soon seek out the "society of the coarse, the obscene and licentious in conversation." Libertines would seduce him into further defilement. Once his mind was "soiled" by their conversation, he would no longer wish to protect the "weaker and dependent sex," considering them instead as objects for "a base, brutal sensuality." Soon after, the young man would find himself at the "threshold of that house whose doors are the passage-way to moral death."[34] If a young man somehow evaded this fate, he would only survive to lay "schemes of seduction and ruin" for young women.[35] These advice guides, then, were helping sustain traditional seduction rhetoric in American print culture.

They also helped broaden its scope. Other sorts of seducers lay waiting for the young man as he entered the city. For example, these authors frequently warned against gambling room operators. Reverend Daniel Wise warned that this "finished seducer" is a "man who will greet a young man with smiles and with flattery," one who will falsely "predict his success at the gaming table."[36] The tables had, in fact, been turned on the young man. Earlier, young women had been warned that male youth would seduce them by offering false promises of marriage. Now young men had to worry about the dishonesty of men, as gamblers put up false fronts. In both situations what loomed was the promise of adulthood. As young women reached adulthood through marriage, so did young men acquire manhood through wealth. In essence, young men were now being feminized, for they too could become victims of seduction.

Wise's ministerial colleague Daniel Eddy tried to expose the gamblers' schemes. He first warned that the deck was already stacked in the sharper's favor. There were "few sources of corruption more fascinating and deceptive" than gambling, he warned, because "all men want money." Such, at least, was the wisdom of the new age. With the "prospect of securing a large sum in a single night," the young man's "eyes" would be "dazzled and blinded." The gambler increased his odds of ensnaring the youth by taking him to the tavern for drinks. The gambler, Eddy warned, would wait until the young man's "brain is on fire" and then lead him back to the gaming table to "rob him of his all."[37] Gambling, Eddy insisted in sensational language, was a "fearful vortex" that "swallows up every vessel" that enters "its fatal circles." He warned that this vice "*intoxicates*" and "*maddens the brain*."[38] Gambling was such a seductive temptation because it offered up those very things that young men were seeking in entering the city. Offering quick riches, it was a shortcut to becoming a bourgeois man. But it was not a singular vice. Authors warned against gambling as part of a wider assault on consumptive temptations of the city. The variety of warnings against the dangers of the brothel, the gambling house, the theater, and the saloon throughout these texts suggests, above all, the reformist strain of these authors.

Having harrowed up fearful prospects, advice writers dramatized the transition into adulthood as a difficult passage through dangerous waters or along a treacherous path, as the "Terra del Fuego of life's journey."[39] The young man had great potential, but he could be easily led astray. Daniel Wise confided "there is a hidden potency" of youth that both "charms and pains me." The pain came with his reflection that the young were "so inexperienced" and therefore "so susceptible of evil." It was hard to steer the young man because he was "so full of stormy feelings" and "so unsettled in opinion." Wise explained how, as a boy, the youth had "sailed upon the calm rivers of a quiet river" because he was carefully guided by a "mother's love" and a "father's skill." Now the young man was "sailing through the winding channels, the rocky straits" that led into the "great sea of active life." And now for the first time the youth was "in *command* of the vessel." The dangers were not merely external; in fact, a young man needed to recognize that "the most potent of all sources of danger" resided "in his own breast." The young man's heart was "a volcano of feeling" that he needed to exert "lordship" over.[40] In Wise's telling, youth was the age of passion, not of reason. Locke had almost been turned on his head. And yet none of these writers ever told the young man to turn back entirely. Wise himself chose a motivational picture of a young man ascending the treacherous Alps, inspired by Longfellow's Excelsior, as the frontpiece to his text (Figure 7). Instead of telling the young man to turn back, these authors would help him on his journey.

*   *   *

If these writers felt some trepidation about the freedoms granted to youth, they nonetheless addressed their audience as independents. If they sometimes gave in to the impulse to preach, these popular advisors still adopted the pose of the Lockean parent. Rather than presenting themselves as superiors exhorting inferiors to perform their duties, these writers portrayed themselves as equals offering friendly counsel. The names of some of their works are quite suggestive along these lines; they include, for example, William Alcott's *Young Man's Guide* and *Familiar Letters to Young Men*, Jared Bell Waterbury's *Considerations for Young Men*, Daniel Wise's *The Young Man's Counsellor*, and A. B. Muzzey's *The Young Man's Friend*. If we contrast these titles to those of more reactionary authors, for example, Joel

Figure 7. Front illustration to Daniel Wise, *Young Man's Counsellor* (1850). Artist unknown. Wise, like other advisors of male youth at this time, imagined the journey into adulthood to be a demanding venture over treacherous paths. Reproduced by permission of The Huntington Library, San Marino, California.

Hawes' *Lectures to Young Men*, the self-positioning is quite evident. They were offering friendly counsel, familiar advice, and considerations for the young to contemplate; they were not demanding obedience. Even more suggestive of the Lockean approach is the motivational strategies employed by these writers. In urging moral behavior, they appealed to the emotions and the reason of their intended readers. They did not simply insist that the reader perform his duty; they offered reasons why it was in his interest to do so. Invoking the specter of the wounded maternal heart or an offended conscience was a popular motivational strategy. Most popular of all, however, was the use of economic incentives. These authors promised that listening to them would result in upward economic mobility. The need for offering such promised rewards was manifest in a competitive market for youth. Other authors and attractions that pandered to the desires of youth were a constant threat to these authors' moral purposes.

One of the first and probably the most successful of the antebellum advice manuals was William Alcott's *Young Man's Guide*. The text, which appeared in at least eighteen editions between 1833 and 1846, undoubtedly served as a model for the flood of similar advice manuals that appeared after its first printing.[41] A close consideration of Alcott's introduction to *The Young Man's Guide* will help illuminate the Lockean orientation that characterized these works. In the early pages of the book, Alcott appears almost as a family counselor, trying to intervene between warring elderly authority and youthful rebelliousness. He makes his first intervention by suggesting there is still room for dialogue between the young and old. Showing sensitivity to the imagined young reader, he suggests that elders who criticize youth for not being open to counsel do not estimate them properly: "The young are often accused of being thoughtless, rash, and unwilling to be advised." Alcott's concedes that perhaps the young might be "thoughtless" or "rash," but such qualities are merely to be explained by the fact that the young are inexperienced or full of youthful energy. If one knows a youth who is "unwilling to be advised," however, it is certain this can be blamed on "parental mismanagement" or an "unfortunate method of advising." Some elders, he insists, cannot handle the task of advising the young, especially those who do not "remember" that they themselves had "once been young." Parents who show "little or no sympathy" for their child cannot be surprised, he chides, if the "habit" of "filial reliance and confidence is destroyed."[42]

Having shown sensitivity to the young by defending them, Alcott then pleads with his readers to reconsider the advice of their elders. He certainly does not expect that they should completely "forsake society or their youthful pastimes" for the purpose of listening to their elders; this would be asking "too much" of them. Nonetheless, the older generation does have valuable advice to offer that is worth listening to. It is important, he insists, that "in some measure" the young "conform" to the "gravity of the aged."

There are times when older people, "however disgusted they may be with the young," are willing to "unbend themselves as to enter into cheerful and instructive conversation." Betraying a position of weakness, Alcott pleads with the reader to listen to his elders, even if they "doubtless will hear much that is uninteresting."[43] Alcott was trying to open a space for elderly counsel.

After creating room for an elder advisor, Alcott offers himself as that counsellor. Since communication between generations is difficult, Alcott offers an easier way to receive guidance than through direct personal contact: "But my young friends, there is one method, besides conversation, in which you may come at the wisdom of the aged; and that is through the medium of books." The advantage of books is that one will not be "prejudiced or disgusted" by the potentially "repulsive" or "chilling manner" of the advisor. If the emergence of a capitalist market had pulled youth away from their parents, books produced by the very same marketplace might serve in their stead. Of the books youth might consider, Alcott humbly recommends his own: "I cannot but indulge the hope that you will find some valuable information and useful advice in *this* little book." He then makes a bid for influence over his readers, asking them to meet his high expectations for them: "in accordance with my own principles, I believe you will try to follow my advice." Of course, an added benefit was that by following Alcott's advice, the reader could prove his parents wrong. Portraying himself as a sympathetic elder, Alcott asked youth to strive to earn his esteem.[44] His introduction betrays the fundamental weakness of his authority over readers. Living on their own, they had no reason to listen to their elders. He had to struggle to win their confidence.

Alcott's tactic of presenting himself as a sympathetic friend of the reader was adopted to varying degrees by all of his contemporary advice writers.[45] At times it was difficult for them to maintain a friendly tone in their moral lectures, but all these writers at least paid some attention to packaging their works in such terms. Another indication of the Lockean orientation of these writers was the means by which they sought to influence their readers. Reaching across an imagined space between reader and writer, they sought to influence the young by appealing to both their reason and their emotions. Unlike past authorities over youth such as parents or pastors, these advisors had little or no leverage to command obedience in their charges. They had to make obedience seem attractive.

To strengthen fictitious bonds between themselves and their readers, some authors invoked the sentimental bonds they presumed connected readers with their flesh-and-blood parents. A. B. Muzzey, in pleading for moral behavior, asked the reader to remember the sentimental debt they owed their mothers: "How many sleepless hours, and with what unequaled anxiety, did the mother that bore us watch over our endearing weakness?" To disappoint her who "weeps for our misfortunes" would be an act of great cruelty.[46] John Angell James emphasized the importance for moral self-control in his readers by telling them that the hearts of parents ached when their child left home: "You know not, you cannot know, what was the deep and silent trouble of your father's heart, the painful solicitude of your mother's gentle spirit, in the prospect of your leaving them." John Todd similarly noted that "scarcely any hour" could be "more anxious to the parent" than the moment of separation.[47]

The moment of separation was so difficult because it marked the moment when youth would have to rely upon themselves in making moral decisions. Lockean child rearing was geared toward this moment of self-government, but these authors displayed considerable anxiety about releasing youth into a world that now seemed so dangerous. Imagining youth to be afloat in a chaotic world full of dangerous temptations, these writers spent considerable energy seeking to locate or create an internal moral monitor in their readers. As a number of historians who have considered this advice literature have already noted, the concepts of conscience and character assumed central places in these texts.[48] These concepts were related and overlapping, but not synonymous. Character seemed more malleable. It was the sum total of the habits and principles that a youth formed when first entering the adult world. A youth could form either a positive or negative character during this crucial life stage. Once fixed, however, character was permanent. If a youth formed a correct character, he would inevitably lead a moral life. Conscience seemed more naturalized and inherently positive. In contrast to the traditional notion of conscience as a state of self-knowledge, the concept of conscience for these writers approximated the definition of the moral sense as described in the moral philosophy of the Scottish Enlightenment.[49] These writers were not alone in popularizing this emergent concept of conscience; popular child rearing manuals at this same time were investing increasing faith in this moral faculty. According to the advice writers, each youth had a natural internal monitor that would point him toward making correct moral choices. Yet these writers also portrayed conscience as open to influence; a young man could cultivate or warp his conscience. While different in these described respects, conscience and character were both understood to be inscribed within the individual.

By investing hope in an inward check on outward behavior, these writers were suggesting a different method to shape moral order than that employed in traditional village communities where public shaming could cultivate dutiful outward behavior.[50] Suggesting that youth possessed an internal monitor represented an important shift in the popular moral philosophy of the nineteenth century. For these advice writers, the prospect of urban anonymity suggested the futility of publicly shaped morality. T. S. Arthur, in his *Advice to Young Men*, provided an instructive discussion of the critical distinction between externally and internally shaped morality. Arthur told his young readers that "there are two kinds of self-government" to control "evil and disorderly propensities." The first sprang merely from a regard to "external considerations such as the love of reputation, ease, or wealth." The other, correct approach to self-government came from an "abstract regard to right principles." The first did not "give a man any real power over himself." His "inward disorders" were merely "caged as wild beasts." Since outward "restraints" on behavior would not always be operative, one's evil propensities would often reappear with "renewed power and activity."[51] A. B. Muzzey drew a similar distinction for his readers. While character consisted in "permanent qualities," reputation was "most fickle." For Muzzey the "foundation of virtue" was above all a "pure conscience."[52] In essence, by urging a turn away from external controls on behavior and toward self-surveillance, these writers were imagining in a rudimentary form what Foucault later described as the internalized gaze promoted by bourgeois society.[53]

These authors tried to deploy the conscience of their readers in a couple of ways. They conjured up a preexisting conscience and encouraged readers to further build their internal monitors. For example, Muzzey tried to activate the conscience of his readers by insisting that one could never stifle the inner moral voice. He warned that even if somehow a reader managed through "art and caution" to "sustain a good name" while really possessing a "hollow and false character," he would not be able to truly enjoy life. In contrast to those who would suppose that people derive happiness merely from pursuing their "interest," Muzzey insisted that the reader could not ignore his internal monitor, asking rhetorically, "Is it nothing to our happiness to enjoy a pure conscience?"[54] John Angell James similarly warned that he who succumbed to temptation would have to "bear" the "pangs of self-reproach."[55] These authors not only warned about inevitable feelings of guilt, they also asked readers to further develop the sensitivity of their moral natures. John Todd stressed the importance of daily attention to fortifying the conscience. If a young man's internal monitor could be "blunted" by regular exposure to profanity or drink, he could just as easily work to recover it, so that it might be "susceptible to divine impressions." As part of his program for the "discipline of the heart" Todd directed the reader to daily "cultivate your conscience."[56]

One of the critical areas where moral self-control would be necessary was in the dangerous marketplace of Jacksonian America. These writers continually criticized those who would put self-interest and wealth above morality.[57] Honesty in business was critical. William Alcott chastised those who would try to "get as 'good a bargain' in trade as possible." In calling for his readers to practice fair dealing in trade, he demanded the "renunciation" of the "spirit of avarice." Alcott provided a list of morally dubious practices. Concealing or misrepresenting the market price, selling defective products, and using false weights and measures were among the practices he criticized.[58] Just as in courtship, a young man was not to deceive those he engaged in business. T. S. Arthur similarly condemned the "cheating of all grades," from the "speculator's overreaching operations" to the "selling of goods by spurious weights," that happened in "these evil and degenerate days."[59] John Angell James agreed. He criticized those who failed to subordinate profits to ethics. Those who sought "wealth for its own sake," he insisted, would suffer the consequences of capitulating to this "absorbing passion." Every "moral principle" that relates to "immortal destiny" would be compromised; the money-making passion would "benumb the conscience."[60] One of the most dangerous forms of money-making passion was the launch onto the "stormy sea of speculation." A. B. Muzzey warned that those to whom "fair profits and reasonable gains" were but "dull words" would find themselves on "the brink of a fearful precipice"; their "moral edifice" would lay in "ruins."[61] George Burnap blamed the overpopularity of mercantile pursuits for a decline in business ethics. Over the preceding decade, he had seen an "inordinate passion for wealth" creep into American culture. Facing "excessive competition," many seemed "too apt to induce unfair means to get and retain customers." He accepted no excuses for such conduct; he felt the "warmest indignation" toward those who suggested it was "impossible for a merchant to be an honest man."[62]

While these writers preached the need for morality in business, they simultaneously, and perhaps paradoxically, upheld the ideal of the self-made man. Each writer saw self-improvement and steady upward mobility as both possible and desirable.[63] T. S. Arthur told his young readers that the "deficiencies of early years" should not "keep them back" from rising in the world. Those trained as mechanics could make the jump into the white-collar world through "self-education." To emphasize the lesson, Arthur provided a detailed story of a young apprentice who managed to rise above his peers, all of whom were "blessed with quicker intellects" and had "greater advantages of education." While his fellow workers "preferred idleness or mere amusement to study," he was "diligently seeking to improve himself." Nothing seemed out of reach for this youth: he soon was raised to the highest clerking position under his employer, later earned a well-paid position as a railroad engineer, and finally became a distinguished professor of mathematics.[64] In summarizing his general wisdom, Arthur insisted that "to rise above the great mass" of men would be the "unfailing result of patient and thorough self-education." William Alcott aptly summarized the prevailing wisdom of self-help and upward mobility: "as a general rule, *you may be whatever you will resolve to be.*"[65]

These writers not only preached the message of upward mobility; they provided tools to accomplish it. Hard work, time management, early rising, prudent spending, saving, and delayed gratification, among many other habits, were urged on young readers. William Alcott, in urging early rising, said that he had "seldom known a man in business thrive" who did not wake up early enough in the morning to plan his day.[66] John Todd, who was especially insistent about the need for hard work, succinctly summarized his work ethic this way: "Every hour should be perseveringly filled up."[67] T. S. Arthur instructed readers that they should not spend all of their income if they wanted to rise in the world: "This habit of living up to the income seems to be the bane of all success. The cause of it is not in a small income, but in unsatisfied desires."[68] Not surprisingly, Benjamin Franklin and his precepts were ubiquitous in these advice books. A. B. Muzzey upheld Franklin's noted time-management skills as an avenue to upward mobility: "Imitate that great economist of time, who by this habit was enabled so to cultivate his intellect, that he rose from being a poor printer's boy to a seat in our Federal Convention."[69]

Franklin, as we have already noted, however, was also a dangerous example; not only did he represent a youth who started on his own too early, but he was known for his willingness to manipulate appearances to get himself ahead. These authors generally were too concerned with inner character and honesty to recommend such duplicity. Nevertheless, their works are clearly rife with contradictory messages. If they did not always recognize the tension between their lessons of self-advancement and their pleadings for honesty, there were moments when the strain was too obvious to ignore.

John Todd, who was insistent about the importance of ambition, recognized the danger it might pose to morals. Todd warned the reader that being an "honest man" in the business world was difficult. Since the reader would be "making bargains" with other men, he would be "strongly tempted" to "cheapen what you buy and overpraise what you sell."[70] George Burnap conceded that it "has never been settled, and perhaps it never can be" how much information a merchant can "avail himself of" about the "value of commodities" and "the state of markets" when others were in "ignorance."[71]

T. S. Arthur even admitted to his readers that the dishonest might outpace the honest in the world. In a business world where "nearly all take undue advantages in trade," a man of high morals would have trouble sustaining himself; he would have to be "wary, active, and energetic" or he would "lose by the dishonesty of others." Nevertheless, the young man should keep moral business practices, even if "he may not grow rich as rapidly as his neighbor." His advance would be "rapid enough" to ensure happiness.[72] William Alcott explicitly addressed the tensions in his text and insisted that youth not misread his message. After recommending watching the market to decide when to buy and sell, he warned the reader not to take this advice as an endorsement of dishonesty: "some dishonest person, under shelter of the rule, in this chapter, may gratify a wish to take unfair advantages of those with whom he deals . . . I should be sorry to give countenance, for one moment, to such conduct."[73]

Ironically, these writers most clearly exposed the conflicted nature of their endeavors when they were preaching moral principles to their readers. These advisors told youth that if they practiced religion, obeyed their consciences, and followed certain moral precepts, they inevitably would enjoy success in the world. By using success as the ultimate reward for good behavior, they threatened to undermine the very practices they wished to encourage. At various junctures, these authors quite frankly admitted their reliance on self-interest to motivate their readers.[74] T. S. Arthur, for example, stated that while "many considerations might be urged upon young men" to inspire them to action, advisors would ultimately have to appeal to selfish impulses. It was good to start with an appeal to a young man's sense of "duties to common society." Yet one could not wholly rely on such a motivational approach: "too few are able to feel so unselfish a consideration as this, and they must be moved by the lower influences of respectability, eminence, or the possession of wealth."[75] Arthur and his fellow writers applied this wisdom.

These popular advisors sold their moral lessons with promises of upward mobility. Alcott instructed his readers that an extended dependency to an employer was not only morally correct, but would pay off as well. After pointing out that the longer he could serve, the "wiser, healthier, and holier" a youth would be, Alcott turned to the ultimate promise of wealth: "Even if your highest aim were to make money, what I have said is worthy of your entire confidence. . . . never have I seen the young man a loser even in a pecuniary point of view, from serving many long years as an apprentice or a journeyman."[76] Muzzey told his readers that a strong devotion to religion would inevitably lead to economic gain. He first anticipated possible objections to his plea for religion: "'But,' says our young objector, 'were I to become personally religious, it would injure me in my *Worldly Business.*'" He insists, however, that far from being "prejudicial to one's business life," religiosity would be rewarded with strong credit. Even the "vicious and irreligious" would "rely on the word" of a religious man. They would "give him credit," even if he were in "unfortunate and destitute circumstances." Thus, "genuine piety" was profitable: "instead of being, as you fear, an obstacle in your worldly affairs, [it] would be a positive advantage to you."[77] James also saw positive market advantages for religion: "religion, by giving diligence and sharpening the faculties, will promote success."[78] Daniel Wise concurred. All "elements of success," he insisted, were available to "every youth who will cordially embrace, and faithfully adhere to, the religion of Christ." John Todd similarly pointed out the advantages of cultivating conscience. If one was seeking a "powerful motive" to impel his work, Todd recommended bolstering one's internal monitor: "conscience is a motive which can be brought to bear upon all, and can be cultivated till she calls every energy, every susceptibility, every faculty of the soul into constant, vigorous, powerful action."[79] And as Todd made clear, strenuous effort yielded material success. Overall, each writer turned to the promise of success to inspire moral behavior. Yet all were acutely aware that devotion to success could compromise morals. What was driving this paradoxical message?

An answer might be found in considering more closely these writers' warnings against consumptive temptations. The theater, the brothel, and the gambling room were all condemned in these texts.[80] These authors saw youth as the intended consumers for the pleasures marketed in these venues. Such attractions thus represented dangerous competition for these authors for influence over youth. A. B. Muzzey demonstrated his recognition of this. He encouraged his readers to resist urban pleasure houses by exposing the snares laid for them by each. He asked the reader to consider the marketing ploy of the gambling house: "The Gaming-table is spread in the retreats of darkness; and for whom is it spread?" He answered his own question: "For *Young Men*. There are vultures looking out from those scenes toward you for their prey." The brothel operator had similar aims: "There are houses of Licentiousness in the secluded alleys and courts of our cities. To whom is the voice of their panders addressed? To *Young Men*. They whisper, they allure; they spare no arts to entice the unwary."[81] Only by following the counsel of advisors and avoiding the pull of such market temptations could youth lead a good life.

While the products of urban pleasure houses attracted much condemnation, there was another type of marketed good that these authors attacked even more strongly: other books. While condemning bad books had been a commonplace in American fiction and advice books since at least the late eighteenth century, these advice books have a more virulent tone and accord an inordinate amount of attention to this issue in comparison to prior publications. This was more than mere convention. David Reynolds has demonstrated that the mid-nineteenth century, with its rapid advances in printing technology, witnessed a tremendous boom in the publication of scandalous novels.[82] Their presence was obviously felt by these authors. As competitors for the attention of readers, authors of licentious literature seemed to pose the greatest threat to the moral purposes of these authors. The stakes were high; the world of publishing was imagined to be quite powerful. John Todd articulated this assumption: every author had "the best possible opportunity to do good or hurt." They could "pen a sentence or a paragraph" and it would "travel through the nation," on to Europe and eventually influence "millions of immortal beings."[83]

Books had to be carefully chosen by youth. A. B. Muzzey attempted to draw a distinction he wished readers to observe between light and serious literature. The "perusal" of the "light and ordinary novel," or the "corrupting poem," was "fraught with inconceivable harm." Reading the "best literary productions," however, was a "great safeguard to our principles." How youth were supposed to make this discrimination is unclear; in fact, these authors' inability to decisively draw this distinction likely heightened their anxieties. John Todd had nothing short of hatred for the authors of "*bad books.*" Such authors had been "permitted" to write works that would "pollute and destroy for generations after they are gone." These men and their agents were nothing short of demonic: "What shall be said of those who print and sell such works to the young?—of those who go out on purpose to peddle them? They are the most awful scourges with which a righteous God ever visited the world."[84] Daniel Wise was hardly less condemning in his judgments. *"Bad books"* such as the "innumerable novels" that were "perpetually issuing from unprincipled presses" threatened to "debase" the young. In a likely reference to anti-masturbation texts, Wise criticized the "class of filthy books, pretending to medical, physiological, and instructive" that he saw as "only disgusting stimulants to unholy, prurient desires."[85]

William Alcott, as a professional writer, understood the problem well. His second advice manual for male youth, *Familiar Letters to Young Men* (conceived as a "Companion to the *Young Man's Guide*"), betrayed some frustration with a growing tide of works that undermined his moral aims. Alcott blamed the publishing industry for pandering to popular tastes: "How few solid books, indeed, are published!" Even books of "real worth" would not gain attention unless *"highly spiced"* in some fashion. Alcott said that many novels, "especially those published first in our catch-penny papers or magazines," are *"intended* to be exciting." They also sold at unbeatable prices. They were published sometimes in "pamphlet form" in "miserable type, upon still worse paper, and sold *cheap*." Alcott wondered how a "true friend of his country" could "repress" the anger he felt at the authors of these licentious publications. At times, Alcott said, he hoped that "Boards of Supervision" might be established at "various points of our wide-spread country." Their duty would be to recommend those books "suitable" for "town, social, district, and private libraries."[86]

Making clear distinctions between books might have been quite difficult to accomplish because these advisors had themselves been forced into pandering. Alcott was protesting too much when he denied his sensitivity to the market: "I have another thing to aim at in these letters besides being popular. I aim to state the truth, according to my views of it, without fear of losing favor, as well as without an overweening desire to receive it."[87] Writing at the end of the 1840s, T. S. Arthur had the perspective to comment on the series of advice books written before his own. He was not pleased. His words nicely encapsulate the tendencies borne out in these texts. According to Arthur, books that were intended to offer moral precepts to the young often failed in their purposes: "There is too great a disposition to offer precepts that regard only temporal well-doing—to furnish the means by which wealth is acquired."[88] Especially troublesome to Arthur were those authors who recommended religious and moral posturing as merely an avenue to advancement in the world. According to Arthur, some writers of "advice to young men" had recommended that youth "assume devout appearances" because it would give them "a much better chance of being taken by the hand, and pushed forward in the world." Such advice was encouraging of dishonesty: "For a young man to do this, we should say, would be for him to act hypocritically."[89] Arthur perceptively noticed his fellow advisors' pandering ways. The competitive market of print was not a friendly place for sound moral advice. These moralist authors had been driven into defeating their own purposes.

*   *   *

Conceived as moral lectures fighting the abuses of the market, the advice books of the Jacksonian era ultimately seemed highly compromised by the market's forces. While their authors certainly shared with many of their contemporaries a hope that the marketplace could produce benefits for all, they also wanted to preserve morality in the business world. If profits were more highly regarded than ethics, such hopes would be lost. Faced with urban anonymity, the advice writers hitched their hopes to modern notions of self-control. The concept of conscience held particular promise. Nurtured in young children by attentive mothers, this internal monitor would check the passion for gain that would bring dishonesty into business. And yet this strategy was not fully satisfying. Active participants in the market economy themselves, these authors knew they had to sell morals in other ways. In trying to fight the market, they actually extended its reach. They displaced parents by offering guidance to young men as they abandoned the home. Moreover, they propagated market values. Ultimately, these authors believed that only seductive promises of material reward were sufficient to compel behavior. These advisors thus told readers that practicing morality would yield success. By using the incentive of success to sell morals to their readers, these writers were performing a dangerous balancing act. The ultimate and unintended lesson of their advice may have been that profit is what matters most in the world.

Chapter 6

Private Libertines:
Emergent Strategies for the Control of
Male Youth in Bourgeois America

While advice manuals intended to guide young men through the urban business world were gaining great popularity in the Jacksonian era, another brand of advice literature preaching chastity was spreading too. And it, too, reflected anxiety about the young man faced with the lures of the market. In this case, sexual temptation was singled out in particular as a threat to a young man's safety. We have seen that the image of the licentious woman, generated in work with prostitutes, lusty Eve reborn, could produce anxiety about the safety of young men. Formerly, male youth had been feared for their sexual aggression; now they began to be seen as sexually vulnerable as well.

The English writer John Angell James in *Young Man From Home*, published in America in 1840, articulated this common set of fears clearly: "VICIOUS WOMEN are as much to be dreaded as bad men, and far more so." Warning that a "young man should be on his guard" around "*female servants*," James was even more insistent about the dangers of "those unhappy women" who "are the victims of seduction." Paralleling the commentary of the Magdalen Society, James warned how seduction could set up a vicious cycle of depravity. Seduced women would "horribly avenge themselves upon the sex of their betrayers, by becoming seducers in *their* turn." Thus male youth helped plant the seeds of their own destruction. To prevent such a sequence, the slightest "temptation" was to be avoided. Dalliance could lead to disaster: "Once yield to temptation and you are undone."[1] With the purity of women less certain, some measure of sexual control had to be assumed by male youth. The safety of both young men and young women depended upon it.

Warnings about prostitutes were part of a new emphasis on male purity, but to fully understand the male chastity ideal in Jacksonian America, one has to turn to the most common sexual advice for young men in this period: writings on the dangers of masturbation. As in warnings about prostitution, traces of the traditional seduction dialogue can be found in this literature. At first consideration, this seems counterintuitive. In conventional tales, female virtue fell victim to male treachery. Masturbation, known popularly as onanism, as a solitary act left no female victim. But sex reformers in this period saw all sex acts as inextricably linked. They subscribed to a wider belief held in reform circles that one small indulgence could create an appetite for sin. Masturbation, the most accessible form of sexual indulgence, was for sex reformers what the first sip of alcohol was for teetotalers. Stopping masturbation was therefore conceived as one way to prevent the downward spiral into sexual sin. This practice, the reformers warned, could lead a young man to seduction and prostitution.

Yet onanism was not simply dangerous because it could lead a male youth into a dark career as a rake. Reformers believed it was inherently harmful to young men. There seem to be at least two other major reasons why reformers were drawn to this topic. One was a fear of the consumptive opportunities of the emerging market economy. Indulgence in masturbation represented the dangers posed by all the stimulating possibilities of urban America. The literature on onanism was here reinforcing the messages of the advice manuals for the young man entering the city. As capitalism and democracy encouraged individualism on an unprecedented scale, as old social controls fell to the wayside, a pressing need emerged to educate youth in self-control. In other words, anti-masturbation literature tapped into the very essence of what it meant to be bourgeois.

As they articulated bourgeois notions of self-control in the marketplace, the writers of anti-masturbation tracts very well could have been writing for themselves. Ostensibly fighting the dangers of the market, they were deeply immersed in it. Their immersion in the world of publishing and reform, in particular, stands out as the second major reason for their preoccupation with masturbation. As writers, these reformers fought with others for attention. They had to battle purveyors of pornography as well as make space for their own reform agenda vis-à-vis other reformers. These writers recognized and capitalized on the sensational opportunities posed by solitary vice. There was something oddly compelling about a crime that no one could see, an act that had no immediately visible victim. By offering graphic, voyeuristic views of the masturbator and his disease, sex reformers could win an audience by unmasking unseen sin for the public. The careers of these self-made men (and at least one woman) would rest on the ruined bodies of young men.

*   *   *

Perhaps the opening salvo of a new concern with the body of the male youth was the American publication of Tissot's famous text *Onanism* in 1832.[2] Over the next two decades (and beyond) a rush of doctors, authors, and popular speakers explored the physical and mental consequences of masturbation in male youth.[3] Certainly the belief that masturbation led to madness and physical ailments was well known to some Americans before the Jacksonian era. The man who left the greatest influence on American medicine in the early nineteenth century, Benjamin Rush, discussed the physical and mental illnesses incurred by masturbation, and sexual indulgence more generally, in his 1812 text *Medical Inquiries and Observations Upon the Diseases of the Mind*.[4] The ideas of such notable European intellectuals as S. A. Tissot and Jean-Jacques Rousseau on the dangers of masturbation must have been familiar to many as well.[5] If not entirely new, fears of masturbation assumed new proportions in the Jacksonian era. There was much broader interest in the topic and an increased moral fervor in the language of the many writers who expounded upon it. The writers on masturbation can collectively be seen as a community of sex reformers who helped construct a new chastity ideal for young men.[6]

Two impulses, in varying proportions for each individual, were present in this body of reformers. Most seem to have had both righteous and worldly, pedantic and popular, motivations propelling their efforts. Appropriate bookends for this range of reformers might be Sylvester Graham and Dr. Frederick Hollick. Each mixed moralistic and market-oriented aims, with Graham the more moralistic and Hollick the more market-driven. Sylvester Graham originally had aimed to be a minister, receiving training at Amherst Academy. Failing to find a pastorate, he obtained a post that allowed him to preach nonetheless at the Pennsylvania Temperance Society in Philadelphia in 1830. Deeply troubled with visions of social apocalypse, Graham would find temperance too narrow a field for his moral vision. Turning to physiological writings to make fuller sense of human actions, he mixed the ideas of Benjamin Rush and new French theories on the body to develop a new vision for healthy living. Creating a "sacralization of personal life," Graham called for a highly disciplined regimen of vegetarian diet, avoidance of luxury, and sexual chastity. In Graham's mind, disease, rather than otherworldly punishment, was the threat that now loomed over those who violated physiological principles. If the religious imprint on Graham was strong, he nonetheless did not shy away from engagement with the secular world. Earning a career as a popular speaker and author, lecturing to crowds as large as 2,000 persons, Graham had a popular touch.[7] As we will see, his writings, in particular, show a real market-savvy, for Graham had a penchant for drama that seized the attention of audiences and readers.

Frederick Hollick seems to have been more interested in building his career and less sweeping in his notions of social and sexual purity. Arriving as a popular lecturer from England in 1842, Hollick quickly established himself as a health lecturer and earned support by selling mail-order medicines, books, and even aphrodisiacs. His abundantly illustrated anatomy books sold very well and Hollick used anatomical models to enliven his lectures. Hollick at times courted controversy and in 1846 was arrested in Philadelphia for the indecency of his books and models. Of all the anti-masturbation writers, Hollick was the most accepting of sexual pleasure. While Graham insisted that marital sex should be as infrequent and unexciting as possible, Hollick saw sex as natural and even necessary for human health. And yet Hollick was no advocate of free love, delineating clear boundaries for the proper avenues of sexual expression. He very clearly expressed his fears about masturbation. To those who might indulge this pleasure, he delivered high-toned warnings about the terrors of disease that awaited them. In addition, he earned respectable audiences who vouched for the propriety of his lessons.[8] Collectively, sex reformers insistently pressed the ideal of chastity on male youth but simultaneously found ways to make their message palatable to a wide audience.

Why did the male chastity ideal emerge so strongly in the Jacksonian era? For one thing, the emergent code for male youth came in reaction to, and in competition with, an emerging rake culture. Fears of seduction were enflamed by celebrations of male sexual aggression, increasingly visible in popular print in the decades approaching midcentury.[9] A public rake culture was not earlier unknown in Anglo-American culture. In fact, it had reached legendary status in the libertine style of the aristocracy of seventeenth- and eighteenth-century England. But the Reformed churches of colonial America had significantly suppressed this cultural expression; it was only now coming into its own in the northern United States.[10] To understand writings on onanism, we must first spend a few pages exploring this rake culture.

The male as "Rover" was now in some circles celebrated rather than condemned. Compare the "Rover" chided in the ballad "The Men are All Rovers Alike" quoted in the first chapter to the "Mr. Rover" in the 1830 ballad "Dr. Stramonium" by popular balladeer Samuel Woodworth. If the first captured the distrust toward young men printed in turn-of-the-century fiction, the second represents an emerging subculture glorifying rakes in Jacksonian America. While the earlier song conjured up sympathy for women, with female readers being invited to condemn men's treachery, the perspective now subtly but surely shifts, with the author winking at the deceptions of its male protagonist.

In Woodworth's ballad, the young man on the make happily skips from town to town with no authorial condemnation of his behavior. This young man invokes the economic and geographic mobility of the period, moving constantly to new occupations after having duped his fellow citizens. This confidence man did not merely leave upset customers in his wake, however, he left pregnant women as well. In a spoken section of the ballad, he quotes the women he has left behind:

"O Tabitha, what will become of me! The dear sweet Mr. Rover (for that was my travelling name), the pedler, is gone, and perhaps I shall never see him again. O dear!" "Your dear sweet Mr. Rover, indeed! I'd have you to know, cousin Keziah, that he is *my* dear sweet Mr. Rover, and he has left me something to remember him by."

While the deceived women call Mr. Rover a "base, wicked deceiver," it is clear that their plight is comic for the author. While these women were despairing their condition, Mr. Rover was heading to the next town, planning "a similar mine to spring in the next village."[11] Woodworth seems to delight in the freedom of Mr. Rover and invites his audience to do the same.

Such lighthearted fare actually pales in comparison to the dark crime literature and pornographic fiction that emerged in the Jacksonian years. The literary scholar David Reynolds, in surveying the long-neglected erotic popular writings of the 1830s and 40s, has judged that this "popular pornography" was characterized by "unbridled sensualism and sadomasochistic violence."[12] Male libertines were encouraged to delight in sexual aggression. The production of such literature represented an important new departure in American publishing. It is not that pornography had not appeared earlier in America. French imports had been making their way into private collections for decades. In addition, *Fanny Hill*, the British story of the sexual escapades of a prostitute, served up in shockingly explicit detail, was published by at least a couple American printers in the 1810s.[13] Still, it was not until the 1830s, and more especially the 1840s, that American publishers and writers tried seriously to match European productions. According to the historian Helen Lefkowitz Horowitz, the Tariff Act of 1842 accelerated the process. When Congress banned the importation of erotic materials, American presses quickly filled the breach, republishing European products, as well as contracting with homegrown writers.[14]

American novelists such as George Lippard and George Thompson wrote stories meant to shock and titillate readers. As in traditional seduction tales, authors would sometimes condemn men's treachery. In fact, male seducers often received their just deserts at the hands of murderous prostitutes. In this new brand of writing, lustful heroines could pursue sex and murder with abandon. So this literature might seem like wish fulfillment for wronged women, but a closer look reveals other purposes. Authors lingered at length on the bodies of their female characters, voyeuristically offering views of their naked "snowy globes" and vaginas. Offering a geography of vice in the booming metropolises of the Northeast, authors guided newcomers from oyster cellars to dance halls, from gambling dens to theaters, from saloons to brothels.[15]

Some literary magazines also began explicitly to court an audience of libertines in these years. In New York, for example, weekly periodicals such as *The Rake, The Whip, The Flash*, and *The Libertine* aimed to cultivate a sporting culture among young men living in the city. The very titles of these periodicals were insider references to an underground world centered on male pastimes and aggression toward women.[16] If the seduction tales of the late eighteenth and early nineteenth centuries had implicitly denied male accountability by giving the responsibility for preventing seduction to young women, some literature of the decades approaching midcentury did much more—it valorized and encouraged male exploits.

Literary rakes surely had real-life counterparts, though they are more difficult to see today. At times, however, the young men who would see their likeness in such printed materials did step into view. Making themselves more visible, male libertines came to be known for their fancy dress. As early as 1819 one urban commentator was noting an emerging devotion to fashion among sexually brazen men that would come to define rake culture in the Jacksonian era. In *Hermit in America on a Visit to Philadelphia*, Robert Waln parodied the scenes of the city, taking particular notice of the many "dandies" who pranced the streets (Figure 8). These young men aped the European aristocracy, paying an inordinate amount of attention to their

Figure 8. *The Walk in Chestnut Street*. From Robert Waln, *The Hermit in America on a Visit to Philadelphia*. Waln ridiculed the young dandies and coquettes who pranced on Philadelphia's fancy avenue. Courtesy of The Library Company of Philadelphia.

appearance. These "ambitious 'fashion mongering boys'" would go to such lengths as to add "pads" to their shoulders and breasts and "corsets" around their waists.[17] Making matters worse, such young men spent much of the rest of their time doting on fashionable coquettes. These men could ruin respectable women simply with their incessant flattery, "'*double-entendres*,'" and "liberties in conversation."[18] Waln never explicitly discusses prostitution, but by the Jacksonian era dandies had clearly become associated with brothels. The perfect embodiment of the dandy-cum-rake was the dubious hero Richard Robinson. Patricia Cline Cohen has demonstrated that his 1836 New York trial for the murder of prostitute Helen Jewett provided an opportunity for young men to revel publicly in their sporting culture. Rallying to Robinson's side during his trial, mimicking his dandified dress, and disrupting the meetings of sex reformers who opposed them, the dandies and rogues of New York's sporting culture proudly staked their place in urban America.[19]

One of the most startling examples of rake culture by the 1840s was the brothel guide.[20] Speaking from experiential knowledge, and therefore blurring the line between representation and reality, these texts offered intimate urban tours. For example, by midcentury young men arriving in Philadelphia could procure a copy of *A Guide to the Stranger, or Pocket Companion for The Fancy*. This sordid brochure offered street addresses and descriptions of the major "gay houses and ladies of pleasure" in Philadelphia. Evidently penned for a middle-class audience, it assessed brothels and houses of assignation on the respectability of their clientele and the polish of their prostitutes. For example, one entry recommended a house where "beautiful and accomplished ladies" never used "disgusting language" but instead used their talents on the piano and their "melodious voices" to entertain clients. "None but gentleman," the writers insisted, visited this "Paradise of Love."[21] And yet the authors did accommodate other tastes. While dismissing most lower-class haunts as low and vulgar, they did mix titillation with disgust in directing the reader to "a brothel occupied by a swarm of yellow girls" who "keep their faces well powdered." Wondering why white men might give business to African American women, instead of their "fairer skinned rivals," the authors concluded there "is no accounting for taste," saying "we have no objection to a white man hugging a negro wench to his bosom, providing his stomach is strong enough to relish the infliction."[22] While the racism herein was perhaps not so shocking for its day, the sarcastic tone of the entry shows a high disregard for emerging standards of chastity.

Living independently of employers in boardinghouses and spending free time frequenting brothels, saloons, oyster cellars, and theaters, young men, many of them middle-class clerks, took to the streets to enjoy their freedom.[23] Faced with such challenges, sex reformers initiated a campaign against the sexual disorder of male youth. While some organizations, like the New York Female Moral Reform Society, turned to an attack on the brothel trade, other reformers turned their attention toward the act of masturbation. One must wonder how masturbation was linked in their minds to this sporting culture.

Writers on onanism saw themselves working against the rake culture of their day, frequently expressing direct concern about sexual aggression toward women. For example, Sylvester Graham lamented the pride displayed by some seducers:

Such is the state of morals at the present day—too frequently, they feel complacency in being thought successful libertines;—and it is much to be feared, that there are those who wear the *form* of man, who can reflect with satisfaction on the blight and lasting desolation, which they have caused to female chastity and happiness.[24]

Sex reformers believed that young men often encouraged one another in their exploits. William Alcott suggested that those who commit seduction often "*glory* in such triumph," giving the example of one man whom he heard "boast of the number of the other sex he had misled."[25] The phrenologist and sex reformer O. S. Fowler similarly noted how libertinism and hostility to women went hand in hand. He asked: "Reader, did you ever hear the libertine speak well of woman as a sex? This fact is apparent; and you may *always* measure the sensuality of a man by his disrespect for the sex."[26] Dr. John Ware insisted that he and other reformers would have to instruct young men on sexual matters, otherwise "teaching on this very important topic" would inevitably be left in the hands of "companions," those "whose ideas in regard to it are low and gross." Instead of learning that the sexes were to come together for "the higher object of a moral and intellectual union," they would learn that women simply existed for the "sensual indulgence" of men.[27] Seemingly drawing on an older discourse of savagery and civility, Ware was calling on young men to subscribe to a more elevated view of women and marriage.[28] In articulating a chastity ideal for men, sex reformers were participating in working out new ways to accomplish a safe coexistence of men and women in a world that granted men increasing social freedoms but had reined in courting behavior for women.[29] No longer would preventing illicit sex be the responsibility of women alone.

How could libertinism be prevented? One answer was to block access to the most accessible form of sexual indulgence, masturbation. Jacksonian sex reformers expressed a vision of the difficulty of containing sexual indulgence once initiated. While the theme of a slippery slope of sin had a long history in American culture, there was a new priority on stopping what the Puritans had called besetting sins, for older community controls had disappeared.[30] The superintendent of the Massachusetts Lunatic Hospital, Samuel B. Woodward, summarized this view well: "The natural consequence of indulgence in this, as in most other vices, is an increased propensity to them." Woodward quickly drew an analogy to drinking: "As the inebriate would probably never conquer his appetite for alcoholic drink if he indulged once a month only—so in this habit, the occasional indulgence will thwart the whole plan of cure."[31] The anonymous author of *Solitary Vice Considered* also turned to the analogy of alcohol addiction. This sex reformer noted that the masturbator "bears many marks in common with the drunkard," concluding that "of all those upon whom vice and sensual indulgence set the seal of their curse, these two are *most* alike." Put simply, onanism, like drinking, was a "seductive vice."[32]

Because masturbation, like alcohol, was so addictive once started, the best chance any young man had was to avoid temptation in the first place. According to the popular lecturer on sex and anatomy Frederick Hollick, one could easily become irresistibly devoted to sexual indulgence: "with each new indulgence the habit strengthens and becomes more confirmed."[33] With the parallel of drink in mind, sex reformers followed the logic of temperance as alcohol reformers pushed toward teetotalism. John Ware expressed this line of thought clearly. He concluded that if masturbation could be "arrested," stopping the "more open form of licentiousness would be comparatively easy." Masturbation was dangerous, Ware explained, because it "creates and establishes at an early age a strong physical propensity, an animal want of the most imperious nature, which like the longing of the intemperate man, is almost beyond human power to overcome."[34]

What did Ware mean by a more "open form of licentiousness"? Specifically, what he had in mind was prostitution. He found ordinary efforts at moral reform wrongheaded in that they failed to address the problem of lust at its source. He rhetorically wondered "what purpose" it served society to "make and execute laws against open licentiousness," to "arm ourselves with policemen and spies," to "prosecute the keepers of brothels," or to "hunt the wretched prostitute from the dram-shop to the cellar, from the cellar to the jail, from the jail to the grave?" All such efforts would not "purify society" because they were geared toward "external" manifestations of a deeper "corruption." As long as the "secret" form of licentiousness, onanism, persisted, moral reform efforts were doomed to fail.[35] Other sex reformers agreed. Samuel Gregory insisted that "solitary vice is the source of social vice," warning that "dalliance" with "lust" would unleash uncontrollable urges. Seduction and prostitution were sure to follow. He was certain that masturbation had "done much to furnish inmates and patrons for houses of ill-fame."[36] The author of *Solitary Vice Considered* offered similar sentiments, asking: "Did ever one become socially vicious, without first learning to be so in solitude?" The answer to this question was "apparent without illustration." Masturbation was "hasting on" young men, "with a daily accelerated speed," to the "degradation of public lewdness and prostitution." This reformer, like Ware, doubted the effectiveness of ordinary public campaigns against prostitution, rhetorically asking, "Where, then, should Moral Reform *begin*?"[37]

The goal, then, was to stop libertinism at its source. How did one learn to masturbate? Most believed that young men initiated one another in the practice. Part of what made the problem of masturbation so intractable is the way it spread among friends. Much as in the seduction of women, sex reformers feared that peers would encourage one another in this vile practice. Frederick Hollick summarized a widely held view: "This practice is most generally acquired from others, and for this reason prevails in nearly all institutions where young persons are congregated."[38] The sex reformers saw boardingschools as the hotbeds of masturbation, thus one can detect a class dimension to their concern with it. Samuel B. Woodward makes it clear that it was bourgeois youth who were most at risk: "I believe that in our High Schools, Academies, and Colleges, the evil is alarming, or more so, than amongst an equal number of young men in any of the humble walks of life. I am confident that the sedentary and inactive are more commonly its victims than the laborious and active."[39]

John Newman described in detail how one of his patients was ruined at school. This young man had been "chaste until the age of nineteen" until one day he went "into a classmate's room in college." Walking in "suddenly and without knocking," he discovered his friend "engaged with two or three others in masturbating." Feeling "curious" about what they were doing, he "allowed them to initiate him into its mysteries." Unfortunately, he "soon exceeded all of them in the eagerness with which he followed the practice."[40] Urban areas were also particularly prone to such dangers. Newman discusses several cases in which young men left the countryside and "entered the city from a mistaken notion of improving their fortune." Finding work in "dry good stores," breathing "impure and heated air" and eating a "stimulating diet," they were soon ready to be "initiated by other clerks into the practice of onanism."[41] Rake culture thus began innocently enough when young men encouraged one another in self-stimulation.

If sexual indulgence in any form could quickly cultivate an inexhaustible appetite for further indulgence—potentially an appetite for seduction and prostitution—then masturbation was especially to be feared because it was so easily accomplished. According to William Alcott, the solitary vice was "practicable whenever temptation or rather imagination solicits."[42] O. S. Fowler expressed similar concerns: "the latter by being so much the more accessible, subjecting its possessor to no expense (but that of life) and no shame, because perpetrated in secret, is therefore more wide-spread, frequent, and ruinous."[43] Another author noted that while "there are many hindrances in the way of social licentiousness," the "*solitary* debauchee is confined by no limits and restrained by no obstacle."[44] In parallel fashion, John Ware noted that those factors that might prevent illicit sex, such as "fear of discovery, regard for character, or a dread of diseases" were not deterrents in the case of masturbation.[45] As Isabel V. Hull finds in her study of anti-masturbation writings in late eighteenth-century Germany, the solitary vice was seen as "sex without society," the nightmare embodiment of severing the egoistic individual from the oversight of community.[46] Urban Jacksonian America had taken this prospect to dramatic new heights. Even if parents or guardians somehow managed to prevent youth from premarital sex or prostitution, they were helpless against this form of sexual vice. The popular health reformer Mary S. Gove lamented that many had "become the victim[s] of self-pollution, who [were] carefully guarded from social licentiousness."[47]

Gove's comments here suggest that masturbation was seen as more than just a gateway to sexual sin. Concern over masturbation cannot merely be understood as an attempt to control the problem of seduction—Gove suggests that preventing "social licentiousness" is not enough. Masturbation was a major problem, in and of itself. In fact, nearly all these authors saw masturbation as the *most* dangerous of sexual vices.[48] While sex reformers endorsed a limited level of procreative marital sexuality, there was no room for moderation in masturbation.[49] If one hoped to cure this vice, it would only be through complete abstinence. O. S. Fowler perhaps stated this position most dramatically, suggesting that the choice was between "ABSTINENCE OR DEATH." Samuel B. Woodward expressed similar sentiments: *"Nothing short of total abstinence from the practice can save those who have become the victims of it."*[50] Concerns beyond seduction must have been at stake for these writers. To make masturbation seem most dangerous of all was, in fact, to risk implicitly recommending illicit sex with women.

How else, then, can one make sense of these writings? What challenges faced young men alone? As cities boomed, new opportunities for self-indulgence appeared. In this context, onanism took on great symbolic weight. To resist masturbation was to master the self. These authors used physiological principles to warn against overstimulation of the body. In the face of temptation from both without and within, young men needed to steel themselves to avoid wasteful indulgences. This meant turning away from women, too. Complicating their calls for respect toward women, these writers often posed women as symbolic of dangerous temptations. Encoding sensual indulgence as a feminine activity, these writers upheld an ideal of sturdy manhood that separated men from the domestic world of female emotion and consumption. But they protested too much. For all their emphasis on manly autonomy, these writers highly indulged their readers. In an effort to win themselves an audience, they turned to the rhetorical excesses of sensational fiction, using fiery language and sexual imagery. Perhaps they fought so hard against the market because they had been so compromised by its forces.

Consider first the fears of market temptations. Embedded in the writings of sex reformers are anxieties about the dangers posed to male autonomy by the emerging market economy. This concern was mostly worked out in the name of science, with reformers exploring the effects of stimulation on the body. Sylvester Graham was the first major American author of the Jacksonian era to write on masturbation and he seems to have shaped subsequent treatments of the topic. While a few authors retained some elements of Tissot's concern with the retention of semen, all of these writers grounded their medical thought on the physiological principles of bodily sympathy that Graham articulates most fully.[51] The historians Charles Rosenberg and Caroll Smith-Rosenberg have referred to this notion of bodily sympathy as the "reflex-irritation" model of disease.[52] According to this theory, any disturbance in one portion of the body would be communicated and felt by other parts of the body through the medium of the nerves. Exposure to exciting city life could wreak havoc on the body. By tracing the genealogy of this medical theory into the eighteenth century, we can see that the "reflex-irritation" model was a product of the culture of sensibility at work in the field of medicine. While the discourse of sensibility had noticeably disappeared in much of American culture by the antebellum era, the model did persist as an underlying principle in the field of medicine.[53]

As discussed in the Chapter 1, literary expressions of the culture of sensibility had offered a model of gender integration. Writers on sensibility had sought to cultivate sensitivity to pain in their readers; the "man of feeling" was upheld as a model to emulate. While it is important to observe to a certain degree the boundaries between the multiple fields in which ideas about sensibility gained sway (including religion, science, conduct literature, and fiction), all shared some basic assumptions and often followed parallel paths. Scientific writing about the physical body mirrored writings concerning the social body.[54] Sylvester Graham's writings on the physical body, then, promise to offer further insights into his and his fellow sex reformers' social thought.

One would expect Graham to support sensibility in men, for he unequivocally condemned male sexual aggression against women, and, as quoted above, considered it a mark of modern degeneracy that there were men who took pride in causing "lasting desolation" to "female happiness."

And yet Graham did no such thing. Instead, he insisted that young men should strive to avoid the "aching sensibility" that characterized the diseased body.[55] His work helps delineate the limits of the new male ideal. As Graham asked men to join women in adopting chaste behavior, he simultaneously constructed sexual difference by marking sensitivity as undesirable and as female. Thus the transformation of sensibility that the seduction tales of the late eighteenth- and early nineteenth-centuries helped achieve—turning sensibility from a potentially gender-neutral model of human sensitivity into a largely feminized code of behavior for women—was only underscored and validated by the work of Graham and his fellow sex reformers who idealized the desensitized male body.

Traditional writing on sensibility had valued integration whether in the body or in society. Through the principle of sympathy, constituent parts of the social or physical body communicated with one another. The medium of body communication was the nervous system, and, for medical writers steeped in sensibility, the nerves were of preeminent importance in determining the health of individuals. A disturbance in one organ would encourage another organ to display a sympathetic response. Social thought about sensibility was built on similar principles. The Enlightenment theorist David Hume clearly articulated the principle of sympathy on which the social thought of sensibility rested: "No quality of human nature is more remarkable, both in itself and its consequences, than that propensity we have to sympathize with others, and to receive by communication their inclinations and sentiments, however different from, or even contrary to our own."[56] The social and physical versions of sensibility often merged in fiction writing. In the work of authors like eighteenth-century novelist Samuel Richardson, characters experienced physical distress throughout their bodies when they observed painful scenes from the outside world. Physical distress emerged in the work of many authors as a positive sign of one's feeling nature.[57]

Sylvester Graham largely maintained the scientific model of sensibility but transformed it in crucial ways by his fixation on the sensibility of one set of organs, the genitals. Graham evinced recognition of this transformation in his suggestion that the genitals possessed "peculiar sensibilities." Yet Graham did not apply the concept of sensibility differently to the rest of the physical body. For Graham, stimulation in nearly any form or location would hurt one's bodily constitution. He insisted on a bland diet that excluded stimulating agents such as spices, meat, or alcohol. Following popular French medical theory then entering America, Graham insisted that the healthiest body was one that had no sensibility at all: "the nerves appertaining to organic life . . . are in their natural and healthy state, entirely destitute of sensibility."[58] Graham warned that masturbation was the most ruinous sexual activity because it set up a cycle of mutual stimulation between the mind and the genitals that led to a debility of the entire body:

The mental action, and the power of the imagination on the genital organs, forcing a vital stimulation of the parts, which is reflected over the whole nervous system, are exceedingly intense and injurious; and consequently the reciprocal influences between the brain and genital organs become extremely powerful, and irresistible and destructive.[59]

Graham spends the greater part of his lecture detailing the wide range of diseases caused by masturbation. One wonders if he has left out a single known disease in this extensive list that goes from diabetes to brittle bones to insanity.[60] If he did leave any out, his fellow sex reformers probably corrected the omission. Graham and his colleagues found their explanation for all such diseases in the same principle, a "morbid irritability and sympathy" was established between the organs of the body, by outside stimulation of the mind and genitals.[61]

By categorizing the stimulation of the sensory system as negative, and by concentrating in particular on the stimulation of the "peculiar sensibilities" of the genital organs, Graham nearly inverted the traditional dialogue on sensibility. While Samuel Richardson had learned from Dr. George Cheyne that his hypochondria was a sign of his emotional sensitivity, of his humanity toward others, Graham declared the same disease to reflect a depraved nature: "Hence hypochondriacs, and those who are afflicted with nervous melancholy, are generally morbidly lecherous; and hence also insanity . . . is generally attended with excessive sexual desire."[62] The man of feeling, once a paragon of virtue, now was seen as prone to fits of lust and madness.

By calling for male insensibility, Graham promoted gender difference. For Graham, the healthy and moral male was the unfeeling male. Meanwhile, nineteenth-century Americans were promoting the view that women were especially sensitive beings.[63] Conventionally, historians have taught that the bourgeois ideology of separate spheres took women's sensitivity as cause for dividing the public and private domains. From this perspective, women's refined virtue could only operate in a domestic space sequestered from the dangerous public world of men. Graham himself, as we have seen, certainly bought into the notion that female virtue needed to be protected from men. Simultaneously, however, we see in his work an alternative rationale for dividing the sexes, one with a very different moral economy. The social implications of Graham's construction of masculinity become clear in his general discussions condemning stimulation in any variety. Overall, Graham encoded indulgence in stimulation as a feminine activity. In his words, he wished for men to avoid all "habits of luxury and effeminacy."[64] According to the terms of Graham's physiology, women were quite dangerous. Since women in the nineteenth century were strongly associated with consumptive urban activities like shopping, tea drinking, and novel reading, they were obviously a threat to young men. One might even imagine that at some level Graham saw women as sexually indulgent or dangerous, though he did not say so explicitly. He did warn readers against "dalliance with females," and he also symbolized the daydreams of the masturbator as "filthy harpies," invoking the half-woman, half-bird character of Greek mythology.[65] Nonetheless, Graham does not directly blame women for the lewd thoughts they might occasion.

Others were less guarded. Dr. John Newman, for his part, felt that one of the great dangers of the city was that it offered too many opportunities for casual contact with women. In seeking causes for masturbation, he blamed social events where women were in attendance: "Attending balls and parties, especially when plays are introduced of which kissing is the forfeit, is always sure to arouse undue amative feelings." Lustful feelings that led to "onanism" would inevitably be "inflamed by the constant intercourse of women."[66] O. S. Fowler went even further. He stated explicitly the implicit message of the work of Graham and his fellow sex reformers: "Well has WISDOM said, '*Give not thy* STRENGTH *unto women.*' And he who does, must expect to be weak every where else."[67] In other words, contact with women was a dangerous drain on male energy. In asking men to barricade themselves from stimulation, Graham and his fellow sex reformers constructed a model of sexual difference that treated sensitivity as ruinous and as feminine.

What attraction was there in this model of sturdy manhood? These writers seemed to believe that men engaged in the struggle of the marketplace had little room for indulgence. A proclivity for excess was dangerous because the overconsumption of luxury goods represented a waste of precious resources in a capitalist economy. A rising urban bourgeoisie faced with new temptations needed to develop habits of self-control and moderation. G. J. Barker-Benfield has explored this line of argument most fully.

His extensive analysis of the reformer Reverend John Todd reveals deep concerns about the market as they were played out on the body. Todd, who embedded an anti-masturbation tract in Latin in his popular text *The Student's Manual*, was obsessed with how young men might waste themselves in masturbation. Denoting Todd's philosophy "the spermatic economy," Barker-Benfield demonstrates how Todd saw masturbation as an expenditure of precious energies that would be best "sublimated" into strenuous work. From this perspective, strict self-discipline and sumptuary control were necessary to success. In calling on young men to fight the masturbatory urge, Todd was building a mind-set and physical regimen for the self-made man.[68] This view has received further corroboration from work on the bourgeoisie in other cultural contexts. Historians of Germany and Russia have found that fears of a pampered urban bourgeoisie haunted writers who warned of the dangers of masturbation. Country youth, they believed, were not prone to the same set of stimulating habits as young men in the city.[69]

We can see other American writers than John Todd expressing such concerns. O. S. Fowler, for example, worried about men's ability to strive hard in the marketplace. According to Fowler, the man who indulges himself sexually "lays down his nobleness, dignity, power, and manhood, and is no longer bold, resolute, determined, aspiring, dignified." He becomes "tamed," "irresolute," and "uncertain in his plans and inefficient in their execution." Ultimately, he is merely a "drone to himself and society."[70] In Fowler's rendering, the self-satisfied man lost the aggression necessary to compete and succeed. Others worried about draining temptations. Samuel Gregory regretted that the young became knowing in the ways of luxury, complaining that parents often "brought up" the young in an "idle, effeminate, and luxurious manner." This, he insisted, courted disaster: "their passions, are, like tinder, ignited by the first spark that falls upon them." Mary S. Gove similarly noted the dangers of the "present unhealthy and stimulating method of living," including "the use of soft feather beds" and "the use of condiments, pepper, spice, and indeed all heating and stimulating substances."[71]

John Newman thought that not all young men should jump into the competitive struggle. He regretted that some "young men fresh from the country air" had ever "entered the city" with the "mistaken notion of improving their fortune." Stimulating city life and the "onanism" it brought on would soon see to it that they were "interred in early graves."[72] Thus the medical advice of the sex reformers may have had wider resonance in a society in which self-sufficient young men had to hoard resources and avoid the costly consumption of luxuries. Here was a physiology built for the competitive economy of Jacksonian America.

*   *   *

These reformers were quite familiar with the dangers lurking in the economy. The more reflective among them had to admit their own complicity in stimulating lascivious desires among youth. By resorting to sensational descriptions of disease and frenzied addiction to masturbation, these authors risked inspiring the very feelings they wished to combat. The dramatic tone and moral fervor of their books is unmistakable. The dire warnings offered in these books were ostensibly written to strike fear in the hearts of would-be masturbators. Might there have been other motives as well? Perhaps above all they wished to be heard. These authors would have to go to dramatic lengths to be heard above the din being generated by the pornography and reform literature of their day. More than feather beds, spicy foods, or even alcohol, these authors recognized books as the most dangerous product vended in cities.

David Reynolds has illustrated how a wide range of reformers, including those combating alcohol and prostitution, were moving toward fiery rhetoric in their publications in the 1830s and '40s. Reynolds further suggests that many writers became so enraptured with their colorful descriptions of sin that they crossed the line into becoming "immoral reformers." By "probing the grisly, sometimes perverse results of vice," these reformers blurred the boundaries between reform and sin. While they "proclaimed they were wallowing in foul moral sewers only to scour them clean," Reynolds observes, "their seamy writings prove they were more powerfully drawn to wallowing than cleaning."[73] Sex reformers writing on the dangers of masturbation were fully immersed in the world of reform and publishing. It seems they too plunged into the sewers. If the primal masturbation text, *Onania*, was born in the publishing gutter of eighteenth-century "Grub Street" England, as Thomas Laqueur has recently argued, American masturbation texts found a similar host environment for their rapid growth in the Jacksonian era.[74]

Jacksonian sex-reform writers recognized that other reformers were competing with them for the public's attention. This can be witnessed in the comments they made about their relationship to other reform efforts and to other masturbation writers. We have seen how some criticized other moral reformers for going after "external" manifestations of lust, such as prostitution, rather than condemning masturbation. Anti-masturbation writers could also claim to be more righteous than other reformers by attacking a sin others had been afraid to expose. Samuel Gregory noted how temperance had gained wide acceptance, while masturbation was ignored. While the "public" was "strongly enlisted to put down the evils of intemperance in the use of intoxicating drinks," he observed, here was "as deadly a foe, insidiously preying upon the vigor, happiness, and virtue, of community," yet it was "scarcely noticed or molested." O. S. Fowler called on "moralists" to make "perverted sexuality" their "*first* work of reform." Seeing sexual indulgence as the root of "all other forms of depravity," he expressed surprise that "so *few* ministers preach against this sin in any of its forms, especially against self abuse."[75]

As sex reformers struggled to be noticed, they took care to establish the legitimacy of their work. Fearful of criticisms they might receive, they displayed considerable defensiveness as they justified their endeavors. They did not need the latter-day insights of Michel Foucault to learn that they risked proliferating sex and sexual discourse.[76] By their own account, many around them regularly accused them of this very offense. Tellingly, they also admitted that some of their fellow writers had gone too far. Nonetheless, each insisted that his or her particular book exercised proper discretion.

John Ware described the battle they had to fight. He admitted that the "opinion of many" is that sexual matters were "too delicate and difficult" to be discussed with the young "with safety." The danger, they imagined, is that by "seeking to enlighten," writers might instead "lead the thoughts where it is always dangerous for them to wander" and "rouse sentiments which might otherwise slumber." Ware diffused this criticism by asserting that youth inevitably would be exposed to such things by peers. It was thus best if they received information from guardians and not just from corrupt youth.[77] Samuel Gregory also seemed defensive about his chosen topic of reform. He congratulated the "few philanthropists" who had possessed the "moral courage to speak out" about masturbation, to "raise their warning voice against this invisible scourge." "Many virtuous people," he noted, had "predicted immense harm from publishing information on a subject so delicate." Corroborating Ware, he suggested that the public feared that "youth, yet pure and uninstructed in vice would be initiated in practices with which they were before unacquainted."[78] He doubted that youth were actually sheltered from sexual sin and put his faith instead in sound instruction. The author of *Solitary Vice Considered*, who failed to reveal his or her own identity, nonetheless called on others to show moral courage. "Friends of purity," this writer insisted, should no longer be "deterred by the fear of charges of indelicacy and indiscretion."[79] Mary Gove similarly played the martyr, presenting herself as part of a "noble band" that had been "reviled and persecuted."[80]

Why did they feel so embattled? One reason is that others had already suffered shame for dredging up the sexual muck of bourgeois society. The example of anti-prostitution crusader John McDowall must have been in the mind of many. This Presbyterian minister had been defrocked and driven into isolation and shame in New York City in 1834 for attacking prostitution too vigorously (or perhaps too delightedly). If any of the masturbation writers followed the McDowall case, they knew that many Americans were unwilling to brook frank discussions of sexual matters in public.[81] Similarly, Robert Dale Owen's *Moral Physiology* had invited controversy because it openly offered advice on contraception.[82] Whether learning from these cases or their own experience, anti-masturbation writers were aware that they faced popular resistance. Their testimony concerning how many saw their writings as offending "delicacy" tells us as much.

But it wasn't simply some amorphous public who stood against them. These writers pointed an accusing finger at one another. Physician Homer Bostwick was critical of his peers. He said that while "many publications" had been offered to educate the public about "the abuses of the procreative organs," most had "emanated from sources not entitled to regard." In fact, many of these books, he concluded, had been "evidently designed to minister to depraved tastes and prurient imaginations."[83] In the second edition of his *Lecture to Young Men*, Sylvester Graham bemoaned the fact that "unprincipled book-publishers" had discovered that "works on this subject will sell rapidly" and had published books of questionable probity, some of which were merely designed to encourage "promiscuous commerce between the sexes" or move sales of "vile patent remedies."[84] John Newman said he had had undergone a change of heart but admitted that he once felt that public discussions of masturbation were inappropriate: "There was a time when I would have been thoroughly ashamed of seeing my name appended to a work of this character."[85]

John Ware held on to more skepticism. He explained that he intended to write a book that was "free from the faults of other works which have recently been written for this purpose." What problems plagued the books of his competitors? Well, unlike other books, his would "never [be] offensive to modesty, nor suggestive of evil thoughts." Furthermore, it would not overly dwell on the effects of vice, thereby obliterating hopes for reform. He insisted his work would not have the "exaggeration which has sometimes prevented reform, by the belief that reform was impossible, or would be useless, and has thus produced despair instead of repentance."[86] But if this was his aim, he recognized that the same charge might be leveled at him. After discussing a wide range of ailments that beset the masturbator, he suggested that when masturbation is "carried to an extreme" the "unhappy victim" might no longer be saved by his own efforts at "repentance." Recognizing his own inconsistency, he quickly offered: "Let no one say that we overstate the extent of this evil, or exaggerate its importance to the health and morals of the young." Coming to terms more fully with his own project, he admitted a few pages later that his was a subject "upon which it is hard to think, to speak, or to write, without seeming to partake in some measure of its pollution."[87]

Samuel Gregory was more positive about anti-masturbation texts, but he was willing to entertain the possibility that some writings on masturbation were offensive. Gregory shored up the reputation of his own work by stocking it full of testimonials. One of the most interesting letters he includes is one by a Mr. Wells, a teacher in Boston. Wells announced up front that he "generally [had] an objection to publications on this subject." It wasn't that "they are not needed," simply that "most" he had seen were "calculated to increase the very practice they are intended to correct." He had become so "disgusted with such works," that he had given up entirely on reading them or presenting them to students. Instead he chose his "own mode of addressing" youth when instructing them on this topic. Gregory seems to have been desperate for approval, for he includes Wells's letter even though Wells admits he had not "read even your little work." He did say he trusted the work was pure since Gregory had appended letters of endorsement by "Dr. Woods and Professor Stuart."[88] Sylvester Graham similarly appended several testimonials to his second edition, including letters from fellow popular advisors Samuel B. Woodward and William A. Alcott. By obtaining the endorsement of others, authors could protect themselves against the charge of arousing lascivious passions. John Ware, who acutely feared charges of impropriety, presented his work not as his alone but as the collective work of a committee of leading lights in New England.[89] John Newman similarly filled his book with cases and examples taken from other authors who corroborated his own conclusions about the dangers of sexual excess and masturbation.[90] These writers intuitively understood the multivalent interpretive possibilities available in their own texts and did their best to stabilize the meaning of their books, insisting that they were respectable guides to sexual self-control. If fiction had earlier proved unstable as a tool of moral reform, didactic literature was showing a mutable character too.[91]

We should not be surprised at the defensiveness of these authors. More than simply bringing up the topic of masturbation, they jumped in with both feet. They served up salacious descriptions that even today have the ability to shock. To be fair, as the recent work of Helen Lefkowitz Horowitz nicely illustrates, and earlier discussion suggests, there were some real differences between these authors. Some were certainly more inflammatory or prurient than others.[92] Nonetheless, all these authors readily turned to the techniques of sensational fiction that, as David Reynolds has demonstrated, dominated popular literature of the day. Mixing the immoral indignation of firebrand evangelists with descriptions of sex and disease, these writers pushed the very metaphorical boundaries of language.

Sylvester Graham, for one, indulged in the evangelical style Reynolds has linked to antebellum sensational fiction. Graham used a tone of moral indignation in describing the power of lust for his readers. Once a masturbator had been rendered a "wreck and desolation of all that *was* a rational and moral being," he would still possess "foul and fiendish lust." This "tyrant of the ruined soul" would push "the miserable and loathsome body" with "maniac instinct" to the "perpetration of the destructive and horridly abominable vice."[93] Samuel B. Woodward also expressed heated indignation in describing how masturbation played into "unhallowed desires." Filling the masturbator's mind with "lewd and corrupt images," the practice "could turn its victim to a filthy and disgusting reptile." Homer Bostwick also posed as an incendiary preacher in passing judgment on masturbation and sexual excess. Reflecting on "the wide and repulsive field of moral and physical disease," he was "painfully impressed" by "the immense weight" that abuses of the genitals had "added to the amount of human guilt and human suffering." The "eternal law of retribution" made certain that the masturbator would be brought to justice: "Often sharp, sudden, and overwhelming do the thunderbolts of justice fall upon the transgressor."[94]

Beyond using the language of moral indignation, these authors engaged in sensational techniques by positioning the reader as spectator. By offering to unmask vice in hidden spaces, or by merely alluding to its presence, authors could make vivid appeals to the reader's voyeuristic imagination. Samuel Gregory characteristically betrayed his ostensible aims when he said he chose not to "draw the veil, to disclose the revolting scenes presented by those who are wholly abandoned to their vicious habit." If he did, he warned, slightly tugging at the curtain, surely the scene would "leave an impression never to be effaced." Readers who were "tempted to this fatal vice," would see "in characters horrid as if traced by the skeleton finger of death—BEWARE!"[95] John Ware similarly alluded to the "terrible secrets" that lurk in the "prison-house of the human heart" and "beneath the fair and even face of society." The author of *Solitary Vice Considered* raised dramatic potential by suggesting that this "vice that seeks darkness and secrecy" was not "confined to the worthless and profligate, but finds its way into high places of respectability."[96] Frederick Hollick invited considerable controversy by more literally positioning his audience as spectators when, in his public lectures, he displayed anatomical models showing the genitalia.[97]

Further evidence of the sensational style lies in the manner in which these writers broke taboos by discussing sexual addiction and by graphically displaying the ravages of disease. The historian Karen Halttunen has discussed how the triumph of the culture of sensibility had put discussions of pain beyond the pale of respectability in the nineteenth-century.[98] If this is so, these writers clearly engaged in what Halttunen refers to as the "pornography of pain," since their texts describe in great detail disease and madness brought on by masturbation. Sylvester Graham set the tone for works to follow. In one passage in his *Lecture to Young Men* he suggested how the "wretched transgressor" would become a "degraded idiot" possessing a "deeply sunken and vacant glossy eye, and livid, shriveled countenance, and ulcerous, toothless gums, and fetid breath." Not stopping there, Graham avowed the masturbator would have a "feeble, broken voice and emaciated and dwarfish and crooked body." His "almost hairless head" might further be covered with "suppurating blisters and running sores."[99] Samuel Gregory certainly must have raised some eyebrows when he quoted a physician to describe masturbatory disease. After detailing how "the hands become tremulous, the knees weak, and the whole muscular system flaccid," his correspondent related how self-abuse could affect the bowels. Masturbation could produce the "most excruciating and obstinate piles." In fact, "after every act of self-pollution" one might find that "blood and fetid matter have been discharged from the intestines, attended, of course, with very great pain." Typically, the physician painted a dismal end for the masturbator: "These wrecks of humanity generally close the scene of their miserable and loathsome existence either as raving maniacs or as epileptic idiots."[100] Addiction to masturbation could drive young men to strange extremes.

Samuel B. Woodward mixed descriptions of sex and pain in his discussion of one young man whose addiction to masturbation "had become irresistible, and the consequences truly deplorable." Feeling the depths of "shame and confusion," this man in "a fit of desperation" tried to "emasculate himself, but succeeded in removing one testicle only."[101]

Descriptions of the actual sex act tended to be less graphic than the descriptions of disease, but the metaphors used by these reformers to describe addiction left little to the imagination. Samuel Gregory, for example, turned to transparently phallic imagery, suggested that "secret dalliance with lust" would raise up uncontrollable "passions" that "rage like the fires of a volcano."[102] Sylvester Graham used precisely the same imagery with his own dramatic flare. Warning against eating stimulating foods and various other habits of luxury, he suggested that once such excitement occurred, "pernicious day dreams" were sure to follow and masturbation became almost inevitable. One might just as well "attempt to prevent the eruption of volcanic mountains, when the internal fires were kindled, and the molten entrails were boiling and heaving like the exasperated ocean!" Pushing the metaphor even further, he warns that one might "think to stand at the gushing mouth of a crater, and roll back the burning tide" as to prevent masturbation.[103] The author of *Solitary Vice Considered*, in warning that masturbation would send men in ever greater numbers to brothels, called for stopping the problem at its phallic source: "The FOUNTAIN, *the fountain*, must be purified; or all evils that result from unrestrained licentiousness, will continue to flow out."[104]

Few could top the graphic displays offered by John Newman. He certainly borders on sadomasochism in his graphic descriptions of masturbatory addiction. He fills his book with case after case of sexual perversion springing from the solitary vice. One story involved a young man named Gabriel Gallien from Languedoc who by the age of fifteen was masturbating "some eight times a day." "Emission at last became so difficult," Newman wrote, that "he would strive for an hour and then procure only the discharge of a few drops of blood." By the age of twenty-six he "could not induce any more emissions." His addiction did not relent. The man now turned to "tickling the internal part of the urethra, by means of a piece of wood six inches long." He would spend "several hours" at a time in this "unnatural occupation." After a number of years "the canal of the penis" became "hard, callous, and insensible," thus the "piece of wood had become as ineffectual as his hand." Because the "tyrant would not even then surrender his slave," the man was driven to take a "blunt knife and cut

Figure 9. Erotica published in the 1848 American edition of Jean Dubois, *Secret Habits of the Female Sex*. Courtesy of The Library Company of Philadelphia.

down on the penis laying open the canal." Rhetorically both a passionate slaveholder and degraded bondsmen, the youth had lost all will. He continued in this occupation until finally he had "split the penis in two equal parts." In case it might be wondered how a masturbator could survive such ordeals, Newman concluded by assuring the reader that the man eventually died of consumption.[105] Little wonder, then, that these books invited scandal.

Discussion of female masturbation was uncommon in American texts during these years; few seemed ready yet to believe that female modesty could be so lost.[106] Therefore, when a French text, *Secret Habits of the Female Sex*, was reprinted in 1848 there had to be some compelling attraction for the anonymous American publishers.[107] Despite its French origins, the book is rather conventional, featuring case study after case study of diseased women destroyed by onanism. It purportedly was written to warn mothers of the dangers that loom for their daughters if they stray into the solitary vice. This book, however, unlike others of this era, contained illustrations. Four erotic engravings, including one with a wholly naked young woman, and two others with pairs of female nudes, were inserted in the book (Figure 9). The book also carried on its back cover advertisements for novels from the pen of the notorious French writer Charles Paul De Kock.[108] Surely the publishers had a male gaze in mind. Their choice to deliver erotic pictures in an anti-masturbation text provides suggestive testimony about how they felt the genre more generally was received.[109] And they had good justification. While authors of the other texts never offered such an open invitation to masturbation, they certainly had broken many taboos in their sordid descriptions. Immersed in a competitive print market, they had to draw attention to themselves. Using the rhetoric and imagery of sensational fiction promised to win them a crowd, but perhaps at the cost of compromising their moral agenda.

Then again, their rhetorical strategies, at least in the long run, may have served their interests. As these authors pandered to the crowd, they ironically came upon a new strategy whereby adults could begin to exert authority over youth. By creating hyperbolic descriptions of weak and diseased youth who suffered under sexual addiction, they helped posit a new image that would eventually, in a less virulent form, become the stereotype for all youth. If these authors were pushing the boundaries of respectability, their descriptions of male youth nonetheless did work their way into the world of medicine and popular culture.[110] It is worth noting that many of the most important late nineteenth- and early twentieth-century writers on adolescence, such as G. Stanley Hall, expressed great concern about the problem of masturbation among the young.[111] The images surrounding the male masturbator infused later descriptions of adolescence. While sex reformers had called on young men to be sturdy for the market, they ultimately found them incapable. Rather than an image of independent manhood, these advisors projected a picture of male youth as vulnerable, weak, and dependent, as feminine.

The young male masturbator clearly could not handle independence. Samuel B. Woodward provided a typical description of male weakness, suggesting that the masturbator "becomes feeble, is unable to labor with accustomed vigor, or to apply his mind to study; his step is tardy and weak, he is irresolute."[112] Homer Bostwick offered a similar portrait: "He is easily startled. The slamming of a door—the firing of a cracker—the fall of a book—a sudden touch, or even the passing or speaking to him unexpectedly, will cause him to start 'like a guilty thing.' Cowardice is a sure consequence of masturbation."[113] Lacking strength or rational control, male youth could not stop themselves from masturbating. John Newman reported that one young man was so overcome with desire that even disease did not "deter him from polluting himself," rather, he "did it more frequently, until he reduced himself to such a state, as rendered death inevitable."[114] According to O. S. Fowler, the masturbator had little in the way of manly independence; he was "timid, afraid of his own shadow . . . Nor will he walk erect or dignified, as if conscious of manhood, and lofty in his aspirations, but will walk and move with a diminutive, crying, sycophantic inferior, mean, self-debased manner."[115]

In destroying his genitals in masturbation, the young man lost his manhood and undoubtedly his ability to compete in capitalist society. Fowler elaborated on how sex drained men of their manliness. He compared the effects of sexual indulgence to the neutering of domestic animals: "Destroy the sexual apparatus of animals by emasculation and witness the effects. Compare the stallion with the gelding. What becomes of the proud and lofty prance, the noble bearing, the perfect form, the physical stamina, the free, bold, neighing resolute horse? . . . His mien humbled. His free spirit chained."[116] This vision of young men who were weak, effeminate, and driven by passion, would become the stereotype for youth writ large in the decades to follow. G. Stanley Hall would masterfully synthesize this image in his landmark 1904 study *Adolescence*. Recapitulating during their own lifetimes the evolution of man, young men were not to mature too quickly, so that they could fully arrive as rational adults. Vulnerable and awkward, male youth, like young women, would need the careful supervision of elders.[117]

Again anticipating the later architects of adolescence, these writers began to imagine ways to contain young men. Sounding like prison reformers such as Jeremy Bentham (as described by Foucault), sex reformers called for various strategies of observation. Frederick Hollick, for example, called for the constant watchful gaze of guardians: "From the nature of the practice it cannot be prevented, when there is a disposition to it, unless the offender is kept under *constant surveillance*."[118] In the absence of real surveillance, he suggested, one might merely use the illusion of it. The solitary vice might be prevented if one could cultivate a "fear of *detection*": "Let them know, that it produces a certain effect upon their appearance, which to a practiced eye, *points them out as certainly as if they had it written on their forheads!*"[119] Masturbation, since it was driven by mutual stimulation between the brain and the genitals, was as much a sin of the mind and imagination as it was of the body, so sex reformers tried to extend control over both.[120] Hollick's solution of real or imagined surveillance was adopted in various forms by many sex reformers. Samuel B. Woodward seemed to take Hollick's advice by assuring his readers that he had the skill to detect masturbators upon interview: "amongst a hundred that I have questioned, I have rarely been mistaken."[121] Homer Bostwick more generally attributed these skills of perception to doctors: "In these times, it is the physician, in extensive practice, who is the depository of the fearful secrets of depraved human indulgence."[122] O. S. Fowler, not surprisingly, saw phrenology as a tool well suited to such detection: "Let every sensualist, especially *private libertine*, remember that he is marked and known, and read by all men who have eyes and know how to use them."[123]

Beyond claiming the powers to read the bodies and minds of masturbators, guardians of youth could create surveillance through architecture. Homer Bostwick suggested that "dormitories should be so arranged as to preclude opportunities of corrupting communications and example." He suggested keeping "light" glowing "in the sleeping apartments." Similar "preventions against privacy," Bostwick urged, "should be adopted in the construction of the water-closets."[124] Bostwick even suggested that if a young man succeeded in stopping himself from masturbating while conscious, he might still try to do it while asleep—such a problem led him to recommend tying patients' hands to their bedposts![125] Imagining the outer limits of subjugating the will, guardians would sometimes have to turn to coercion. Thus, to prevent masturbation, these advisors were calling for the intervention of guardians who could protect male youth from themselves. In portraying male youths as vulnerable, sex reformers were crafting a new response to sexual disorder—male youth would need to be treated as dependents in need of the stewardship of parents, teachers, and medical advisors. While one could hope that youth would internalize the watchful gaze of guardians, the prospect of self-control was in fact being abandoned. In the late nineteenth-century this trend would be fully realized as various educational and monitoring institutions such as high schools and the Young Men's Christian Association spread across America.[126] The independent youth would become the dependent adolescent.

* * *

The advice on masturbation is full of contradictions. To a certain extent, this literature can be understood as an attempt to protect women by preventing the act of seduction. At another level, it can be understood as a caution against entering the female world of consumption and emotional entanglements that would cause the loss of vital energies that were needed for competition in the marketplace. Simultaneously, however, these works pandered to the consumption habits of the reading public by serving up sensational descriptions of sex, addiction, and disease. Perhaps responsible for weakening the nerves of their audience, the authors of these works questioned the ability of male youth to stand alone and urged the intervention of elders. Collectively, these works suggest a new chastity ideal for young men, even if it was one that was imperiled by their seamy writings. One might resolve these seeming tensions more fully, if not completely. The writings of the sex reformers urged a new respect for women, but it was at the expense of most forms of sexual relations.[127] If men were to respect the bodily integrity of women, they had to avoid connection in any form. The threat of sexual conquest decried in late eighteenth-century seduction literature was blocked but a new model of gender integration was not offered as a replacement. According to the advice of the sex reformers, sexual expression became dangerous not merely to women (as it had been in traditional seduction fiction) but to men as well. Facing sexual danger, whether in prostitution, illicit relationships, or simply masturbation, at-risk male youth would need the careful oversight of guardians.

By midcentury, then, both young women and men of the bourgeoisie were being urged to a chastity ideal. Subscription to this ideal made one bourgeois. For women, the roots of this ideal can be traced to at least the late eighteenth-century, with the seduction tale of that period being one of its most important exponents. To the degree that this narrative was undermined as the nineteenth-century progressed, the assumption of chastity for women had become more structured by class. If the seduction narrative was undermined in some locales, such as in the Magdalen Society, bourgeois women were largely unaffected, because this departure had been carried out in class-specific ways. In fact, the image of working-class depravity could actually reinforce notions of bourgeois propriety, with working-class women serving as a cultural foil for bourgeois women. For bourgeois male youth a new chastity ideal appeared in the decades approaching midcentury. Scientific sex reformers warned young men of the dangers of sexual indulgence and suggested that they too, like young women, would need close supervision in social and sexual encounters. By midcentury, in the realm of sexuality, both young men and women appeared quite unable to handle the independence promised in the wake of the Revolution.

Conclusion

In 1849 William Alcott reflected on the changes in age relations in America. Formerly the young had been "treated with too much reserve" and "kept at too great a distance." In fact, "not a few" had been "treated more like servants and menials than like sons." But things had changed. He wondered now whether Americans had reached "the other extreme" and if there was "not danger of going too far."[1] Alcott looked forward to a day when the pendulum might be steadied. There was a certain rough, if overstated, truth to his observations and prescience to his anticipations. Framing change in age relations over a broad sweep of time, from the colonial era to the end of the nineteenth century, one can better appreciate the unique qualities of the early national era. Youth in the colonies generally experienced a protracted dependency, while young adults during the early national era enjoyed expanding claims to adulthood. The independence of youth would in turn be curtailed in the late nineteenth century, as the architects of adolescence developed institutions to contain the young.

In colonial subsistence farm communities, parents held tight to their children as they aged, waiting to confer property until their final years. With few alternatives for achieving economic competency, youth understood that it behooved them to pay respect to their elders. A young man or woman married against the wishes of a parent or had sex outside of wedlock at their own risk. Northern courts and churches were vital to upholding the patriarchal order, with fines, whippings, and excommunication served to subversive youth. The era of the American Revolution witnessed a challenge to the standing patriarchal order. In the decades approaching and following the war, Americans approvingly consumed English novels by authors such as Samuel Richardson who decried the interference of fathers in marriage. Overthrowing a patriarchal king delegitimized patriarchy in the young country. In addition, fathers had been losing much of their leverage over children as land supplies were depleted by successive partible patrimonies in older village communities. Just as importantly, community churches and courts forsook oversight of courting and sexual behavior, decreasingly punishing the sin of fornication. Declining patriarchal and community control is clearly revealed in the booming rates of pregnancy before marriage in these years. As we have seen, American elders began to pen seduction tales that expressed growing misgivings about the ability of youth to negotiate marriage on their own. While parents and neighbors in the early republic never regained old powers over marriage decisions, they did succeed in curtailing premarital pregnancy among the young.

If the late eighteenth century left a mixed legacy in courtship, the early nineteenth-century witnessed developments that would further propel the empowerment of the young. Especially in urban centers such as Philadelphia, youth became empowered consumers, as cultural vendors sold them access to adulthood at every turn. As the number of colleges proliferated too rapidly, professors were forced to cater to the young. Imbibing notions of democracy, male youth were increasingly impatient under their professors' stern rule. Some students boldly demanded that they receive their degrees and independence in fewer years; schools competing for students had little choice but to give in to their requests. Religious revivalists sold piety freely, telling the young to forsake the wisdom of elders and to seek God on their own. Standing as spiritual independents, young men and women no longer had to rely on the mediation of ministers. Moralist authors also had to pander to youth to win their attention. Trying to stand in the place of parents, some authors offered advice to young men who left home to chase fortunes in the cities. These youth aspired to fulfill the dream of the self-made man. In their books, authors such as William Alcott and Daniel Eddy had to give up the posture of superiors addressing inferiors. Instead, they told young men that they were merely friends, men who might provide some useful counsel for the independent young man.

If elders trying to guide the young in the antebellum era had to acknowledge the independence of their youthful readers, they also began to devise strategies to control youth. By exaggerating how precarious it was to cross the threshold from the home into the world, antebellum moralists made the passage through youth seem like a dangerous journey that demanded their guidance. With seductive confidence men hawking sex, alcohol, and dangerous books on every corner, young men might lose their self-mastery to flights of fancy and passion. As writers and moralists increasingly depicted youth as a dangerous age, they were laying the groundwork for the late nineteenth-century concept of adolescence. Writers on the dangers of masturbation took these images of youth to the most dramatic heights. Authors such as Sylvester Graham and Samuel B. Woodward depicted masturbation's victims as weak, emaciated, and effeminate.

During the late nineteenth and into the twentieth century, self-styled youth savers began to build institutions to contain the young. As high schools and urban rescue institutions like the Young Men's Christian Association segregated youth from the world of adults, the image of the immature, awkward adolescent replaced the independent youth in American culture. Youth were pushed out of the job market, as middle-class occupations increasingly demanded high school and college diplomas. As a result, youth came to spend an extended dependency preparing for adulthood. Such dependency became all the more necessary as scientists became convinced of the mercurial nature of young adults. G. Stanley Hall's 1904 tome *Adolescence*, an extended meditation on the volatility and immaturity of young adults, would crystallize intellectual trends well under way in the late nineteenth century.[2] From a long-term perspective, then, youth stood more outside adult guidance and control in the early national era than in the eras that preceded and followed it.

The consequences of the empowerment of youth for the middle class were many. Expanding freedoms for youth produced cultural backlash. Conservative commentators had trouble influencing youth, but their words did have impact. As bourgeois society took form, Americans adopted a range of values and institutions that had been forged in dialogues centered on problems presented by youth. Chastity, domesticity, meritocracy, conscience, and respectable piety—each was trumpeted as a means to control disorder occasioned by youth. Their hold was only partial. An expanding marketplace of goods, ideas, and influences subverted efforts to impose bourgeois order. Urban prostitution coexisted nervously alongside bourgeois sexual propriety. Male peers encouraged one another in sexual indulgences and student disorders. Young men found opportunities to pursue upward mobility without the credentials of higher learning. Publishers pandered to dangerous tastes. Religious revivalists gave spiritual authority freely. Those looking to control youth had to battle against these sources of competition. Youth gained bargaining power as a result. Liberal, free-market values would gain a foothold because of this competition. Still, conservative moralists did have their say; they impressed their notions on a coalescing bourgeoisie.

The talk began in earnest soon after the Revolution. Writers of seduction tales expressed fears of a marriage market out of control. These authors saw mobile male youth as a danger to vulnerable young women. Bemoaning the wiles of deceptive male youth who might seduce their daughters, authors urged chastity to stem the tide of sex and pregnancy among the young. While writers of seduction tales cast young men as predators, they asked young women to assume responsibility for sexual control. They urged chastity upon young women as a self-protective strategy. In addition, the dangerous outside world these authors imagined recommended the haven of home. The writings of seduction moralists were critical to forming bourgeois notions about gender. Chastity and domesticity came to stand for bourgeois femininity, even if some women's claim to these totems was challenged in the early nineteenth century.

As the nineteenth century unfolded, the sexual disorder of youth continued to influence sexual ideals for an emerging bourgeoisie. Moralist commentators became particularly frustrated with prostitutes. The seduction narrative proved too weak to support the challenges heaped upon it by disorderly young women. Bourgeois moralists who took up institutional ventures informed by the seduction narrative, such as the operators of the Philadelphia Magdalen Society, decided that not all women deserved sympathy. Many young women refused to give up their trade or to play the pure victim, challenging the initial assumptions of these reformers. Still, middle-class notions of female purity did prevail. Moral reformers protected bourgeois ideals by stigmatizing prostitutes as members of a degraded urban lower class. If notions of sensibility had promised to bridge class divides with sympathy in the early nineteenth century, by midcentury a chasm separated the bourgeoisie from working-class women.

Youth not only informed bourgeois sexual codes; they influenced bourgeois educational and vocational values as well. College education had never been a primary means for bringing youth into maturity in colonial America. Nevertheless, Americans inspired by republican ideals hoped it could become one in the new nation. Despite these hopes for an expanding education in virtue, early nineteenth-century colleges struggled to find students. The students who did come provided further disappointment, as riots and disorders plagued colleges in the early republic. College authorities combated student disorder by developing a strategy to better command loyalties to themselves. Differentially rewarding students with grades encouraged competition among peers. Merit awards distributed unevenly in schools would confirm the justness of an uneven distribution of resources in bourgeois society at large. Only a select portion of youth would directly experience college values in the early nineteenth century, but as higher learning became a bastion of middle-class legitimacy in the late nineteenth and twentieth centuries, notions of meritocracy would sweep through bourgeois culture.

Competition for young souls during the Second Great Awakening forced changes in Protestant Christianity. Admission into the church of one's elders had been an important rite into adulthood in colonial America. But as religious competition intensified among denominations and churches in the early nineteenth century, it became less certain that youth would follow the lead of their parents and pastors. Revivalists offered youth spiritual rebirth into communities where their voices could more readily be heard. Worship in established churches had served to preserve, not upset, hierarchies. In order to regain some measure of moral control, ministers had to soften orthodoxies and relax their monopoly on religious authority. Fearing the depletion of their churches, religious conservatives began to offer youth positions of authority in Sunday schools in the 1820s. With the assistance of Sunday schools staffed by youth, long-established churches managed to prosper anew. The new theological bent of these churches reflected these compromises. A softer and more accessible God who reveled in the piety of obedient children emerged from bourgeois churches.

The Second Great Awakening was also clearly registered in two new brands of didactic literature for youth that entered American culture in the Jacksonian era. The emphasis on temptation and danger, long the stock rhetoric of evangelical preachers, emerged in manuals written to guide young men through cities and in anti-masturbation tracts. The Market Revolution had thrust youth into strange new work relationships. In colonial America most youth had followed the path into the vocations of adulthood through service under fathers and masters. In the decades approaching midcentury, young men seeking riches forged occupational paths on their own. Efforts at self-making undermined the moral stewardship of the apprenticeship system. If elders no longer housed and watched over the young, then perhaps moral regulation could be situated in the self. Seeking to stem ambition, bourgeois writers urged the cultivation of conscience. The promises of the market, however, were too attractive to be withstood entirely. Thus self-help writers for male youth would leave a mixed legacy. On the one hand, their persistent fear mongering about the seducers awaiting the young man at the threshold of the city would help contain the young. On the other hand, these writers abetted self-making by offering a way for youth to get advice free of parental influence and by propping up profit as a legitimate goal for men in public. While certainly not unambiguous exponents of laissez-faire doctrine, these self-help writers did nudge the bourgeoisie in the direction of free-market values. They would help make material success the hallmark of the American dream.

Books warning against onanism also bore an ambivalent relationship to the marketplace. These texts both cautioned and titillated. As a rake culture became more visible in antebellum urban America, authors more forcefully urged a chastity ideal on young men. These authors saw a slippery slope for those who would dabble in sexual sin. In attacking masturbation, they tried to block sexual transgression in its most accessible form. Using heated sensational rhetoric, language so steamy that it threatened to provoke prurient desires, sex reformers warned of the dangers of masturbation. By the means of such rhetoric, the bourgeoisie by midcentury had applied notions of sexual purity to men, even if their loudest exponents sometimes endangered these ideals, even if a double standard that granted more sexual license to men persisted.

Moral guardians voiced concerns about youth that came to define the emerging bourgeoisie. In trying to control the rising generation, they articulated class identity. Certainly changing material relations in urban America were important in helping the middle class recognize itself, but aspiring Americans also bonded as they worried about the young. Critical bourgeois values and institutions were forged as elders tried to teach young adults how to exercise self-control. In their efforts to transfer young adults into respectable stations, reformers learned lessons of their own. The bourgeoisie came to know itself—one might say it almost called itself into being—in endless discussions about the young. In reacting to the prospect of seduced and abandoned youth, aspiring Americans were reborn as a coherent middle class.

Notes

The names of the archives have been abbreviated as follows:

HSP   Historical Society of Pennsylvania
HUA   Harvard University Archives
LCP   Library Company of Philadelphia
PHS   Presbyterian Historical Society
PUA   Princeton University Archives
UPA   University of Pennsylvania Archives

Introduction

1. Alexis de Tocqueville, *Democracy in America*, ed. Phillips Bradley (New York: Vintage Books, 1945), 2: 202.

2. Tocqueville's use of the word "adolescent" appears in the original French text. The term had begun to gain wider currency in eighteenth- and nineteenth-century France but, tellingly, did not receive wide usage in America until the late nineteenth and twentieth centuries; see Philippe Ariès, *Centuries of Childhood: A Social History of Family Life*, trans. Robert Baldick (New York: Knopf, 1962), 25–32; Howard P. Chudacoff, *How Old Are You?: Age Consciousness in American Culture* (Princeton, N.J.: Princeton University Press, 1989), 20–28, 45–46, 61–62, 66–72.

3. Richard Godbeer, *Sexual Revolution in Early America* (Baltimore: Johns Hopkins University Press, 2002), 52–83, esp. 56, 74, 83; see also Roger Thompson, *Sex in Middlesex: Popular Mores in a Massachusetts County, 1649–1699* (Amherst: University of Massachusetts Press, 1986), 17–109.

4. For a fuller overview of patriarchy in colonial families, see Rodney Hessinger, "Problems and Promises: Colonial American Child Rearing and Modernization Theory," *Journal of Family History* 21 (April 1996): 125–43. The most important study of patriarchy in colonial New England is Philip Greven, *Four Generations: Population, Land, and Family in Colonial Andover, Massachusetts* (Ithaca, N.Y.: Cornell University Press, 1970); the closest study of Quaker family dynamics is Barry Levy, *Quakers and the American Family: British Settlement in the Delaware Valley* (New York: Oxford University Press, 1988).

5. Ashbel Green, "To the Trustees of the College of New Jersey," April 9, 1816, Box 1, Folder 14, Ashbel Green Papers, PUA.

6. Green, "Letter to the Young Gentleman," [1812], Box 1, Folder 12, Ashbel Green Papers, PUA.

7. Ashbel Green, "Report to the Faculty," n.d., Box 1, Folder 13, Ashbel Green Papers, PUA.

8. Burton Bledstein, *The Culture of Professionalism: The Middle Class and the Development of Higher Education in America* (New York: Norton, 1976), 205–7.

9. Carroll Smith-Rosenberg, "Sex as Symbol in Victorian America: An Ethnohistorical Analysis of Jacksonian America," in John Demos and Sarane Spence Boocock, eds., *Turning Points: Historical and Sociological Essays on the Family* (Chicago: University of Chicago Press, 1978), 212–47; Karen Halttunen, *Confidence Men and Painted Women: A Study of Middle-Class Culture in America, 1830–1870* (New Haven, Conn.: Yale University Press, 1982), chap. 1.

10. Glenn Wallach has argued that American youth until the Civil War era did not rebel, that they showed reverence for their elders. In a certain limited sense, Wallach is correct—there was no outward rhetoric of rebellion (with the exception of college campuses and revival meetings)—but he defines his notion of generational discourse too narrowly. In the absence of generational conflict, tension still can surround youth's coming of age. See Wallach, *Obedient Sons: The Discourse of Youth and Generations in American Culture, 1630–1860* (Amherst: University of Massachusetts Press, 1997). On tensions surrounding courtship and the sexuality of youth in the early republic, see Cathy Davidson, *Revolution and the Word: The Rise of the Novel in America* (New York: Oxford University Press, 1986), esp. chap. 6; Carroll Smith-Rosenberg, "Sex as Symbol in Victorian America," 212–47; Smith-Rosenberg, "Beauty, the Beast, and the Militant Woman: A Case Study in Sex Roles and Social Stress in Jacksonian America," *Disorderly Conduct: Visions of Gender in Victorian America* (New York: Oxford University Press, 1985), 109–28; G. J. Barker-Benfield, *The Horrors of the Half-Known Life: Male Attitudes toward Women and Sexuality in Nineteenth-Century America* (New York: Harper and Row, 1976), part 3. On concerns surrounding college education, see David F. Allmendinger, Jr., *Paupers and Scholars: The Transformation of Student Life in Nineteenth-Century New England* (New York: St. Martin's Press, 1975); Steven J. Novak, *The Rights of Youth: American Colleges and Student Revolt, 1798–1815* (Cambridge, Mass.: Harvard University Press, 1977); Bledstein, *The Culture of Professionalism*, chap. 6. On tensions surrounding youth and religious revival, see Mary Ryan, *Cradle of the Middle Class: The Family in Oneida County, New York, 1790–1865* (New York: Cambridge University Press, 1981), chap. 2; Christine Leigh Heyrman, *Southern Cross: The Beginnings of the Bible Belt* (Chapel Hill: University of North Carolina Press, 1997), chaps. 2, 3. On fears about youth entering the city, see Halttunen, *Confidence Men and Painted Women*, chap. 1; Allan Stanley Horlick, *Country Boys and Merchant Princes: The Social Control of Young Men in New York* (Lewisburg, Pa.: Bucknell University Press, 1975). Joseph Kett looks most broadly at all of these concerns in his *Rites of Passage: Adolescence in America, 1790 to the Present* (New York: Basic Books, 1977), chaps. 1–4.

11. See Greven, *Four Generations*, 175–258; Kenneth Lockridge, "Land, Population and the Evolution of New England Society, 1630–1790," *Past and Present* 39 (April 1968): 62–80; Robert A. Gross, *The Minutemen and Their World* (New York: Hill and Wang, 1976), 74–89.

12. The fullest and most influential statement on the revolution against patri-

archy in American culture is Jay Fliegelman, *Prodigals and Pilgrims: The American Revolution against Patriarchal Authority, 1750–1800* (New York: Cambridge University Press, 1982). For a convincing substantiation of Fliegelman's thesis, see C. Dallett Hemphill, "Age Relations and the Social Order in Early New England: The Evidence from Manners," *Journal of Social History* 28, no. 2 (Winter 1994): 271–94. A salutary corrective to exaggerated notions of generational rebellion in the eighteenth century is Anne Lombard, *Making Manhood: Growing Up Male in Colonial New England* (Cambridge, Mass.: Harvard University Press, 2003). By considering the rule of the patriarch over his entire household, the recent work of Carole Shammas suggests enduring patriarchy in the revolutionary and early republic eras, particularly in the realm of property management. Her broad perspective, considering women and slaves, along with children, is helpful. However, a close inspection of cultural developments in the early republic does reveal expanding power and choices for youth. It is not surprising that youth enjoyed liberation before other dependents, for Shammas shows that parental influence over marriage decisions had always been relatively tenuous, relying on wider community support. See Shammas, *A History of Household Government in America* (Charlottesville: University of Virginia Press, 2002).

13. See Daniel Scott Smith, "Parental Power and Marriage Patterns: An Analysis of Historical Trends in Hingham, Massachusetts," *Journal of Marriage and the Family* 35 (August 1973): 419–28; Ellen Rothman, *Hands and Hearts: A History of Courtship in America* (New York: Basic Books, Inc., 1984), chap. 1; Gross, *The Minutemen and Their World*, 98–104; Stephanie Graham Wolf, *As Various as Their Land: The Everyday Lives of Eighteenth-Century Americans* (New York: Harper Perrenial, 1994), 71–77; Lisa Wilson, *Ye Heart of a Man: The Domestic Life of Men in Colonial New England* (New Haven, Conn.: Yale University Press, 1999), 37–71; Godbeer, *Sexual Revolution in Early America*, part 3.

14. See Terry Bilhartz, *Urban Religion and the Second Great Awakening: Church and Society in Early National Baltimore* (Rutherford, N.J.: Farleigh Dickinson University Press, 1986); Richard Carwardine, "The Second Great Awakening in the Urban Centers: An Examination of Methodism and the 'New Measures,'" *Journal of American History* 59 (September 1972): 327–40; Chapter 4 below.

15. See Ryan, *Cradle of the Middle Class*, chap. 2; Marion Bell, *Crusade in the City: Revivalism in Nineteenth Century Philadelphia* (Lewisburg, Pa.: Bucknell University Press, 1977), chap. 4; and Heyrman, *Southern Cross*, chaps. 2, 3; Chapter 4 below.

16. On market competition between colleges, see Chapter 3 below. On student disorders in the early nineteenth century, see Allmendinger, *Paupers and Scholars;* Novak, *The Rights of Youth;* Bledstein, *The Culture of Professionalism*, 223–47; Kett, *Rites of Passage*, 51–61.

17. Cf. Patricia Cline Cohen, *The Murder of Helen Jewett: The Life and Death of a Prostitute in Nineteenth-Century New York* (New York: Knopf, 1998), 10–12, 302–4, 309–10; Timothy Gilfoyle, *City of Eros: New York City, Prostitution, and the Commercialization of Sex, 1790–1920* (New York: Norton, 1992), 92–116; Haltunnen, *Confidence Men and Painted Women*, 1–32.

18. Helen Lefkowitz Horowitz, *Rereading Sex: Battles over Sexual Knowledge*

and Suppression in Nineteenth Century America (New York: Alfred A. Knopf, 2002), 169–72, 210–48; David Reynolds, *Beneath the American Renaissance: The Subversive Imagination in the Age of Emerson and Melville* (Cambridge, Mass.: Harvard University Press, 1988), 211–24.

19. Davidson, *Revolution and the Word*.

20. M. M. Bakhtin, *The Dialogic Imagination*, ed. Michael Holquist, trans. Caryl Emerson and Michael Holquist (Austin: University of Texas Press, 1981), esp. 259–422. In this section I deliberately conflate periodical fiction and the novel. The two, however, are not synonymous. In chapter 1 I will observe how novels did seem more open to competing voices than the fiction appearing in late eighteenth-century magazines.

21. On the high regard for Richardson's moralism, see Herbert Ross Brown, *The Sentimental Novel in America, 1789–1860* (Durham, N.C.: Duke University Press, 1940), 28–51. Bakhtin himself acknowledges the more closed quality of Richardson's didactic novels; see *Dialogic Imagination*, 9–10. Cathy Davidson emphasizes the suspicion toward novels in her *Revolution and the Word*, esp. 42–54.

22. Cohen, *The Murder of Helen Jewett*, 38–68.

23. On the Lucretia Chapman trial, see Karen Halttunen, " 'Domestic Differences': Competing Narratives of Womanhood in the Murder Trial of Lucretia Chapman," in Shirley Samuels, ed., *The Culture of Sentiment: Race, Gender, and Sentimentality in Nineteenth-Century America* (New York: Oxford University Press, 1992), 39–57. On the Singleton Mercer trial, see David Reynolds, "Introduction" in George Lippard, *The Quaker City, or the Monks of Monk Hall*, ed. David Reynolds (Amherst: University of Massachusetts Press, 1995), xii–xiii, and Chapter 2 below. On the trial of Amelia Norman for attempted murder, see Barbara Meil Hobson, *Uneasy Virtue: The Politics of Prostitution and the American Reform Tradition* (New York: Basic Books, 1987), 74–75. On the Jereboam Beauchamp trial, part of the so-called Kentucky Tragedy, see J. W. Cooke, "Portrait of a Murderess: Anna Cook(e) Beauchamp," *Filson Club History Quarterly* 65, no. 2 (April 1991): 209–30, and Cooke, "The Life and Death of Colonel Solomon P. Sharp, Part 2: A Time to Weep and a Time to Mourn," *Filson Club History Quarterly* 72, no. 2 (April 1998): 121–51. Matt Schoenbachler is exploring the Beauchamp case in depth; his manuscript-in-progress is tentatively entitled " 'To Make Madness *Beautiful*': The Kentucky Tragedy in Time and Memory." The case of Elizabeth Wilson, convicted of killing her infant twins in 1786, was also cast in a similar light in the early nineteenth-century; see Daniel A. Cohen, *Pillars of Salt, Monuments of Grace: New England Crime Literature and the Origins of American Popular Cutlure, 1674–1860* (New York: Oxford University Press, 1993), 148–49.

24. Quoted from Davidson, *Revolution and the Word*, 46–47.

25. Reynolds, *Beneath the American Renaissance*, esp. 212–24. On sensationalism in nonfiction print forms, see Karen Halttunen, *Murder Most Foul: The Killer and the American Gothic Imagination* (Cambridge, Mass.: Harvard University Press, 1998).

26. The classic treatment of the self-indulgent tendencies in the sentimental novel is Ann Douglas, *The Feminization of American Culture* (New York: Knopf, 1977).

27. Those works that have been most successful have treated Locke more as emblematic, rather than as determinative, of social and cultural change. The most direct and satisfying exploration of Lockean pedagogy in popular and devotional literature is Fliegelman, *Prodigals and Pilgrims*. What is particularly useful about Fliegelman's treatment of the Lockean legacy is that he demonstrates how in successive reappropriations, Lockean ideas were given an increasingly liberal, antipatriarchal tinge. Invaluable in tracing Lockean educational thought in manners advice and social life into the antebellum era is C. Dallett Hemphill, *Bowing to Necessities: A History of Manners in America, 1620–1860* (New York: Oxford University Press, 1999). Also useful are Jacqueline Reinier, *From Virtue to Character: American Childhood, 1775–1850* (New York: Twayne Publishers, 1996), and Lawrence Cremin, *American Education: The Colonial Experience, 1607–1783* (New York: Harper and Row, 1970). Some more tenuous claims for Lockean influence have recently been advanced in Gillian Brown, *Consent of the Governed: The Lockean Legacy in Early American Culture* (Cambridge, Mass.: Harvard University Press, 2001).

28. This dynamic was not restricted to the American republic, or even to youth. It was unleashed across the Western world as Enlightenment writers explored the social implications of greater individual freedoms. Isabel V. Hull provides an illuminating account of how a greater emphasis on education over coercion in legal thinking emerged in the shift from an absolutist to a liberal state in eighteenth century Germany; see her *Sexuality, State, and Civil Society in Germany, 1700–1815* (Ithaca, N.Y.,: Cornell University Press, 1996).

29. John Locke, *Some Thoughts Concerning Education*, ed. R. H. Quick (Cambridge: Cambridge University Press, 1913), 129.

30. Ibid., 30–31, 56–65, quoted 59, 62. Melvin Yazawa explores the more coercive dimensions of Locke's writings in *From Colonies to Commonwealth: Familial Ideology and the Beginnings of the American Republic* (Baltimore: Johns Hopkins University Press, 1985), esp. 41–44. While Locke certainly wishes to have children obey parents, what is most surprising about his pedagogy is the degree to which he seeks to respect children's desire for liberty, urging parents to deploy a wide range of strategies meant to prevent any contest of wills. His strategies for rearing children without coercion would become all the more important in the early republic when youth garnered a growing share of freedoms in family and society.

31. Locke, *Some Thoughts Concerning Education*, 129–30.

32. Ibid., 32, 60–61.

33. Ibid., 51–52, 61–62.

34. Ibid., 51.

35. Ibid., 34.

36. Ibid., 78–79.

37. Ibid., 27–28.

38. Ibid., 28.

39. Ibid., 133–34.

40. Locke himself recognized the risk of being forced into pandering in using rewards to goad behavior. His particular concern was that material rewards would subvert a parent's aims in child rearing; see Locke, *Some Thoughts Concerning Education*, 32–35.

41. Michel Foucault, *Discipline and Punish: The Birth of the Prison* (New York: Vintage Books, 1995); idem, *The History of Sexuality*, vol. 1 (New York: Vintage Books, 1990); idem, *Foucault Live* (Interviews, 1961–1984), ed. Sylvère Lotringer, trans. Lysa Hochroth and John Johnston (New York: Semiotexte(e): 1996), 207–40; see also Hull, *Sexuality, State, and Civil Society in Germany*, 142, 167–69.

42. Later in his career, after the publication of *Discipline and Punish* and *The History of Sexuality*, vol. 1, Foucault began to emphasize more the potential for resistance. One can see this in a three-way conversation between Foucault, Jean-Pierre Barou, and the historian Michelle Perrot in 1977. Perrott is particularly interested in the gaps in power, the considerable opportunities for resistance, in emerging bourgeois societies. See Foucault, *Foucault Live*, 226–40.

43. Like this study, Mary Ryan's *Cradle of the Middle Class* placed changing notions of child rearing at the center of its analysis of the material and cultural formation of the bourgeoisie. While Ryan's classic book has been inspirational, and in many ways remains compelling, her focus on upstate New York does place some important limits on her study. We must remember what Oneida County was—a collection of small, if growing, frontier towns far removed from the urban centers of the East where the bourgeoisie was most fully taking form. This is not to say that a bourgeois class and bourgeois values did not come to Oneida County. Still, many of the ideas and values that Ryan ties to a specific set of economic developments in Oneida had been explored in the long-settled East years before their birth in upstate New York; cf. Nancy F. Cott, *The Bonds of Womanhood: "Woman's Sphere" in New England, 1780–1835* (New Haven, Conn.: Yale University Press, 1977); Ruth H. Bloch, "American Feminine Ideals in Transition: The Rise of the Moral Mother, 1785–1815," *Feminist Studies* 4, no. 2 (1978): 101–26.

44. G. J. Barker-Benfield, *The Culture of Sensibility: Sex and Society in Eighteenth-Century Britain* (Chicago: University of Chicago Press, 1992).

45. The term "early republic" will be used to encompass the entire era under consideration in this study. A useful survey of the some of the best literature on the Market Revolution is Sean Wilentz, *Society, Politics, and the Market Revolution, 1815–1848*, 2d ed. (Washington: American Historical Association, 1997).

46. Bruce Dorsey, *Reforming Men and Women: Gender in the Antebellum City* (Ithaca, N.Y.: Cornell University Press, 2002), 10.

47. Especially useful were Cohen, *The Murder of Helen Jewett*; Gilfoyle, *City of Eros*; Christine Stansell, *City of Women: Sex and Class in New York, 1789–1860* (Urbana: University of Illinois, 1987); Sean Wilentz, *Chants Democratic: New York City and the Rise of the American Working Class, 1788–1850* (New York: Oxford University Press, 1984).

48. It is important to recognize that this group of youth should not be seen as representative of the whole. As Harvey J. Graff has ably demonstrated, many youth in the early republic continued to live lives remarkably similar to the lives of their colonial forbears. See Graff, *Conflicting Paths: Growing Up in America* (Cambridge, Mass.: Harvard University Press, 1995). Also, I do not mean to imply that working-class youth were wholly ignored. Cf. Paul Boyer, *Urban Masses and Moral Order in America, 1820–1920* (Cambridge, Mass.: Harvard University Press, 1978),

3–53; Joseph Hawes, *Children in Urban Society: Juvenile Delinquency in Nineteenth-Century America* (New York: Oxford University Press, 1971).

49. Jared Waterbury, *Considerations for Young Men* (New York: Jonathan Leavitt, 1832), vii.

50. Among the most important studies that address middle-class formation are Stuart Blumin, *The Emergence of the Middle Class: Social Experience in the American City, 1760–1900* (New York: Cambridge University Press, 1989); Ryan, *Cradle of the Middle Class*; Paul Johnson, *A Shopkeeper's Millennium: Society and Revivals in Rochester, New York, 1815–1837* (New York: Hill and Wang, 1978); Burton Bledstein, *The Culture of Professionalism*; Boyer, *Urban Masses and Moral Order in America, 1820–1920*; Gary Kornblith, "From Artisans to Businessmen: Master Mechanics in New England, 1789–1850" (Ph.D. diss., Princeton University, 1983).

51. Studies of the American working class are legion. Probably the most influential is Wilentz, *Chants Democratic*. For a synthetic overview see Bruce Laurie, *Artisans into Workers: Labor in Nineteenth-Century America* (New York: Hill and Wang, 1989).

52. C. Dallett Hemphill, for one, has demonstrated in the American context that key middle-class values began to take form prior to changes like the development of white-collar labor. See her "Middle Class Rising in Revolutionary America: The Evidence from Manners," *Journal of Social History* 30, no. 2 (Winter 1996): 317–44.

53. Dror Wahrman, *Imagining the Middle Class: The Political Representation of Class in Britain, 1780–1840* (New York: Cambridge University Press, 1995).

54. Ibid., 371–75.

55. Michael Sappol, *A Traffic of Dead Bodies: Anatomy and Embodied Social Identity in Nineteenth-Century America* (Princeton, N.J.: Princeton University Press, 2002), 9–12.

56. Even in England matters other than pitched political battles helped forge the bourgeoisie. As Leonore Davidoff and Catherine Hall have shown, gender and evangelical religion were central to class formation in England. See their *Family Fortunes: Men and Women of the English Middle Class, 1780–1850* (Chicago: University of Chicago Press, 1987).

57. See Hemphill, *Bowing to Necessities*, and Richard Bushman, *The Refinement of America: Persons, Houses, Cities* (New York: Knopf, 1992).

58. See William W. Cutler, "Status, Values and the Education of the Poor: The Trustees of the New York Public School Society, 1805–1853," *American Quarterly* 24, no. 1 (March 1972): 69–85. The broadest statement on the middle-class origins of reform is Boyer, *Urban Masses and Moral Order in America, 1820–1920*.

59. For similar formulations of "bourgeois" that have benefited this study, see David Hogan, "The Market Revolution and Disciplinary Power: Joseph Lancaster and the Psychology of the Early Classroom System," *History of Education Quarterly* 29, no. 3 (Fall 1989): 381–417; Laura Engelstein, *The Keys to Happiness: Sex and the Search for Modernity in Fin-de-Siècle Russia* (Ithaca, N.Y.: Cornell University Press, 1992), 1–13; Sappol, *A Traffic of Dead Bodies*, 9–12.

60. Davidoff and Hall, *Family Fortunes*.

61. Hull, *Sexuality, State, and Civil Society in Germany*, 267–69, 280–83; Ian

Watt, *The Rise of the Novel: Studies in Defoe, Richardson, and Fielding* (Berkeley: University of California Press, 1967), 158–59, 166–68, 220–22.

62. The classic example of this is Royall Tyler's play *The Contrast* (1787), which pitted the virtuous American Colonel Manly against the British aristocratic fop Billy Dimple; see Michael Kimmel, *Manhood in America: A Cultural History* (New York: Free Press, 1996), 15–16. See also Elliott J. Gorn, *The Manly Art: Bare-Knuckle Prize Fighting in America* (Ithaca, N.Y.: Cornell University Press, 1989), 22–32, 54–68.

63. For the impact of the working class on bourgeois identity, see Boyer, *Urban Masses and Moral Order*; Johnson, *A Shopkeeper's Millennium*; Stansell, *City of Women*, chap. 4; Carroll Smith-Rosenberg, *Religion and the Rise of the American City: The New York City Mission Movement, 1812–1870* (Ithaca, N.Y.: Cornell University Press, 1971).

64. See Jeanne Boydston, "The Woman Who Wasn't There: Women's Market Labor and the Transition to Capitalism in the United States," *Journal of the Early Republic* 16 (Summer 1996): 183–206; Mary Ryan, *Women in Public: Between Banners and Ballots, 1825–1880* (Baltimore: Johns Hopkins University Press, 1990); Susan Branson, *These Fiery Frenchified Dames: Women and Political Culture in Early National Philadelphia* (Philadelphia: University of Pennsylvania Press, 2001).

65. See Cott, *The Bonds of Womanhood*, 63–100; Katheryn Kish Sklar, *Catharine Beecher: A Study in American Domesticity* (New York: Norton, 1976); Jeanne Boydston, *Home and Work: Housework, Wages, and the Ideology of Labor in the Early Republic* (New York: Oxford University Press, 1990), 142–63. This is not to suggest that separate-spheres ideology was the only cultural prescription for women's place in antebellum society. On a countervailing set of prescriptions in manners literature, see C. Dallett Hemphill, *Bowing to Necessities*, chap. 9.

Chapter 1

1. *Lady's Magazine and Musical Repository* (New York), January 1801, 40.

2. On the intended audience of seduction fiction, see Cathy N. Davidson, *Revolution and the Word: The Rise of the Novel in America* (New York: Oxford University Press, 1986), 111–25. On the redefinition of womanhood as innately virtuous, see Ruth H. Bloch, "The Gendered Meanings of Virtue in Revolutionary America," *Signs* 13 (Autumn 1987): 37–58 and Nancy F. Cott, "Passionlessness: An Interpretation of Victorian Sexual Ideology, 1790–1850," *Signs* 4 (Winter 1978): 219–36.

3. Bloch, "The Gendered Meanings of Virtue," 37–58.

4. Leonore Davidoff and Catherine Hall, *Family Fortunes: Men and Women of the English Middle Class, 1780–1850* (Chicago: University of Chicago Press, 1987); G. J. Barker-Benfield, *The Culture of Sensibility: Sex and Society in Eighteenth-Century Britain* (Chicago: University of Chicago Press, 1992).

5. This happened, paradoxically, at a time when all women's voices were losing credibility in courts; see Kathleen M. Brown, *Good Wives, Nasty Wenches, and Anxious Patriarchs: Gender, Race, and Power in Colonial Virginia* (Chapel Hill: Uni-

versity of North Carolina Press, 1996), esp. chaps. 4, 6; Cornelia Hughes Dayton, *Women before the Bar: Gender, Law, and Society in Connecticut, 1639–1789* (Chapel Hill: University of North Carolina Press, 1995), chap. 5.

6. Barbara Welter, "The Cult of True Womanhood, 1820–1860," *American Quarterly* 18 (Summer 1966): 151–74; Kathryn Kish Sklar, *Catharine Beecher: A Study in American Domesticity* (New Haven, Conn.: Yale University Press, 1973); Mary P. Ryan, *Cradle of the Middle Class: The Family in Oneida County, New York, 1790–1865* (New York: Cambridge University Press, 1981). Post-structural theorists have added further emphasis to the importance of binary oppositions or dichotomies in the creation of ideologies; see Joan C. Williams, "Domesticity as the Dangerous Supplement of Liberalism," *Journal of Women's History* 2 (Winter 1991): 69–88.

7. Thomas Laqueur, *Making Sex: Body and Gender from the Greeks to Freud* (Cambridge, Mass.: Harvard University Press, 1990), 43–51, 161–63.

8. Brown, *Good Wives, Nasty Wenches, and Anxious Patriarchs*, chaps. 4, 6; Dayton, *Women before the Bar*, chap. 5.

9. Cott, "Passionlessness."

10. For a precise explanation of the designation of "best-seller" and a listing of the same, see Frank Luther Mott, *Golden Multitudes: The Story of the Best Sellers in the United States* (New York: Macmillan, 1947). On the popularity of *The Coquette*, see Cathy Davidson, *Revolution and the Word: The Rise of the Novel in America* (New York: Oxford University Press, 1986), 149–50. The most thorough study of the popularity of *Charlotte Temple* is R. W. G. Vail, *Susanna Haswell Rowson, the Author of Charlotte Temple: A Bibliographic Study* (Worcester, Mass.: Davis Press, 1933).

11. On the popularity of seduction tales in periodicals, see Mildred Doyle, "Sentimentalism in American Periodicals, 1741–1800" (Ph.D. diss., New York University, 1941), 55–61; see also Jan Lewis, "The Republican Wife: Virtue and Seduction in the Early Republic," *William and Mary Quarterly* 3rd ser., 44 (October 1987): 689–721; Rodney Hessinger, "'Insidious Murderers of Female Innocence': Representations of Masculinity in the Seduction Tales of the Late Eighteenth-Century," in Merril Smith, ed., *Sex and Sexuality in Early America* (New York: NYU Press, 1998), 262–82. On seduction in ephemeral literature in Philadelphia, see Clare Lyons, "Sex among the 'Rabble': Gender Transitions in the Age of Revolution, Philadelphia, 1750–1830" (Ph.D. diss., Yale University, 1996), chap. 5. Richard Godbeer has recently added more evidence of the popularity of this theme across the young nation. Particularly valuable is his finding that newspapers pursued this theme as well. The content of those articles seems to have been consistent with that of periodical stories and novels. See his *Sexual Revolution in Early America* (Baltimore: Johns Hopkins University Press, 2002), chap. 8.

12. C. Dallett Hemphill, *Bowing to Necessities: The History of Manners in America, 1620–1860* (New York: Oxford University Press, 1999), chap. 6.

13. Joel Perlmann and Dennis Shirley, "When Did New England Women Acquire Literacy?," *William and Mary Quarterly* 3rd ser., 48 (January 1991): 50–67. For a more general consideration of literacy in the late eighteenth-century, see Davidson, *Revolution and the Word*, 55–79.

14. Davidson, *Revolution and the Word*, 17.

15. Ibid., 27–29. Davidson also notes that lending was prevalent among acquaintances.

16. Ibid., 28, 65, 114. For the ways in which novels entered social circles in nineteenth-century America, see Ronald J. Zboray and Mary S. Zboray, "Books, Reading, and the World of Goods in Antebellum America," *American Quarterly* 48, no. 4 (December 1996): 587–622.

17. Michael Kimmel, *Manhood in America: A Cultural History* (New York: Free Press, 1996), 15–16; Andrew Burstein, *Sentimental Democracy: The Evolution of America's Romantic Self-Image* (New York: Hill and Wang, 1999), 289–91. On adaptations of seduction tales for the stage, see Ann Douglas, "Introduction," in Susanna Rowson, *Charlotte Temple: A Tale of Truth*, ed. Ann Douglas (New York: Penguin Books, 1991; 1st American ed., Philadelphia: M. Carey, 1794). *The Coquette* was transformed into a play as early as 1802; see Nichols J. Horatio, *The New England Coquette: From the history of the celebrated Eliza Wharton: A tragic drama in three acts* (Salem, Mass.: N. Coverly, 1802).

18. Philip Greven, *Four Generations: Population, Land, and Family in Colonial Andover, Massachusetts* (Ithaca, N.Y.: Cornell University Press, 1970); Daniel Scott Smith, "Parental Power and Marriage Patterns: An Analysis of Historical Trends in Hingham, Massachusetts," *Journal of Marriage and the Family* 35 (August 1973): 419–28; Ellen Rothman, *Hands and Hearts: A History of Courtship in America* (New York: Basic Books, Inc., 1984), chap. 1; Robert Gross, *The Minutemen and Their World* (New York: Hill and Wang), chap. 4.

19. Jay Fliegelman, *Prodigals and Pilgrims: The American Revolution against Patriarchal Authority, 1750–1800* (New York: Cambridge University Press, 1982); C. Dallett Hemphill, "Age Relations and the Social Order in Early New England," *Journal of Social History* 28 (Winter 1994): 271–94.

20. The classic text describing the effects of the declining prospects of land inheritance in one community, where these changes were in full swing by the mid-eighteenth century, is Greven, *Four Generations*, 175–258. See also Kenneth Lockridge, "Land, Population and the Evolution of New England Society, 1630–1790," *Past and Present* 39 (April 1968): 62–80; Gross, *Minutemen and Their World*, chap. 4. On the decline of the apprenticeship system during the early republic, see Sean Wilentz, *Chants Democratic: New York City and the Rise of the American Working Class, 1788–1850* (New York: Oxford University Press, 1984), 23–60; Gordon Wood, *The Radicalism of the American Revolution* (New York: Vintage Books, 1993), 185–86. For a general description of the geographic mobility of youth in the early republic, see Joseph Kett, *Rites of Passage: Adolescence in America, 1790 to the Present* (New York: Basic Books, 1977), 11–110.

21. Carole Shammas has made the case that it was declining community involvement, more than lessening parental control, that best explains problems such as rising premarital pregnancy in the late eighteenth-century; see her *A History of Household Government in America* (Charlottesville: University of Virginia Press, 2002), chap. 4. For an overview of the decline of community influence in family affairs in the mid- to late eighteenth century, see Helena M. Wall, *Fierce Communion: Family and Community in Early America* (Cambridge, Mass.: Harvard University Press, 1990).

22. Laurel Thatcher Ulrich, *Good Wives: Image and Reality in the Lives of Women in Northern New England* (New York: Knopf, 1980), 94–105, 118–23; Barry Levy, "'Tender Plants': Quaker Farmers and Children in the Delaware Valley, 1681–1735," *Journal of Family History* 3 (1978): 116–35; Godbeer, *Sexual Revolution in Early America*, 84–101; Lisa Wilson, *Ye Heart of a Man: The Domestic Life of Men in Colonial New England* (New Haven, Conn.: Yale University Press, 1999), chap. 2. Wilson suggests that by the late colonial period a failed courtship for men could prove quite embarrassing because it was largely up to young men rather than their parents to arrange a marriage; yet the oversight of the community and the young woman's family remained, thus a thwarted courtship was seen in public. This seems an intermediary stage before male youth more easily escaped both parental control and community notice.

23. Cornelia Hughes Dayton, "Taking the Trade: Abortion and Gender Relations in an Eighteenth-Century New England Village," *William and Mary Quarterly* 3rd ser., 48 (January 1991): 19–49; Dayton, *Women before the Bar*, chap. 4; Godbeer, *Sexual Revolution in Early America*, 227–36, 245–63. For a more general discussion of the shift away from patriarchal responsibility toward the community, see E. Anthony Rotundo, *American Manhood: Transformations in Masculinity from the Revolution to the Modern Era* (New York: Basic Books, 1993), 10–30.

24. Daniel Scott Smith and Michael S. Hindus, "Premarital Pregnancy in America, 1640–1971," *Journal of Interdisciplinary History* 5 (Spring 1975): 537–70; Robert V. Wells, "Illegitimacy and Bridal Pregnancy in Colonial America," in Peter Laslett, Karla Oosterveen and Richard M. Smith, eds., *Bastardy and Its Comparative History* (Cambridge, Mass.: Harvard University Press, 1980), 349–61; Susan E. Klepp, *Philadelphia in Transition: A Demographic History of the City and Its Occupational Groups, 1720–1830* (New York: Garland Publishing, 1989), 62–137. Smith and Hindus track an eighteenth-century climb in premarital pregnancy and locate its peak around the time of the Revolution; they also suggest that bastardy rates probably followed this same pattern. Wells's suggestive work on bastardy generally concurs with Smith and Hindus' findings. Susan Klepp in her thorough demographic study of Philadelphia locates the peak of illegitimacy in the post-Revolution years with a subsequent drop in the early nineteenth century. Clare Lyons has also suggested that late eighteenth-century Philadelphia witnessed a boom in bastardy, noting a rapid increase in recorded cases of bastardy in the records of various public institutions for this period. This approach probably overstates the increase in bastardy in Philadelphia because it assumes that authorities were as likely to intervene in one time period as another. However, what these findings do more conclusively suggest is that more informal interventions, such as the application of familial pressure, were no longer proving sufficient in securing support for unwed mothers. See Lyons, "Sex Among the 'Rabble,'" chap. 1.

25. For convincing statements of this position, see Cott, "Passionlessness," 228–31; Christine Stansell, *City of Women: Sex and Class in New York, 1787–1860* (Urbana: University of Illinois Press, 1987), 23–27.

26. Davidson, *Revolution and the Word*, 66–74; Patricia L. Parker, "Susanna Haswell Rowson: America's First Best-Selling Author," in Kriste Lindenmeyer, ed., *Ordinary Women, Extraordinary Lives* (Wilmington, Del.: SR Books, 2000), 25–38.

Even Judith Sargent Murray, perhaps the most outspoken advocate of women's rights in this era and whose "Story of Margaretta" featured a heroine who avoided seduction, still asked young women to seek parental guidance in courtship; see Sheila L. Skemp, *Judith Sargent Murray: A Brief Biography with Documents* (Boston: Bedford Books, 1998), 64.

27. One might see such narratives as a call for reforms that would protect women. Susan Klepp has suggested that late eighteenth- and early nineteenth-century women indulged in a "cult of fear" in which they used traditional concepts of dependency to call on men to assume the role of protector of women. C. Dallett Hemphill has suggested that the "ladies first" etiquette doctrine of the antebellum era, a doctrine that asked men to grant women protective privileges, might in part trace its origins to this feminism of fear. While these tales might be understood as a collective call for help, there are some obvious limits to the gains that can be made under such a strategy. Most fundamentally, women would have no claims on individual freedoms. Their gains would rest wholly on the goodwill of men. See Klepp, "'Heroines whose courage had risen superior to sex': Women, Fear, and Autobiography in the Early Republic," paper presented to the Festive Culture and Public Ritual in Early America conference, April 1996, held by the McNeil Center for Early American Studies; Hemphill, *Bowing to Necessities*, chap. 9.

28. Cathy Davidson and Jan Lewis both suggest that novels and periodical fiction were read by men, as well as women. See Davidson, *Revolution and the Word*, 8, 98, and Lewis, "The Republican Wife," 692.

29. Discussion of the culture of sensibility has boomed in recent years, most fully for Britain. For two wide-ranging accounts of sensibility, see Markman Ellis, *The Politics of Sensibility: Race, Gender and Commerce in the Sentimental Novel* (Cambridge: Cambridge University Press, 1996), and Barker-Benfield, *The Culture of Sensibility*. For accounts of sensibility in American culture, see Karen Halttunen, "Humanitarianism and the Pornography of Pain in Anglo-American Culture," *American Historical Review* 100 (April 1995): 303–34; Sarah Knott, "A Cultural History of Sensibility in the Era of the American Revolution" (Ph.D. diss., Oxford University, 1999); Burstein, *Sentimental Democracy*.

30. Rowson, *Charlotte Temple*, 11–12.

31. William Hill Brown, *The Power of Sympathy, or, The Triumph of Nature. Founded in Truth*, 2 vols. (Boston: Isaiah Thomas, 1789), 2: 29.

32. Hannah W. Foster, *The Coquette*, ed. Cathy N. Davidson (New York: Oxford University Press, 1986; 1st ed., Boston: Samuel Etheridge, 1797), 35, 72, 164.

33. Rowson, *Charlotte Temple*, 4–5.

34. For rhetoric about conscience within family life, see Carl Degler, *At Odds: Women and the Family in America from the Revolution to the Present* (New York: Oxford University Press, 1980), 86–110; Rodney Hessinger, "Problems and Promises: Colonial American Child Rearing and Modernization Theory," *Journal of Family History* 21 (April 1996): 125–43.

35. Brown, *The Power of Sympathy*, 2: 64–65.

36. Ibid., 59–60.

37. "Sorrows of Amelia," *The Baltimore Weekly Magazine*, July 5, 1800, 87.

38. "The Fatal Effects of Seduction," *The Gentlemen and Ladies Town and Country Magazine* (Boston), June 1789, 250–51.

39. "Matilda," *The Key* (Fredericktown, Md.), April 14, 1798, 106.

40. Brown, *The Power of Sympathy*, 2: 105.

41. "Melancholy Tale of Seduction,"*Massachusetts Magazine* (Boston), April 1795, 40–42.

42. For an extended example of this lesson, see Brown, *The Power of Sympathy*, 1: 69–80.

43. *The Gentlemen and Ladies Magazine*, November 1789, 547.

44. Merchants in this era also worried about their relationships with increasingly mobile men. On their concerns about fellow merchants' personal character, and more specifically their fear of being "seduced" by other men, see Toby Ditz, "Shipwrecked; or Masculinity Imperiled: Mercantile Representations of Failure and the Gendered Self in Eighteenth-Century Philadelphia," *Journal of American History* 81, no. 1 (June 1994): 51–80.

45. Lewis, "The Republican Wife," 715–21.

46. Davidson, *Revolution and the Word*, 140–50; Smith-Rosenberg, "Domesticating 'Virtue': Coquettes and Revolutionaries in Young America," in *Literature and the Body*, ed. Elaine Scarry (Baltimore: Johns Hopkins University Press, 1988), 160–84.

47. See especially 26–27, 31, 38, 99, 105, 145.

48. See "Sorrows of Amelia," 86–87; "Sobrina and Flirtirella," *The Key*, April 14 1798, 108–9; "Gossip LIV," *The Boston Weekly Magazine*, February 18, 1804.

49. "Story of Philenia," *Massachusetts Magazine*, December 1791, 729–30.

50. "Matilda," 106.

51. "On the Seduction of Young Women," *The Boston Magazine*, October 1783, 19.

52. *The American Museum* (Philadelphia), August 1787, 106; also reprinted in *The New York Magazine*, July 1791, 419–20; *The Literary Miscellany* (Philadelphia), vol. 1, 1795, 26–27; *The Lady and Gentleman's Pocket Magazine* (New York), September 15, 1796, 122–23.

53. See "Fatal Effects of Seduction," *The New York Magazine*, January 1790, 22–23; "The Prostitute: A Fragment," *New York Magazine*, April 1793, 216–17; "The Ruined Girl," *Lady's Magazine* (Philadelphia), February 1793, 147–48; "Story of a Poor Girl," *Ladies Museum* (Philadelphia), February 25, 1800, 1. In portraying prostitution as an outcome of seduction, Americans were closely following British fictive practice (in fact many American periodical articles were reprints from British sources). On the seduction into prostitution theme in British sensibility literature, see Ellis, *The Politics of Sensibility*, chap. 5.

54. For an excellent exploration of the complications and potential for subversion within one text, see Michael Zuckerman, "Charlotte: A Tale of Sentiment, Seduction, and Subversion," paper presented to the Philadelphia Center for Early American Studies Seminar, September 11, 1992. The novels do seem to subvert themselves more, and to be geared more toward "consumption," than the periodical pieces are. Yet while the novels seem to be potentially more enjoyable from the reader's standpoint, they are to a surprising degree steeped in the same stock lan-

guage one finds in the magazine articles—moral warnings to women of the depraved nature of men were endemic to the form. One might note here, also, that not all fiction in this period engaged in such moralizing; it was precisely the fictive forms that did not which were condemned by the writers of seduction tales. For a discussion of the discriminatory judgments made by American writers, see Herbert Ross Brown, *The Sentimental Novel in America, 1789–1860* (Durham, N.C.: Duke University Press, 1940), 28–29, 75–76; Doyle, "Sentimentalism in American Periodicals," 68–74.

55. See "Speech of Miss Polly Baker," *The American Museum*, March 1787, 212–14; "Friendly Hints; or a Letter to a beloved young lady," *Lady's Magazine*, April 1793, 227–29; "The Dying Prostitute," *The Lady and Gentleman's Pocket Magazine*, September 15, 1796, 122–23; "Seduction—An elegy," *The American Museum*, August 1787, 205–6; "Treachery and Infidelity Punished," *The New York Magazine*, February 1793, 93; "The Seduced Female," *The New York Magazine*, January 1796, 13–14; "Story of Amelia," *The New York Magazine*, April 1797, 210–5; "Seduction," *Weekly Magazine* (Philadelphia), March 16, 1799, 290.

56. Doyle, "Sentimentalism in American Periodicals," 50–55.

57. "Almira and Alonzo," *Massachusetts Magazine*, June 1789, 361–64.

58. Barker-Benfield, *The Culture of Sensibility*; Foster, *The Coquette*, 57.

59. Godbeer, *Sexual Revolution in Early America*, 259–63.

60. See "Amelia: or the Faithless Briton," *Columbian Magazine* (Philadelphia), October 1787, 677; "Fatal Effects of Seduction," *The New York Magazine*, 22; "Story of Amelia," April 1797, 210. The three major novels considered in this chapter not only claimed to be based on fact; there is ample evidence that they in fact were. See Brown, *The Sentimental Novel in America*, 9–10, n. 26; Davidson, *Revolution and the Word*, 140–44; Daniel Cohen, *Pillars of Salt, Monuments of Grace: New England Crime Literature and the Origins of American Popular Culture, 1674–1860* (New York: Oxford University Press, 1993), 168–69.

61. Ellis, *The Politics of Sensibility*, 12–14.

62. Ibid., 43–48.

63. William Hill Brown provides a highly illuminating lecture on the various types of novels, rejecting some, recommending others; see *Power of Sympathy*, 1: 40–61.

64. Rowson, *Charlotte Temple*, 26.

65. Mary P. Ryan, "The Power of Women's Networks: A Case Study of Female Moral Reform in Antebellum America," *Feminist Studies* 5 (Spring 1979): 66–85; Carroll Smith-Rosenberg, "Beauty, the Beast, and the Militant Woman: A Case Study in Sex Roles and Social Stress in Jacksonian America," *Disorderly Conduct: Visions of Gender in Victorian America* (New York: Oxford University Press, 1985), 109–28.

66. The encouragement of parental involvement in marriage decisions in seduction fiction marked a serious departure from the antipatriarchal trends in eighteenth-century Anglo-American literature; see Fliegelman, *Prodigals and Pilgrims*.

67. "Story of Philenia," 730.

68. "Sorrows of Amelia," 86.

69. *The Gentleman and Ladies Town and Country Magazine*, November 1789, 547–48.

70. Rowson, *Charlotte Temple*, 26.

71. Foster, *The Coquette*, 94.

72. "Almira and Alonzo," 361–64.

73. Brown, *The Power of Sympathy*, 1: 119.

74. Ibid., 137.

75. "Felicia to Her Unfortunate Friend," *The New York Magazine*, October 1795, 611–12.

76. Foster, *The Coquette*, 151; "Amelia: or the Faithless Briton," 677–82, 877–80.

77. Rowson, *Charlotte Temple*, 55.

78. Such passages showing the pain of others were also likely part of the unspoken pleasure of reading Rowson's novel; on this potential in sensibility writing, see Haltunnen, "Humanitarianism and the Pornography of Pain," 303–34.

79. "The Ladies Friend. Number IV," *Lady's Magazine*, November 1792, 263–65.

80. Foster, *The Coquette*, 163.

81. "The Duelist and Libertine Reclaimed," *Massachusetts Magazine*, April 1789, 205–7.

82. Clare Lyons demonstrates the cultural narrowing of women's sexual options resulting from seduction tales in her "Sex among the 'Rabble,'" chaps. 2, 5.

83. Foster, *The Coquette*, 163. Following this same line of reasoning, Keith Thomas has suggested that seduction fiction represented the strongest attempt at protecting men's property in women. This deliberate cultural strategy suggested by Thomas seems an overly harsh judgment on writers such as Samuel Richardson; nonetheless, it is clear that seduction fiction did help erect a double standard, even if born out of a concern for women's vulnerability; see his "The Double Standard," *Journal of the History of Ideas* 20 (1959): 195–216.

84. Rothman, *Hands and Hearts*, chap. 1.

85. Ibid., 44–55.

86. Boydston thus sees seduction tales as part of a larger cultural cover-up of women's participation in the economy of the early republic, see her "The Woman Who Wasn't There: Women's Market Labor and the Transition to Capitalism in the United States," *Journal of the Early Republic* 16 (Summer 1996): 183–206.

87. Dayton, "Taking the Trade," 19–49. In larger historical perspective, it appears that this shift toward the double standard represented a reemergence of a standard that had been much muted by the vigorous brand of Protestant Christianity brought by many northern colonial communities in the seventeenth-century.

88. On the rejection of the "man of feeling" in the early nineteenth-century, see Burstein, *Sentimental Democracy*, 308–19. On sentimentalism as feminized, see Ann Douglas, *The Feminization of American Culture* (New York: Knopf, 1977).

Chapter 2

1. William Alcott, *The Young Man's Guide*, 15th edition (Boston: T. R. Marvin, 1843; 1st edition, 1833), 306–8.

2. Sharon Block has recently argued that the seduction narrative was always less tenable than the rape narrative because women in seduction were necessarily more complicit in the crime. This point is undoubtedly true; what I wish to emphasize, however, is that blame toward women in seduction narratives was quite historically variable. See Block, "Rape without Women: Print Culture and the Politicization of Rape, 1765–1815," *Journal of American History* 89, no. 3 (December 2002): 849–68.

3. An incredible amount of ink has been spilt on the topic of the centrality of female chastity to antebellum bourgeois ideology. Two of the most important and convincing statements of this position are Mary Ryan, *Cradle of the Middle Class: The Family in Oneida County, New York, 1790–1865* (New York: Cambridge University Press, 1981), and Nancy Cott, "Passionlessness: An Interpretation of Victorian Sexual Ideology, 1790–1850," *Signs* 4 (Winter 1978): 219–36.

4. Mary Ryan and Carroll Smith-Rosenberg have both indirectly demonstrated the participation of male bourgeois youth in urban prostitution in their depictions of middle-class women retrieving errant sons from brothel visiting. Timothy Gilfoyle most clearly demonstrates the participation of bourgeois youth in a sporting culture centered on prostitution. He also suggests that working-class men shared in this sporting culture. See Ryan, *Cradle of the Middle Class*, 116–30; Smith-Rosenberg, "Beauty, the Beast, and the Militant Woman: A Case Study in Sex Roles and Social Stress in Jacksonian America," *Disorderly Conduct: Visions of Gender in Victorian America* (New York: Oxford University Press, 1985), 109–28; Gilfoyle, *City of Eros: New York City, Prostitution, and the Commercialization of Sex, 1790–1920* (New York: Norton, 1992), 92–116.

5. A number of works have considered the development of a code of bourgeois male sexual propriety. For a synthetic overview of such past scholarship, see John D'Emilio and Estelle B. Freedman, *Intimate Matters: A History of Sexuality in America* (New York: Harper and Row, 1988), esp. chap. 4. Most works have treated this ethic of male chastity as largely the concern of a fringe of midcentury sex reformers; for a recent convincing demonstration of the centrality of male chastity to the antebellum bourgeois mentality, see C. Dallett Hemphill, *Bowing to Necessities: The History of Manners in America, 1620–1860* (New York: Oxford University Press, 1999), chap. 9.

6. Christine Stansell pursues the theme of a class-based view of womanhood with respect to the ideology of domesticity, suggesting bourgeois home-visiting reformers were disturbed by the boisterous community life of working-class women. Stansell also suggests that young working-class women seemed to reject bourgeois sexual standards by adopting a flashy clothing style that accentuated sexual appeal. See Stansell, *City of Women: Sex and Class in New York, 1787–1860* (Urbana: University of Illinois Press, 1987), chaps. 4, 5.

7. In the diary of a late nineteenth-century young bourgeois man, E. Anthony Rotundo has discovered a clearly articulated sexual code that demanded chaste conduct with class peers but allowed sexual indulgence with "chippies," women of the lower class. While no such document has been discovered for an earlier period, there is ample evidence that within mid-nineteenth-century bourgeois society, males had adopted a standard of male sexual propriety and yet simultaneously fre-

quented prostitutes. See Rotundo's *American Manhood: Transformations in Masculinity from the Revolution to the Modern Era* (New York: Basic Books, 1993), 119–28.

8. African Americans, who did not appear in such stories, were undoubtedly less eligible for such conventional assumptions. See Kathleen Brown, *Good Wives, Nasty Wenches, and Anxious Patriarchs: Gender, Race, and Power in Colonial Virginia* (Chapel Hill: University of North Carolina Press, 1996); Deborah Gray White, *Ar'n't I a Woman? Female Slaves in the Plantation South* (New York: Norton, 1985).

9. *Magdalen Society Constitution*, Historical Society of Pennsylvania (hereafter HSP), 1800.

10. *Poulson's American Daily Advertiser* (Philadelphia), January 23, 1801.

11. On the status of the founders and the managers of the Magdalen Society, see Marcia Roberta Carlisle, "Prostitutes and Their Reformers in Nineteenth-Century Philadelphia" (Ph.D. diss., Rutgers University, 1982), 155–62. On the readership of seduction fiction, see Cathy Davidson, *Revolution and the Word: The Rise of the Novel in America* (New York: Oxford University Press, 1986), 11–125.

12. Bruce Dorsey has clearly demonstrated that Philadelphia's reform community prior to 1820 did not see the poor as socially or morally distinct; they saw poverty as a fate that might befall any member of society. See his "City of Brotherly Love: Religious Benevolence, Gender, and Reform in Philadelphia, 1780–1844" (Ph.D. diss., Brown University, 1993), esp. 83–86 and *Reforming Men and Women: Gender in the Antebellum City* (Ithaca, N.Y.: Cornell University Press, 2002), chap. 2. By emphasizing the link between poverty and prostitution, Clare Lyons ignores the plot progression of seduction narratives. Seduction preceded poverty in such tales. As subsequent discussion will demonstrate, the linking of class concerns and prostitution by Society managers did not truly emerge until the middle decades of the century. See Lyons, "Sex Among the "Rabble": Gender Transitions in the Age of Revolution, Philadelphia, 1750–1830" (Ph.D. diss., Yale University, 1996), 369–406. The notion that poverty, if only following family abandonment, could cause a woman to turn to prostitution, at least appeared in some form; the more convention-defying notion that some women were attracted to prostitution because it proved a lucrative occupation was given no consideration at all. For a discussion of the economic opportunities and independence that prostitution offered early nineteenth-century Philadelphia women, see Marcia Roberta Carlisle, "Prostitutes and Their Reformers in Nineteenth-Century Philadelphia" (Ph.D. diss., Rutgers University, 1982); for the same view of New York's prostitutes, see Stansell, *City of Women*, chap. 9.

13. See Minutes of the Board of Managers, 12/7/07 (Vol. 1, 87–88); Minutes, 3/7/08 (Vol. 1, 98–99); Minutes, 2/7/09 (Vol. 1, 131), Philadelphia Magdalen Society (hereafter PMS), HSP.

14. *Poulson's* (Philadelphia), January 23, 1801.

15. For an insightful account of the crucial role that sensibility literature played in the founding and promotion of the Magdalen Hospital in London, see Markman Ellis, *The Politics of Sensibility: Race, Gender, and Commerce in the Sentimental Novel* (Cambridge: Cambridge University Press, 1996), chap. 5.

16. *Poulson's* (Philadelphia), January 23, 1801.

17. Billy Smith documents poverty in late eighteenth-century Philadelphia

and suggests that prostitutes were frequenting the almshouse; see his *The "Lower Sort": Philadelphia's Laboring People, 1750–1800* (Ithaca, N.Y.: Cornell University Press, 1990), 168–69. Between 1807 and 1811 half of the women in the Magdalen asylum entered the institution from the almshouse; see Lyons, "Sex among the 'Rabble,'" 395. While economic considerations alone do not explain the decision of many women in nineteenth-century America to enter prostitution, there clearly was a correlation between working-class status and prostitution, at least by the mid-nineteenth century; see Barabara Meil Hobson, *Uneasy Virtue: The Politics of Prostitution and the American Reform Tradition* (New York: Basic Books, 1987), chap. 4, and Stansell, *City of Women*, chap. 9.

18. Minutes, 7/20/07 (Vol. 1, 83), PMS, HSP.

19. Minutes, 1/15/05 (Vol. 1, 38); Minutes, 2/11/05 (Vol. 1, 41); Minutes, 4/25/05 (Vol. 1, 46), PMS, HSP.

20. Admittance figures are contained in the Society's *Annual Reports*, HSP. For statistical summaries of this information, see Carlisle, "Prostitutes and Their Reformers," 168, 175, 187, and Lyons, "Sex Among the 'Rabble,'" 393, 395.

21. Primary care of the Magdalens was given to a matron hired by the Society, while the managers regularly visited the asylum to ensure that operations were progressing smoothly. Giving daily care to the matron might have helped resolve some of the obvious ideological tensions inherent in a male-led institution geared to helping fallen women who, according to the writings of the Society, had reached their lowered state because of the seductive schemes of men. Another attempt to resolve these tensions may have been the Society's rule that no board member could visit a Magdalen unattended: "No member of the board shall hold any private conversation with any of the Magdalens, nor visit any of their apartments alone." In all visits board members had to be joined by either the steward, matron, her assistant, or a fellow board member. See Minutes 7/20/07 (Vol. 1, 79b-80); Minutes 11/7/09 (Vol. 1, 160), PMS, HSP.

22. Clare Lyons has noted that the entry narratives seemed to mimic popular print. The more extended analysis of the narratives in the pages that follow will more firmly establish this connection. In addition, I wish to suggest several lessons beyond the narratives' similarity to popular print. First, I aim to demonstrate that these narratives were not simply imposed; rather, they were negotiated. Women seeking entry to the asylum recognized that playing the role of the seduced woman availed them sympathy and material benefits. Second, I wish to expose the long-term dynamics of this negotiation. Gradually, the seduction narrative was eroded. In its place emerged a less sympathetic and more class-bound critique of the women who entered the asylum. See Lyons, "Sex Among the 'Rabble'," 403–5.

23. On the fundamental similarity of asylums and prisons in the early republic, see David Rothman, *The Discovery of the Asylum: Social Order and Disorder in the New Republic* (Boston: Little, Brown, 1971). On the deep regulation of daily life in prisons, see Michel Foucault, *Discipline and Punish: The Birth of the Prison* (New York: Vintage Books, 1995). For an in-depth consideration of how the policies of the Magdalen Society resembled the policies of Philadelphia penal institutions, see Michael Meranze, *Laboratories of Virtue: Punishment, Revolution, and Authority in*

Philadelphia, 1760–1835 (Chapel Hill: University of North Carolina Press, 1996), esp. 272–79, 287–88.

24. Minutes, 7/20/07 (Vol. 1, 79b); Minutes, 11/7/09 (Vol. 1, 161), PMS, HSP.

25. Minutes, 7/20/07 (Vol. 1, 80); Minutes, 3/7/08 (Vol. 1, 102), PMS, HSP.

26. Carlisle, "Prostitutes and Their Reformers," 168; Lyons, "Sex Among the 'Rabble,'" 393, 395.

27. Minutes, 2/2/08 (Vol. 1, 91–2), PMS, HSP.

28. Ibid.

29. The manipulation of life histories to present a more sympathetic self by the prostitutes who entered the asylum have much in common with the various efforts at self-invention by the famed prostitute Helen Jewett, as wonderfully demonstrated by Patricia Cline Cohen; see her *The Murder of Helen Jewett: The Life and Death of a Prostitute in Nineteenth-Century New York* (New York: Knopf, 1998), 38–68. On the reformer Charles Loring Brace's suspicions of prostitutes stories, see Stansell, *City of Women*, 192.

30. Minutes, 12/6/08 (Vol. 1, 126), PMS, HSP.

31. Ibid., 127.

32. Minutes, 2/7/09 (Vol. 1, 131), PMS, HSP.

33. Susanna Rowson, *Charlotte Temple: A Tale of Truth*, ed. Ann Douglas (New York: Penguin Books, 1991; 1st American ed., 1794), 106.

34. Cornelia Hughes Dayton and Sharon Block have both emphasized how women's claims about rape were viewed suspiciously in the eighteenth-century. Such suspicion seems to linger here, yet what is most remarkable about the early records of the Magdalen Society is the sympathy, not the suspicion, expressed toward the women admitted. See Dayton, *Women Before the Bar: Gender, Law, and Society in Connecticut, 1639–1789* (Chapel Hill: University of North Carolina Press, 1995), 231–84; Block, "Rape without Women," *Journal of American History* 89, no. 3 (December 2002): 849–68.

35. Minutes, 3/7/08 (Vol. 1, 99–100), PMS, HSP.

36. Rowson, *Charlotte Temple*, 30.

37. Ibid., 70.

38. *Magdalen Society Constitution*, HSP.

39. Minutes, 2/1/04 (Vol. 1, 30); Minutes 4/25/05 (Vol. 1, 43); Minutes 3/4/06 (Vol. 1, 54); Minutes 2/9/07 (Vol. 1, 69); Minutes 3/7/08 (Vol. 1, 99); Minutes 5/3/08 (Vol. 1, 108), PMS, HSP; *Annual Report* 1819, 3; *Annual Report* 1824, 3, HSP.

40. Minutes, 3/7/08 (Vol. 1, 98–99), PMS, HSP.

41. Minutes, 3/4/06 (Vol. 1, 54), PMS, HSP.

42. Minutes, 1/11/08 (Volume 1, 89–90), PMS, HSP.

43. Hobson, *Uneasy Virtue*, chaps. 3, 4; Stansell, *City of Women*, 179–80.

44. Carlisle, "Prostitutes and Their Reformers," 168.

45. Minutes, 9/6/08 (Vol. 1, 130), PMS, HSP. For similar cases of career prostitutes, see the notes for "Magdalen No. 12," Minutes, 5/3/08 (Vol. 1, 109); "Magdalen No. 25," Minutes, 12/6/09 (Volume 1, 167); "Magdalen No. 27," Minutes, 5/1/10 (Volume 2, 13), PMS, HSP.

46. Minutes, 2/7/09 (Vol. 1, 131), PMS, HSP.

47. Minutes 7/3/10 (Vol. 2, 13), PMS, HSP.

48. Minutes 8/1/09 (Vol. 1, 152), PMS, HSP.

49. Minutes, 9/5/09 (Vol. 1, 152–3), PMS, HSP.

50. For popular writers, elopement marked a critical moment when parental counsel in courtship had fatefully been abandoned. For a full discussion of the frequent expulsions and elopements of women at the Magdalen Society, see Carlisle, "Prostitutes and their Reformers," chap. 6. Carlisle discovered that for the period between 1821 and 1836, about one-third of all women admitted quickly fled or were discharged for insubordination.

51. Minutes, 2/2/08 (Vol. 1, 92–94), PMS, HSP.

52. For comparisons between the number of prostitutes practicing in Philadelphia and the number of women who entered the asylum in its early years, see Lyons, "Sex Among the 'Rabble'," 401–2.

53. Carlisle, "Prostitutes and Their Reformers," 175.

54. Gilfoyle, *City of Eros*, 58–59, 344; Diane Lindstrom, "Economic Structure, Demographic Change, and Income Inequality in Antebellum New York," in John Hull Mollenkopf, ed., *Power, Culture, and Place: Essays on New York City* (New York: Russell Sage Foundation, 1988), 5.

55. Particularly useful are the impressions of George G. Foster, who wrote about the underworld of both Philadelphia and New York. See his 1848 writings, "Philadelphia in Slices," ed. George Rogers Taylor, *Pennsylvania Magazine of History and Biography* 93 (January 1969): 23–72, esp. 38–42; see also *A Guide to the Stranger, or Pocket Companion for The Fancy, Containing A List of the Gay Houses and Ladies of Pleasure in the City of Brotherly Love and Sisterly Affection* (Philadelphia, 1849); *An Enquiry into the Condition and Influence of The Brothels in Connection with the Theatres of Philadelphia, Intended to Awaken the Attention of Parents and Guardians, and Those Who are Opposed to the Nightly Practice of Turning our Theatres into Assignation-Houses* (Philadelphia, 1834).

56. *Annual Report* 1834, 6–7, HSP. See also *Annual Report* 1829, 5–6; *Annual Report* 1831, 5; *Annual Report* 1835, 5; *Annual Report* 1839, 5; *Annual Report* 1847, 4, HSP.

57. Minutes 2/15/11 (Vol. 2, 3), PMS, HSP.

58. *Annual Report* 1845, 4, HSP.

59. Quoted *Annual Report* 1836, 7, HSP. For further examples of such a preference and attempts to encourage such a population, see Minutes, 7/6/13 (Vol. 2, 90), PMS; *Annual Report* 1820, 3; *Annual Report* 1843, 3–4; *Annual Report* 1848, 7–8; *Annual Report* 1849, 11–13; White-Williams Foundation Manual Book 1, 2, HSP. Steven Ruggles traces a marked drop in the admittance of older women into the asylum in the second half of the nineteenth-century. See his "Fallen Women: The Inmates of the Magdalen Society Asylum of Philadelphia, 1836–1908," *Journal of Social History* 16 (Summer 1983): 65–82, esp. 67.

60. Gilfoyle, *City of Eros*, 64–65.

61. Minutes, 9/12/17 (Vol. 2, 164), PMS, HSP.

62. Cf. *Annual Report* 1819, 2–3; *Annual Report* 1829, 4; *Annual Report* 1837, 4–5; *Annual Report* 1843, 3–4, HSP.

63. *Annual Report*, 1820, 3, HSP.

64. Ibid., 3.

65. See *Annual Report* 1823, 2; *Annual Report* 1827, 7; *Annual Report* 1832, 6; *Annual Report* 1836, 4; *Annual Report* 1845, 5, HSP. On alcohol and class conflict, see Paul Johnson, *A Shopkeeper's Millennium: Society and Revivals in Rochester, New York, 1815–1837* (New York: Hill and Wang, 1978); Sean Wilentz, *Chants Democratic: New York City and the Rise of the American Working-class, 1788–1850* (New York: Oxford University Press, 1984), 145–53. The post-1820 tendency of the Magdalen Society to blame their charges for their own downfall was a trend shared by most Philadelphia charitable organizations. See Dorsey, "City of Brotherly Love," 110–37.

66. *Annual Report* 1837, 7, HSP.

67. *Annual Report* 1845, 4, HSP.

68. See *Annual Report* 1842, 3–4; *Annual Report* 1845, 4, 6; *Annual Report* 1848 3–5; *Annual Report* 1849, 11, HSP. The turn to parent-blaming, while marking a significant shift from the original seduction narrative, may to a certain extent have allowed some renewed faith in the original innocence of these women. The Society managers' growing concentration on class-based cultural differences was mirrored by similar developments in the thought of bourgeois Americans more generally. For one especially relevant account of the class values embedded in such condemnations, see Stansell, *City of Women*, esp. chaps. 4, 8, 10.

69. *Annual Report* 1841, 5, HSP.

70. *Annual Report* 1834, 8; Annual Report 1835, 5, HSP.

71. *Annual Report,* 1849, 14–15, HSP.

72. *Annual Report* 1826, 8, HSP.

73. *Annual Report* 1831, 5, HSP. For a detailed analysis of the changing architecture and material culture of the asylum, see Lu Ann De Cunzo, "Reform, Respite, Ritual: An Archaeology of Institutions: The Magdalen Society of Philadelphia, 1800–1850," *Historical Archaelogy* 29, no. 3 (1995): 1–168.

74. Foucault, *Discipline and Punish*; *Annual Report* 1849, 6–7, HSP.

75. The society decided against coercively entering prostitutes into their institution, but did hire someone to more actively recruit Magdalens. See *Annual Report* 1847, 5–6, HSP. Eventually, by the 1880s, the Magdalen Society did have court-ordered placements of young women in their asylum. See Carlisle, "Prostitutes and Their Reformers," 191–93.

76. *Annual Report* 1846, 6, HSP. An extended harangue against prostitutes for seducing young men can be found in *An Enquiry into the Condition and Influence of The Brothels in Connection with the Theatres of Philadelphia* (Philadelphia, 1834).

77. *Annual Report* 1827, 7; *Annual Report* 1829, 4; *Annual Report* 1832, 6–8; *Annual Report* 1834, 6–7; *Annual Report* 1840, 5; *Annual Report* 1844, 8; *Annual Report* 1845, 3; *Annual Report* 1850, 11–12, HSP. A number of explanations might be offered for the vestigial image of the seduced woman in the later publications of the Magdalen Society. One possibility might be the Society's lingering awareness of the founding ideology of their institution; another might be the practical consideration of attracting donations for seemingly worthy subjects. My primary concern is with the highly noticeable shift to a negative portrait of the prostitute. The seduction narrative remained far more prominent in popular literature than in the writings of the Society. For a consideration of that persistence of the narrative, see the discussion below.

78. *Annual Report* 1851, 9–10, HSP.

79. This is not to suggest economic causations were wholly absent from the thought of the Society, one can find occasional discussion of such problems. However, the Society failed to address such a perceived problem in any significant way— they instead were more interested in reforming the habits of their subjects; for one discussion of economic problems in relation to prostitution, see *Annual Report* 1849, 11, 15, HSP.

80. Paul Boyer, among others, has noted the tendency of antebellum reformers to understand class as a cultural category rather than as an economic structure. See his *Urban Masses and Moral Order in America, 1820–1920* (Cambridge, Mass.: Harvard University Press, 1978), chaps. 1–4.

81. On these opposing portrayals, see Daniel Cohen, *Pillars of Salt, Monuments of Grace: New England Crime Literature and the Origins of American Popular Culture, 1674–1860* (New York: Oxford University Press, 1993), 202–16; Adrienne Siegel, *The Image of the American City in Popular Literature* (Port Washington, N.Y.: Kennikat Press, 1981), 38–40, 49, 87–88, 112–13, 170–71; Gilfoyle, *City of Eros*, 97–98, 143–61; Hobson, *Uneasy Virtue*, 70–75; David S. Reynolds, *Beneath the American Renaissance: The Subversive Imagination in the Age of Emerson and Melville* (Cambridge, Mass.: Harvard University Press, 1989), 361–65; Herbert Ross Brown, *The Sentimental Novel in America, 1789–1860* (Durham, N.C.: Duke University Press, 1940), 320–21; Ronald G. Walters, *Primers for Prudery: Sexual Advice to Victorian America* (Englewood Cliffs, N.J.: Prentice-Hall, 1974), 50–51, 69–71; Helen Lefkowiz Horowitz, *Rereading Sex: Battles over Sexual Knowledge and Suppression in Nineteenth-Century America* (New York: Alfred A. Knopf, 2002), 146–47, 153–54. The life of Mary Rogers, not a prostitute, but a sexually available cigar girl who died of a botched abortion was rendered in similar fashion in 1840's New York; see Amy Gilman Srebnick, *The Mysterious Death of Mary Rogers: Sex and Culture in Nineteenth-century New York* (New York: Oxford University Press, 1995), 80–82, 148–51, 153–57.

82. Smith-Rosenberg's claims for the originality of the NYFMRS is more persuasive as she describes the Society visiting brothels in order to expose male clients and its policy of hiring only women. Such activities may have been more fully consistent with the implications of the seduction motif than the basic program of the Philadelphia society. One should note however, that the NYFMRS also followed the lead of the Philadelphia Magdalen Society by establishing an asylum (which proved short-lived); see Smith-Rosenberg, "Beauty, the Beast, and the Militant Woman," 109–128. The fullest treatment of the NYFMRS is Larry Whiteaker, *Seduction, Prostitution, and Moral Reform in New York, 1830–1860* (New York: Garland Publishing, 1997). On the class dynamics of Boston's New England Female Reform Society, see Hobson, *Uneasy Virtue*, 49–76.

83. Hobson, *Uneasy Virtue*, 72–74.

84. Cohen, *The Murder of Helen Jewett*; see also Gilfoyle, *City of Eros*, 92–99.

85. Quoted from Gilfoyle, *City of Eros*, 151.

86. Cohen, *Pillars of Salt, Monuments of Grace*, 195–246, 204; Hobson, *Uneasy Virtue*, 72–75.

87. On the class protest at work in this novel, see Reynolds, *Beneath the American Renaissance*, 83–84. For reports on the trial by the *Public Ledger* (Philadelphia),

see issues from March 29, 1843, to April 7, 1843. Another famous trial that inspired heated dialogue about seduction was that of Lucretia Chapman in 1832. This trial has been explored by Karen Halttunen in "'Domestic Differences' : Competing Narratives of Womanhood in the Murder Trial of Lucretia Chapman," in Shirley Samuels, ed., *The Culture of Sentiment: Race, Gender, and Sentimentality in Nineteenth-Century America* (New York: Oxford University Press, 1992), 39–57.

88. Interestingly, legislators added a clause to the law that may have been intended to restrict its application in class terms. Men could only be prosecuted for seduction if the women were of "good repute." See Carlisle, "Prostitutes and Their Reformers," 120. Pennsylvania seems to have been the first state to have an explicit antiseduction statute passed, but antiseduction suits had become quite popular in New York courts at this time. See Cohen, *Murder of Helen Jewett*, 209–10. On the failed attempt to pass an antiseduction law in Massachusetts in 1845, see Hobson, *Uneasy Virtue*, 67–68. On the passage of an antiseduction law in New York in 1848, see Whiteaker, *Seduction, Prostitution, and Moral Reform*, 143–44.

89. Block, "Rape without Women," 849–68.

90. *Public Ledger* (Philadelphia), November 10, 1843.

91. George Lippard, *The Quaker City, or The Monks of Monk Hall: A Romance of Philadelphia Life, Mystery, and Crime*, ed. David S. Reynolds (Amherst: University of Massachusetts Press, 1995; 1st ed., 1845), vii.

92. *Public Ledger*, March 29, 1843.

93. Ibid., April 1, 1843.

94. Lippard, *Quaker City*, 1. Lippard does subsequently soften his conclusion, noting that if such a claim constituted a "sophism," it was one that "errs on the right side."

95. Ibid., *Quaker City*, 132–34.

96. Ibid., 146.

97. Ibid., 544.

98. Ibid., 117, 147, 541–44. This reading of Lippard should be contrasted with that offered by David Reynolds who is more willing to assign a subversive purpose to Lippard's handling of gender issues. *Quaker City* is a dense, polyvocal, text, no doubt. But on balance Lippard is more willing to ride rather than buck conventions when it comes to the figure of the female victim. He mostly seems to be using popular conventions for their dramatic worth, but he reifies them nonetheless. See Reynolds' "Introduction," xxii–xxiii, in Lippard, *Quaker City*.

99. Lippard, *Quaker City*, xiii.

100. Ibid., 417.

101. Gilfoyle, *City of Eros*, 92–116.

102. According to Mary Ryan's work on Oneida County, those who supported moral reform came from diverse classes, but Ryan found that the bulk of support came from the older artisan ranks, not the emergent white-collar bourgeoisie. Most clerks in Oneida stood against the Female Moral Reform Society. See Ryan, *Cradle of the Middle Class*, 117–27.

103. Christine Stansell notes this estrangement as well; see *City of Women*, 171–72, 190–91.

104. Because the conventional narrative often posited prostitutes as coming

from rural backgrounds, one could say that the original narrative was also class-specific. It was class-specific, however, in the sense that it ignored the working-class reality of urban poverty, not in the sense that it portrayed the working-class as possessing a specific moral character. Two notable departures from this blindness to class were iconoclastic social commentators Mathew Carey in Philadelphia and William Sanger in New York. Both stressed environmental factors such as poverty in explaining prostitution. See Roberts, "Prostitutes and Their Reformers," 56–58; Stansell, *City of Women*, 176–77.

Chapter 3

1. Lawrence Cremin discusses the range of consensus on educational goals among the leaders of the revolutionary generation in his *American Education: The National Experience, 1783–1876* (New York: Harper and Row, 1980), 103–28.

2. Samuel Harrison Smith, "Remarks on Education" in *Essays on Education in the Early Republic*, ed. Frederick Rudolph (Cambridge, Mass.: Belknap Press, 1965), 167–223; quoted 220, 221–22.

3. Benjamin Rush, "A Plan for the Establishment of Public Schools," in *Essays on Education*, ed. Rudolph, 1–24; quoted, 18.

4. On the attempts to establish a federal university, see David W. Robson, *Educating Republicans: The College in the Era of the American Revolution, 1750–1800* (Westport, Conn.: Greenwood Press, 1985), 227–36.

5. Robson, *Educating Republicans*, 227–53; Daniel Walker Howe, "Church, State, and Education in the Young American Republic," *Journal of the Early Republic* 22, no. 1 (Spring 2002): 1–24.

6. The most influential analysis of the great retrogression is Richard Hofstadter, *The Development of Academic Freedom in the United States* (New York: Columbia University Press, 1955), vol. 1; also important is Frederick Rudolph, *The American College and University: A History* (New York: Knopf, 1962). Various later scholars have challenged the great retrogression thesis; for a synthetic overview of much of their work, see James McLachlan, "The American College in the Nineteenth Century: Toward a Reappraisal," *Teachers College Record* 80 (December 1978): 287–306. The fullest statement of this position is Colin B. Burke, *American Collegiate Populations: A Test of the Traditional View* (New York: New York University Press, 1982). While earlier histories suggesting a great retrogression may have given too much credence to college authorities, accepting their expressions of desperation as sober descriptions of reality, later work challenging the retrogression thesis has suffered from giving too little attention to what college leaders felt and believed—important determinants of their behavior. In a crucial respect, the two points of view are not mutually exclusive. An important distinction must be drawn: the perceptions and expectations of historical actors must be differentiated from the statistical and particularizing portraits reconstituted by historians. Entering their endeavors in higher education with high expectations informed by republican ideals and European examples, many college leaders saw their hopes frustrated. Of

particular interest here are the issues of student population and curricula. While the total number of students increased at a greater rate than the population itself, enrollments at individual colleges remained at low levels because of the high number of new colleges being founded; consequently, college leaders across the country were continually disappointed by low enrollments. Concerning curricula, there may have been diversification at some colleges, but in relation to Enlightenment-era expectations, American colleges appeared to stagnate. While revolutionary-era expectations did recede in memory, the European, particularly the German, example produced a persistent impression that American colleges were in a beleaguered state.

7. Jefferson to Ticknor, July 16, 1823, in *American Higher Education: A Documentary History*, ed. Richard Hofstadter and Wilson Smith (Chicago: University of Chicago Press, 1961), 267; and Jennings L. Wagoner Jr. "Honor and Dishonor at Mr. Jefferson's University: The Antebellum Years," *History of Education Quarterly* 26 (Summer 1986): 165–66. For a complete picture of student disorder at the University of Virginia, see Philip Alexander Bruce, *History of the University of Virginia, 1819–1919* (New York: Macmillan, 1920), 2: 246–317.

8. Quoted from Novak, *The Rights of Youth*, 168. For discussions of corporal punishment in the colonial college and its decline in the mid-eighteenth century, see James Axtell, *The School upon a Hill: Education and Society in Colonial New England* (New Haven, Conn.: Yale University Press, 1974), 204–5, 235–36; Kett, *Rites of Passage*, 52.

9. Novak, *The Rights of Youth*, 127–28.

10. The careers of two other prominent college educators, Charles Nisbet and Samuel Stanhope Smith, would stand equally well for the failure of the republican educational vision; for portraits of their crushed hopes, see David W. Robson, "Enlightening the Wilderness: Charles Nisbet's Failure at Higher Education in Post-Revolutionary Pennsylvania," *History of Education Quarterly* 37 (Fall 1997): 271–89; Mark A. Noll, *Princeton and the Republic, 1768–1822: The Search for a Christian Enlightenment in the Era of Samuel Stanhope Smith* (Princeton, N.J.: Princeton University Press, 1989).

11. A wide range of literature exists describing student riots and disorder in the early republic. Much information can be found in individual histories of colleges. For helpful overviews of this broad phenomenon in this era, see Joseph Kett, *Rites of Passage: Adolescence in America, 1790 to the Present* (New York: Basic Books, 1977), 51–61; David Allmendinger Jr., *Paupers and Scholars: The Transformation of Student Life in Nineteenth Century New England* (New York: St. Martin's Press, 1975); Steven Novak, *The Rights of Youth: American Colleges and Student Revolt, 1798–1815* (Cambridge, Mass.: Harvard University Press, 1977); Burton J. Bledstein, *The Culture of Professionalism: The Middle Class and the Development of Higher Education in America* (New York: Norton, 1976), 223–47; John Frisch, "Youth Culture in America, 1790–1865" (Ph.D. diss., University of Missouri, 1970), 121–91.

12. On Locke's ideas regarding the management of youth and their popularization through American culture in the revolutionary and early republic periods, see Jay Fliegelman, *Prodigals and Pilgrims: The American Revolution against Patriarchal Authority, 1750–1800* (New York: Cambridge University Press, 1982); C. Dallett

Hemphill, *Bowing to Necessities: The History of Manners in America, 1620–1860* (New York: Oxford University Press, 1999), chap. 5.

13. Tensions surrounding colleges' paternalistic control of students first appeared in the mid-eighteenth-century. Resistance to paternalism became far more widespread and severe during the years of the early republic. Some important student politicization occurred in the years immediately preceding the Revolution and during the Revolution itself, but student activity in these instances most often comprised demonstrations for the American colonial resistance cause and gained the approbation of college leaders; see Axtell, *The School upon a Hill*, chap. 6; Robson, *Educating Republicans*, chaps. 3, 4.

14. For a full portrait of the University of Pennsylvania during this era, see Edward Potts Cheyney, *History of the University of Pennsylvania, 1740–1940* (Philadelphia: University of Pennsylvania Press, 1940), chap. 5.

15. *Report on the Existing State of Abuses in the University*, June 2, 1824, file 1824 College Duties and Discipline, Archives General Collection (hereafter AG), University of Pennsylvania Archives (hereafter UPA).

16. Minutes, Board of Trustees (hereafter BTM), November 6, 1827, June 3, 1828, UPA.

17. Ages ($n = 32$) were computed from General Alumni Society, University of Pennsylvania, *Biographical Catalogue of the Matriculates of the College* (Philadelphia: Published for the Society, 1893).

18. Burke, *American Collegiate Populations*, chap. 3.

19. Hofstadter, *The Development of Academic Freedom*, 224; For a survey of similar criticisms and comparisons, see Hofstadter, *American Higher Education*, part 4. The most sustained critique of American colleges was Francis Wayland, *Thoughts on the Present Collegiate System in the United States* (Boston: Gould, Kendall, and Lincoln, 1842).

20. Frederic Beasley (hereafter FB) to board of trustees (hereafter BoT), October 11 1813, file 107, AG, UPA.

21. Between 1780 and 1810 the number of colleges in America more than tripled, growing from 9 to at least 32. In the next 30 years, the number would more than triple again, reaching at least 106 by 1840. This rapid rate of college founding kept enrollments low at individual colleges, despite an expansion in collective attendance; see Burke, *American Collegiate Populations*, chap. 1. The strain on colleges during this period in many ways resembled the pressures felt by established religious denominations in the face of proliferating sects; see Nathan O. Hatch, *The Democratization of American Christianity* (New Haven, Conn.: Yale University Press, 1989).

22. For more in-depth discussions of student motivations relevant here, see Wagoner, "Honor and Dishonor," 155–79; and Kathryn McDaniel Moore, "Freedom and Constraint in Eighteenth-Century Harvard," *Journal of Higher Education* 47, no. 6 (1976): 649–59.

23. On shortened programs, see Novak, *Rights of Youth*, 10; Hofstadter, *Academic Freedom*, 212. Another strategy was to offer partial course programs that awarded certificates of proficiency rather than degrees; see Rudolph, *The American*

College, 113–16. On cost reductions, see Allmendinger, *Paupers and Scholars,* 80–96; Rudolph, *The American College,* 193–200.

24. Robson, "Enlightening the Wilderness," 281–85.

25. John Todd, *The Student's Manual* (New York: Columbian Publishing Co., 1893; 1ˢᵗ ed., 1835), 126.

26. Beasley's defense of Locke was his *A Search of Truth in the Science of the Human Mind* (Philadelphia: S. Potter and Co., 1822). For brief characterizations of Beasley's moral philosophy, see Noll, *Princeton and the Republic,* 63–64; and *Dictionary of American Biography,* ed. Allen Johnson (New York: C. Scribner's Sons, 1929), 2: 98.

27. On the Lockean distinction between childhood and youth, see Hemphill, *Bowing to Necessities,* chap. 5; Fliegelman, *Prodigals and Pilgrims,* 14–23. This distinction was breaking down over the course of the early nineteenth century as techniques Locke had deemed most appropriate for youth were now also being applied to children. For a consideration of some of the emergent attitudes, see Myra C. Glenn, *Campaigns against Corporal Punishment: Prisoners, Sailors, Women, and Children in Antebellum America* (Albany: State University of New York Press, 1984); David Hogan, "The Market Revolution and Disciplinary Power," *History of Education Quarterly* 29 (Fall 1989): 381–417.

28. *Laws Relating to the Moral Conduct, and Orderly Behaviour of the Students and Scholars of the University of Pennsylvania,* September 19 1801, Society Collection, Historical Society of Pennsylvania.

29. For useful discussions of Lockean sensational psychology and its popularization, see Fliegelman, *Prodigals and Pilgrims,* 12–29; G. S. Rousseau, "Nerves, Spirits, and Fibres: Toward Defining the Origins of Sensibility," in *Studies in the Eighteenth Century,* vol. 3, ed. R. F. Brissenden and J. C. Eade (Toronto: University of Toronto Press, 1976), 137–57.

30. FB to BoT, October 11 1813.

31. This trial, *Commonwealth v. Pullis* (Pa. 1806), was the first of a series of American trials against labor combinations; see Christopher Tomlins, *Law, Labor, and Ideology in the Early American Republic* (New York: Cambridge University Press, 1993), 128–79. On Princeton's laws of 1802, see Noll, *Princeton and the Republic,* 223–24. For examples of the application of this term to student groupings, see Novak *Rights of Youth,* 27, 31, 32, 80, and discussion below.

32. *New England Palladium* (Boston), October 3, 1823.

33. Ibid., October 7, 1823.

34. Kett, *Rites of Passage,* 51–61; Novak, *Rights of Youth,* 16–26.

35. The first quote is from Harvard student William Austin's 1807 book *Strictures on Harvard University,* the latter from the *Troy Gazette,* May 19, 1807; quoted Novak, *Rights of Youth,* 49, 87.

36. Michel Foucault, *Discipline and Punish: The Birth of the Prison* (New York: Vintage Books, 1995), 180–84.

37. On Locke's concepts of parental esteem and disgrace, see Jacqueline S. Reinier, "Rearing the Republican Child: Attitudes and Practices in Post-Revolutionary Philadelphia," *William and Mary Quarterly* 3rd ser., 39 (January 1982): 150–63. For

Beasley on the parental model, see FB to BoT, February 1, 1814, file 108; July 2, 1816, file 115; December 7, 1824, file 1824 Trustees, AG, UPA.

38. For broad descriptions of the changing thought about parenting and pedagogy in the early nineteenth century, see Mary P. Ryan, *Cradle of the Middle Class: The Family in Oneida County, New York, 1790–1865* (New York: Cambridge University Press, 1981); Carl F. Kaestle, *Pillars of the Republic: Common Schools and American Society, 1780–1860* (New York: Hill and Wang, 1983). For an excellent exploration of the meritocratic schemes of Joseph Lancaster, which reveals his use of market values for disciplinary ends, see David Hogan, "The Market Revolution and Disciplinary Power," 381–417.

39. FB to BoT, October 11 1813, file 107, AG, UPA.

40. FB to BoT, January 3 1815, file 109, AG, UPA.

41. Samuel Eliot Morison has argued that merit may initially have been used at Harvard and that the use of the prestige of birth to assign rank either evolved or was imported from Yale; see his *Harvard College in the Seventeenth Century* (Cambridge, Mass.: Harvard University Press, 1936), 58–64.

42. Axtell, *School upon a Hill*, 201–44; quoted 219.

43. Novak, *Rights of Youth*, 11–14; Axtell, *School upon a Hill*, 219–44.

44. FB to BoT, July 2 1816, file 115, AG, UPA. Bledstein, *The Culture of Professionalism*, 225, 235–37, 265, 271–73; Allmendinger, *Paupers and Scholars*, 121–25; Noll, *Princeton and the Republic*, 275; Mary Lovett Smallwood, *An Historical Study of Examinations and Grading Systems in Early American Universities* (Cambridge, Mass.: Harvard University Press, 1935); Robert F. Pace, *Halls of Honor: College Men in the Old South* (Baton Rouge: Louisiana State Press, 2004), 88–89.

45. Cf. *A Brief Appeal to the Good Sense of The University of Oxford on Classification of Merit: With Some Hints to the Rev. H. A. Woodgate on Logic by Philodicæus* (Oxford: H. Cooke, 1829); *Reasons for the Suggestion of Certain Alterations in the Examination Statute, Lately Submitted to the Vice-Chancellor and Head of Houses by the Public Examiners* (Oxford: Baxter, 1832).

46. Hogan, "The Market Revolution and Disciplinary Power," 381–417.

47. Smallwood, *An Historical Study*, 27.

48. Allmendinger's argument on this point rests on the use of report cards in conjunction with grading. As he admits, however, not all schools initially sent grades home. What Allmendinger fails to address is how school authorities thought grades might influence students themselves, that is, how school authorities were trying to create internal motivations to scholarly exertions and proper behavior. See Allmendinger, *Paupers and Scholars*, chap. 8.

49. Smallwood, *An Historical Study*, 70–74; Bledstein, *The Culture of Professionalism*, 235–36.

50. FB to BoT, March 4, 1822, File 1822 Trustees, AG, UPA.

51. While the board did suggest some Latin requirements in 1813, they did not enact an age requirement until 1820 and then only the age of fourteen, which was two years below Beasley's initial request. A fourth class was not added to Penn, despite Beasley's persistent lobbying, until 1824; see BTM, November 23, 1813; October 3, 1820, June 2, 1824, UPA.

52. For evidence of resistance to the medal plan, see FB to BoT, January 3 1815,

file 109; July 2, 1816, file 115, AG, UPA; The board formally ended Beasley's plan in 1819; see BTM, May 4, 1819, UPA.

53. On the social composition of the board of trustees, see Cheyney, *History of the University of Pennsylvania*, 188–89; C. Seymour Thompson, "The Provostship of Dr. Beasley: 1813–1828," *The General Magazine and Historical Chronicle* 33 (October 1930): 79–93, esp. 79–80. On the position of provost and the dominance of the trustees, see Cheyney, 177–78, 187–88, 285–86; on the similar frustrations of Charles Nisbet at Dickinson, see Robson, "Enlightening the Wilderness," 271–89.

54. Elite Philadelphia families represented in the student population during Beasley's term included Coxe, Rush, Wharton, Chew, Cadwalader, Morris, Norris, Ingersoll, and Biddle; for biographical and genealogical information on the student population, see General Alumni Society, *Biographical Catalogue*, 51–79; For a useful categorization of traditional elite Philadelphia families, see Nathaniel Burt, *The Perennial Philadelphians: The Anatomy of an American Aristocracy* (Boston: Little, Brown, 1963).

55. FB to BoT, May 6 1817, file 117, AG, UPA.

56. FB to BoT, July 14 1823, file 1823 Trustees, AG, UPA.

57. BTM, July 2 1822, UPA. On the development of this blacklisting arrangement, see Novak, *Rights of Youth*, 24–25.

58. *A Statute recommended by the provost*, January 6 1824, file 1824 College Duties and Discipline, AG, UPA.

59. *Report on the Existing State of Abuses*, June 2, 1824.

60. FB to BoT, November 2, 1824, file 1824 Trustees, AG, UPA.

61. FB to BoT, December 7, 1824, file 1824 Trustees, AG, UPA.

62. Implicit in this description of rowdy students disrupting the activities of the Philomathean Society are divisions within the student body itself, with some students more riotous, and others more willing to please their professors. For a discussion of divisions within college populations with particular reference to student societies, see Leon Jackson, "The Rights of Man and the Rites of Youth: Fraternity and Riot at Eighteenth Century Harvard," *History of Higher Education Annual* 15 (1995): 5–49.

63. FB to BoT, December 7 1824, file 1824 Trustees, AG, UPA.

64. BTM, December 7, 1824, UPA; When he was readmitted is uncertain, but it must not have been long thereafter, as he graduated in 1825.

65. For examples of required faculty reports, see Robert Patterson (hereafter RP) to BoT, March 1 1825; July 30, 1825; August 5, 1825; file 1825 Trustees, AG, UPA. A large investigation of the school was carried out by a "Committee on the Collegiate Department" in 1825, which requested, created, and compiled a large number of documents and printed a final report on November 15, 1825; see file 1825–6 Trustees and State of College, AG, UPA. The "Committee on the State of the University," which called for Beasley's dismissal, offered its findings in closed minutes; see Trustee Minutes, December 4, 1827, file 1826–7 Trustees, AG, UPA.

66. Trustee Minutes, December 4, 1827, file 1826–7 Trustees, AG, UPA. The university did seem on the verge of collapse: attendance had dropped from sixty to thirty-three in little over a year's time; see RP to BoT, 27 July 1826, file 1826–7 Trustees; RP to BoT, October 2, 1827, file 1827 Students, AG, UPA.

67. DeLancey had joined the board two years before being appointed provost. Earlier he had been trained at Yale and served as a minister in New York. DeLancey had been working in Philadelphia since 1822 as an assistant to Bishop William White, a trustee of the school. For a brief biographical sketch of DeLancey, see *Dictionary of American Biography*, ed. Allen Johnson and Dumas Malone (New York: Scribner's Sons, 1930), 5: 215–16.

68. DeLancey, *Inaugural Address*, 1828 file UPG 70.2 DE 337, UPA, 19, 23.

69. *Inaugural Address*, 23.

70. Within the first three academic years under DeLancey there were at least eight student dismissals and fourteen student suspensions. For accounts of these proceedings, see Faculty Minutes, 1828–31, UPA.

71. *An Address Delivered Before the Trustees, Faculty, and Students*, September 1830, file 1830–3 Addresses by Provost, UPA, 11.

72. Faculty Resolutions, December 22 1828, file 1828 College Students and Activities, AG; *Catalogue of the Officers and Students of the University of Pennsylvania*, 1831, UPA.

73. *An Address Delivered*, 11.

74. Bledstein, *The Culture of Professionalism*, 236, 272–73; Rudolph, *American College and University*, 217; Smallwood, *An Historical Study*, 35, 38; Jackson, "The Rights of Man and the Rights of Youth," 20–21.

75. On Harvard's 1825 statutes, see Bernard Bailyn, "Why Kirkland Failed," *Glimpses of the Harvard Past* (Cambridge, Mass.: Harvard University Press, 1986), 19–44.

76. Kirkland to Committee of the Overseers, 11 May 1826, Reports to the Overseers, vol. 2, HUA.

77. Levi Hedge to Chairman Thomas Winthrop, October 30 1826, Reports to the Overseers, vol. 2, HUA.

78. Paul Beck Jr. to BoT, July 4 1820, file 129, AG, UPA.

79. BTM, May 4 1819, UPA.

80. On the influence exerted by the advent of professionalism in American colleges and society, see Bledstein, *The Culture of Professionalism*.

Chapter 4

1. Alexander, *Suggestions in Vindication of Sunday-Schools* (Philadelphia: American Sunday School Union, 1832; 1st ed., 1829), 14. On the theological positioning of Archibald Alexander and Princeton Theological Seminary more generally, see George M. Marsden, *The Evangelical Mind and the New School Presbyterian Experience: A Case Study of Thought and Theology in Nineteenth-Century America* (New Haven, Conn.: Yale University Press, 1970), esp. 42–43.

2. Alexander, *Suggestions in Vindication*, 14–15.

3. The theme of a religious marketplace in the early republic has been widely explored. For two of the most important and formative discussions of this idea, see Terry Bilhartz, *Urban Religion and the Second Great Awakening: Church and Society*

in Early National Baltimore (Rutherford, N.J.: Farleigh Dickinson University Press, 1986); Nathan O. Hatch, *The Democratization of American Christianity* (New Haven, Conn.: Yale University Press, 1989). On the orientation of revival activity toward youth in this period, see Mary Ryan, *Cradle of the Middle Class: The Family in Oneida County, New York, 1790–1865* (New York: Cambridge University Press, 1981), chap. 2; Marion Bell, *Crusade in the City: Revivalism in Nineteenth Century Philadelphia* (Lewisburg, Pa.: Bucknell University Press, 1977), chap. 4; Christine Leigh Heyrman, *Southern Cross: The Beginnings of the Bible Belt* (Chapel Hill, N.C.: The University of North Carolina Press, 1997), chaps. 2, 3.

4. Alexander, *Suggestions in Vindication*, 7, 15.

5. Ibid., 12, 4, 11; Terry Bilhartz and Bruce Dorsey have both provocatively suggested that religious moderates and conservatives felt an attraction to benevolent activity, such as the Sunday school movement, as a more acceptable alternative to revival activity. Neither, however, explore this connection in the writings of Sunday school supporters. This chapter will substantiate the ideological attraction of the Sunday school cause to religious moderates and conservatives (while not denying its attraction to the more revivalist-oriented as well). In addition, I wish to highlight the heavy preoccupation with youth in this emerging religious counteroffensive. See Bilhartz, *Urban Religion*, 114; Dorsey, "City of Brotherly Love: Religious Benevolence, Gender, and Reform in Philadelphia, 1780–1844," (Ph.D. diss., Brown University, 1993), 98–99.

6. The literature on the religious experience of the Burnt-Over District is too voluminous to detail here. Upstate New York has attracted much attention, at least in part because it was the site of such a wide range of spiritual revivals and experimentations, ranging from Mormonism to Adventism, from the Shakers to the Oneida community of John Humphrey Noyes. The book most responsible for setting the agenda in the religious history of the early republic for the last half-century is Whitney Cross, *The Burned-Over District: The Social and Intellectual History of Enthusiastic Religion in Western New York, 1800–1850* (New York: Harper and Row, 1965). Most germane to this chapter are studies of Charles G. Finney's revivals. The two most influential works on Finney's labors in upstate New York are Paul Johnson, *A Shopkeeper's Millennium: Society and Revivals in Rochester, New York, 1815–1837* (New York: Hill and Wang, 1978); Mary Ryan, *Cradle of the Middle Class*. The best survey of religion in early nineteenth-century Philadelphia is Dorsey, "City of Brotherly Love." More exclusively focused on reform, but also tremendously useful in documenting Philadelphia's religious experience is Dorsey, *Reforming Men and Women: Gender in the Antebellum City* (Ithaca, N.Y.: Cornell University Press, 2002).

7. Marsden, *The Evangelical Mind*, 54, 57; Charles E. Hambrick-Stowe, *Charles G. Finney and the Spirit of American Evangelicalism* (Grand Rapids, Mich.: William B. Eerdmans, 1996), 79.

8. For the upstate New York context of this letter, see Hambrick-Stowe, *Charles G. Finney*, 55–56.

9. Mark A. Noll, *Princeton and the Republic, 1768–1822: The Search for a Christian Enlightenment in the Era of Samuel Stanhope Smith* (Princeton, N.J.: Princeton University Press, 1989), 276–80; Steven J. Novak, *The Rights of Youth: American Col-*

leges and Student Revolt, 1798–1815 (Cambridge, Mass.: Harvard University Press, 1977), 159–63. For Green's own characterization of his revival in which he emphasizes how it had no extravagances associated with it, see his *The Life of Ashbel Green*, ed. Joseph H. Jones (New York: Robert Carter and Brothers, 1849), 618–22.

10. "Pastoral Letter," *The Christian Advocate* (Philadelphia), vol. 5, June 1827, 244–45.

11. "Pastoral Letter," *The Christian Advocate*, June 1827, 252, July 1827, 295.

12. "Pastoral Letter," *The Christian Advocate*, June 1827, 248.

13. "Pastoral Letter," *The Christian Advocate*, July 1827, 293, 295, 297, 302.

14. "Pastoral Letter," *The Christian Advocate*, July 1827, 298, June 1827, 246–47, 250.

15. For secondary treatments of Patterson's ministry, see Bruce Laurie, *The Working People of Philadelphia, 1800–1850* (Philadelphia: Temple University Press, 1980), chap. 2; Bell, *Crusade in the City*, chap. 3; Dorsey, "City of Brotherly Love," 93–99; Hambrick-Stowe, *Charles G. Finney*, 77–79.

16. Thomas James Shepherd, *History of the First Presbyterian Church, Northern Liberties* (Philadelphia: n.p., 1882), 36–37, 57; Charles G. Finney, *The Memoirs of Charles G. Finney*, ed. Garth M. Rosell and Richard A. G. Dupuis (Grand Rapids, Mich.: Academie Books, 1989), 246, n. 19; *Minutes of the General Assembly of the Presbyterian Church in the United States of America* (Philadelphia), 1826, 77, 1829, 462–64. In 1829, when Patterson had 1,026 communicants, the closest church beneath him was the Second Presbyterian of Philadelphia, which had 655. For the 37 churches reporting for the entire Philadelphia Presbytery in that year, there were 6,763 members.

17. Robert Adair, *Memoir of Reverend James Patterson* (Philadelphia: Henry Perkins, 1840), 31–32.

18. Shepherd, *History of the First Presbyterian*, 41. While the district in which Patterson worked was mostly populated by poor and working-class people, his ministry likely attracted more middling folk as well. His original audience, at least, had moderate incomes. Bruce Dorsey, in looking into the backgrounds of the original fifty-three communicants in Patterson's church, found that most of them were "middling shopkeepers." This finding contradicts Shepherd's characterization of Patterson's original congregation as "3/4 of them women, 9/10 of them poor." See Dorsey, "City of Brotherly Love," 93–94.

19. Letter from Rev. Thomas Brainerd in William B. Sprague, *Annals of the American Pulpit* (New York: Robert Carter and Bros., 1868), 4: 426–28. Copies of a good number of James Patterson's skeletons are held at the Presbyterian Historical Society.

20. Finney, *Memoirs of Charles G. Finney*, 262; Brainerd in Sprague, *Annals of the American Pulpit*, vol. 4; Adair, *Memoir of Reverend James Patterson*, 140–41. Patterson not only spoke to the level of his audience, he used a variety of other techniques to gain attention, such as circulating advertisements for his services and pasting religious placards on walls. Patterson's style of preaching resembled that of Methodist and other more popularly oriented denominations and sects. On "democratic" preaching, see Hatch, *The Democratization of American Christianity*.

21. Adair, *Memoir of Reverend James Patterson*, 45, 134–47, 148, 150–51, 156, 162, 175–76, 199–209, 222–23, 228.

22. Ibid., 70, 128, 50–51.

23. Marsden, *The Evangelical Mind*, 52–55.

24. Adair, *Memoir of Reverend James Patterson*, 108, 250, 259. On Patterson's break from Calvinism in sermons, see Dorsey, "City of Brotherly Love," 96. Charles Finney in his *Memoirs* suggests that Patterson was orthodox in his thinking when he arrived in the city. As Charles E. Hambrick-Stowe correctly points out, Finney misread (or perhaps for his own advantage misrepresented) Patterson and his intentions. See Hambrick-Stowe, *Charles G. Finney*, 78.

25. The abrogation of the Plan of Union not only struck at the Synods of Western Reserve in Ohio and the New York Synods of Utica, Geneva, and Genesee; it also dissolved the Third Presbytery of Philadelphia, the presbytery to which Patterson and other Philadelphia New School men belonged. See Marsden, *The Evangelical Mind*, 62–63; Adair, *Memoir of Reverend James Patterson*, 235.

26. On the class constituency of the New School in Philadelphia, see Robert W. Doherty, "Social Bases for the Presbyterian Schism of 1837–8: The Philadelphia Case," *Journal of Social History* 2 (Fall 1968): 68–79. On the same throughout the northern United States, see Charles Sellers, *The Market Revolution: Jacksonian America, 1815–1846* (New York: Oxford University Press, 1991), chap. 7. For a highly instructive example of the vision of respectable revivals that came to dominate New School thinking, see Albert Barnes, "Revivals of Religion in Cities and Large Towns," *The American National Preacher* 15, nos. 1–3 (January–March 1841).

27. Adair, *Memoir of Reverend James Patterson*, 67–68, 74–75.

28. Ibid., 62, 69.

29. Ibid., 62–63.

30. Ibid., 69. Patterson similarly disrupted marriages, encouraging wives to adopt religion against the wishes of their husbands; see 79–80, 231.

31. Ibid., 131.

32. Ibid., 77.

33. Ibid., 46, 49, 51.

34. Ibid., 46–52; Shepherd, *History of the First Presbyterian*, 51–52, 57; Dorsey, "City of Brotherly Love," 98.

35. Adair, *Memoir of Reverend James Patterson*, 48; Dorsey, "City of Brotherly Love," 94, 103; Anne Boylan, *Sunday School: The Formation of An American Institution, 1790–1880* (New Haven, Conn.: Yale University Press, 1988), 7–8. Patterson and the Union Sabbath School Association likely drew inspiration from Robert May, an Englishman who had spent three months in Philadelphia in 1811 and 1812 conducting Sunday school classes using evangelical methods. See Jacqueline Reinier, *From Virtue to Character: American Childhood, 1775–1850* (New York: Twayne Publishers, 1996), 80–82.

36. Dorsey, "City of Brotherly Love," 208–9.

37. Adair, *Memoir of Reverend James Patterson*, 174. Patterson encouraged young men in at least one way that he could not encourage young women. Throughout his career he prodded and financially supported young men to train for the ministry. Adair claims that Patterson convinced more than sixty young men

to enter the ministry. To Old School critics who may have supposed that Patterson was prone to encouraging young men "prematurely," Adair insisted that "few ministers were more diligent than he, in bringing forward young men of the requisite qualifications." See ibid., xx, 29, 36, 155, 174, 217–20, 233.

38. Hambrick-Stowe, *Charles G. Finney*, 77–78.

39. Finney, *Memoirs of Charles G. Finney*, 246 n. 19; ibid., 218 n. 87

40. Hambrick-Stowe, *Charles G. Finney*, 68–70.

41. Finney, *Memoirs of Charles G. Finney*, 250–51.

42. *The Christian Advocate*, vol. 5, December 1827, 553–68; vol. 6, January 1828, 29–36. Hambrick-Stowe, *Charles G. Finney*, 79. Bell, *Crusade in the City*, 52–53.

43. Hambrick-Stowe, *Charles G. Finney*, 73, 102.

44. Suggestive of this realization is Green's handling of the Oneida "Pastoral Letter." In his endorsement of the letter Green defensively stressed to his readers that he and his brethren were not opponents of revivals, only extravagances in them; see *Christian Advocate*, vol. 5, June 1827, 245.

45. Finney, *Memoirs of Charles G. Finney*, 249–50 n. 29.

46. This acquiescence to the religious moderates' strategy of dealing with revivalists would change in a few years. Old School men would soon turn on the Congregationalists and New School men for their willingness to compromise with and tolerate the excesses and theological innovations of revivalists like Finney. See Marsden, *The Evangelical Mind*, chap. 3.

47. For a more complete view of Finney's stay in Philadelphia and estimations of his success, see Bell, *Crusade in the City*, chap. 3.

48. Finney, *Memoirs of Charles G. Finney*, 257.

49. Finney claimed that the church could hold 3,000. Marion Bell suggests it is unlikely that it held many more than 1,000. See Finney, *Memoirs of Charles G. Finney*, 255; Bell, *Crusade in the City*, 31.

50. Finney, *Memoirs of Charles G. Finney*, 254 n. 45; ibid., 255 n. 49. No membership figures survive for the German Reformed Church for the year Finney was there. Patterson also noted attendance from people of differing denominations at his church while Finney was there. See Bell, *Crusade in the City*, 73; Finney, *Memoirs of Charles G. Finney*, 248 n. 25.

51. Finney, *Memoirs of Charles G. Finney*, 255–56.

52. Ibid., 257–60.

53. *The Christian Advocate*, vol. 8, September 1830, 471–75; October 1830, 517–20; vol. 9, January 1831, 20–25; February 1831, 80–84; April 1831, 189–91; May 1831, 246–51.

54. On Methodist revival activity in the eastern United States and Philadelphia more particularly in the early nineteenth century, see Richard Carwardine, "The Second Great Awakening in the Urban Centers: An Examination of Methodism and the 'New Measures,'" *Journal of American History* 59 (September 1972): 327–40; Bilhartz, *Urban Religion and the Second Great Awakening*, chap. 6; Bell, *Crusade in the City*, 83, 108–20. For a traveler's account of a camp meeting in Chester County, Pennsylvania, see Francis Lieber, *The Stranger in America* (Philadelphia: Carey, Lea, and Blanchard, 1835).

55. Christine Heyrman suggests these tendencies began to decline in the nine-

teenth-century South, but as the discussion below demonstrates, these Methodist characteristics must still have been in evidence to social observers. See Heyrman, *Southern Cross*, chaps. 2, 3; see also Dee Andrews, *The Methodists and Revolutionary America, 1760–1800: The Shaping of an Evangelical Culture* (Princeton, N.J.: Princeton University Press, 2000), 107–11.

56. *The Christian Advocate*, vol. 9, January 1831, 20–23; April 1831, 190.

57. *The Christian Advocate*, vol. 9, April 1831, 191; January 1831, 24. See also May 1831, 250.

58. William White, *An Episcopal Charge, on the Subject of Revivals, Delivered Before the Forty-Eighth Convention of the Diocese of Pennsylvania* (Philadelphia, 1832), 5–6. White's notions of "animal sensibility" seem to anticipate the physiological philosophy of Sylvester Graham that will be discussed in Chapter 6.

59. White, *An Episcopal Charge*, 8–9. On sexual tensions surrounding eighteenth-century revivals, see Cedric Cowing, "Sex and Preaching in the Great Awakening," *American Quarterly* 20 (Autumn 1968): 625–44; Richard Godbeer, *Sexual Revolution in Early America* (Baltimore: Johns Hopkins University Press, 2002), 240–45. In the nineteenth century, revival gatherings such as camp meetings were often accused of rousing sexual feelings and being sites of seduction. In addition, revivalist preachers, especially itinerants, were often accused of being sexually lecherous. See Heyrman, *Southern Cross*, 182–84; William G. McLoughlin, "Untangling the Tiverton Tragedy: The Social Meaning of the Terrible Haystack Murder of 1833," *Journal of American Culture* 7 (Winter 1984): 75–84; Lieber, *The Stranger in America*, 311, 313, 320; Frances Trollope, *Domestic Manners of the Americans* (New York: Knopf, 1949; 1st ed., 1832), 80–81, 169, 276–77.

60. White, *An Episcopal Charge*, 13–16.

61. *The Christian Advocate*, vol. 5, December 1827, 554.

62. For a description of traditional evangelical child rearing, see Philip Greven, *The Protestant Temperament: Patterns of Childrearing, Religious Experience, and the Self in Early America* (New York: Knopf, 1977). On the threat to Calvinism posed by a more sentimental view of children, see Ann Douglas, *The Feminization of American Culture* (New York: Knopf, 1977).

63. *The Christian Advocate*, vol. 5, June 1827, 255–58.

64. On the initial clientele of Sunday schools, see Paul Boyer, *Urban Masses and Moral Order in America, 1820–1920* (Cambridge, Mass.: Harvard University Press, 1978), chap. 3. On its transformation, see Boylan, *Sunday School*, 16–18.

65. Alexander, *Suggestions in Vindication of Sunday-Schools*, 6–7. On the preference for affectionate over coercive training of children in Sunday schools, see Boylan, *Sunday School*, chap. 5.

66. Isaac Ferris, *An Appeal to Ministers of the Gospel in Behalf of Sunday-schools* (Philadelphia: ASSU, 1834), 16–19. See also Stephen H. Tyng, *The Connexion between early Religious Instruction and Mature Piety* (Philadelphia: ASSU, 1837).

67. Cf. Isaac Ferris, *An Appeal to Ministers*, 12; James B. Taylor, *The Exigencies and Responsibilities of the present Age* (Philadelphia: ASSU, 1836), 21–22; Francis Wayland Jr., *Encouragements to Religious Effort* (Philadelphia: ASSU, 1830), 34.

68. Boylan, *Sunday School*, 11.

69. Ibid., 63.

70. Ibid.

71. Twenty years after James Patterson died, and the Presbyterian schism had passed, New School minister Thomas Brainerd could perhaps more frankly admit the assessment of many of Patterson. Brainerd recalled, to Patterson's credit, that the pastor harbored antipathy for preachers who humored the "taste and refinement of their more wealthy and fashionable congregations." But Brainerd then suggests that it was Patterson's flaw to fall "into the opposite extreme of raw denunciation and semi-rudeness, if not recklessness, in the pulpit." At times, his sermons were "marked by crudeness and bad taste." See Sprague, *Annals of the American Pulpit*, 427.

72. *Third Annual Report of the ASSU* (Philadelphia, 1827), 15–17.

73. Boyer, *Urban Masses and Moral Order*, 49.

74. *Plans and Motives* (Philadelphia: ASSU, n.d.; 1st ed., 1829), 4, 13, 15.

75. Boylan, *Sunday School*, 109–14.

76. *Second Annual Report of the ASSU* (Philadelphia, 1826), 15–16, 93.

77. J. P. K. Henshaw, *The Usefulness of Sunday-Schools* (Philadelphia: ASSU, 1833), 14–15.

78. Frederick Packard, *The Teacher Taught* (Philadelphia: ASSU, 1839), 3, 146–47.

79. Taylor, *Exigencies and Responsibilities* (Philadelphia: ASSU, 1836), 21–22.

80. Henshaw, *The Usefulness of Sunday-schools*, 15.

81. Statistics on conversions were reported in the ASSU *Annual Reports* for every year. For a more general discussion of this preoccupation, see Boylan, *Sunday School*, 112–13, 135–41.

82. Alexander, *Suggestions in Vindication*, 7.

83. Henshaw, *The Usefulness of Sunday-Schools*, 16–17.

84. Charles Hodge, *A Sermon, Preached in Philadelphia, at the Request of the ASSU* (Philadelphia: ASSU, 1832), 19–20.

85. Cf. *Seventh Report of the Philadelphia Sunday and Adult School Union, With an Account of the Formation of the ASSU* (Philadelphia, 1824), 17–18; Alexander, *Suggestions in Vindication*, 5, 29–30; Ferris, *An Appeal to Ministers*, 26–27.

86. Wayland, *Encouragements to Religious Effort*, 19, 25.

87. *Second Annual Report of the ASSU*, 4–5. This stated aim was quickly called into question. For a defense against such criticisms, see Willard Hall, *Defence of the American Sunday School Union, Against the Charges of Its Opponents* (Philadelphia: ASSU, 1831; 1st ed., 1828).

88. Lawrence Cremin, *American Education: The National Experience, 1783–1876* (New York: Harper and Row, 1980), 69, 304.

89. Taylor, *Exigencies and Responsibilities of the present Age*, 24.

90. Alexander, *Suggestions in Vindication*, 18–19, 21. For similar analysis of the dilemma facing ASSU publishing, see Boylan, *Sunday School*, 76.

91. Boylan, *Sunday School*, 11, 31, 115.

92. Ibid., 16–18, 160–64.

93. On the decline of the ASSU, see Boylan, *Sunday School*, 77–88.

94. The exact number is 69,508; tabulated from table 6 in Boylan, *Sunday School*, 32–33.

95. Ferris, *An Appeal to Ministers of the Gospel*, 12.

Chapter 5

1. Quoted in Ronald Preston Byars, "The Making of the Self-Made Man: The Development of Masculine Roles and Images in Ante-Bellum America" (Ph.D. diss., Michigan State University, 1979), 97. For an excellent overview of the utilitarian impulse in American education during the early republic, see Lawrence Cremin, *American Education: The National Experience* (New York: Harper and Row, 1980), 249–97.

2. Cremin, *American Education: The National Experience*, 276.

3. William DeLancey, *An Address Delivered Before the Trustees, Faculty, and Students* (Philadelphia, 1830), 12–13.

4. See Bruce Laurie, *Artisans into Workers: Labor in Nineteenth-Century America* (New York: Hill and Wang, 1989); Sean Wilentz, *Chants Democratic: New York City and the Rise of the American Working-Class, 1788–1850* (New York: Oxford University Press, 1984); Sharon V. Salinger, "Artisans, Journeymen, and the Transformation of Labor in Late Eighteenth-Century Philadelphia," *William and Mary Quarterly* 3rd ser., 40 (January 1983): 62–84. For an exception to this general trend, see Gary J. Kornblith, "Self-Made Men: The Development of Middling-Class Consciousness in New England," *Massachusetts Review* 26 (Summer–Autumn 1985): 461–74.

5. Joyce Appleby, "New Cultural Heroes in the Early National Period," in Thomas Haskell and Richard Teichgraeber, eds., *The Culture of the Market: Historical Essays* (New York: Cambridge University Press, 1993), 163–88. Appleby's own sources can not fully answer this problem. She draws upon autobiographies written in the late nineteenth century to find the values that had spurred on efforts made early in the century. These works may have merely been mirroring the congratulatory books of the era in which they were published. As discussion below will reveal, the advice manuals from earlier in the century seemed much more conflicted about the idea of the self-made man; how the writers of these autobiographies would have felt about their entrepreneurial behavior at the time they were working is still unknown.

6. My notions of the Market Revolution and the conflicted relationship of bourgeois Americans to its spread in the Jacksonian era are largely informed by the work of Charles Sellers; see his *The Market Revolution: Jacksonian America, 1815–1846* (New York: Oxford University Press, 1991).

7. A good number of historians have explored this literature (which continued to proliferate through the 1850s and 60s). See Karen Halttunen, *Confidence Men and Painted Women: A Study of Middle-Class Culture in America, 1830–1870* (New Haven, Conn.: Yale University Press, 1982), 1–55; Allen Stanley Horlick, *Country Boys and Merchant Princes: The Social Control of Young Men in New York* (Lewisburg, Pa.: Bucknell University Press, 1975), 147–78; Burton Bledstein, *The Culture of Professionalism: The Middle-class and the Development of Higher Education in America* (New York: Norton, 1976), 214–22; Richard Wohl, "The 'Country Boy' Myth and Its Place in American Urban Culture: The Nineteenth-Century Contribution," in *Perspectives in American History* (New York: Cambridge University Press),

3: 77–156; Byars, "The Making of the Self-Made Man"; Joseph Kett, *Rites of Passage: Adolescence in America, 1790 to the Present* (New York: Basic Books, 1977), chap. 4; G. J. Barker-Benfield, *The Horrors of the Half-Known Life: Male Attitudes toward Women and Sexuality in Nineteenth-Century America* (New York: Harper and Row, 1976); Bruce Dorsey, "City of Brotherly Love: Religious Benevolence, Gender, and Reform in Philadelphia, 1780–1844" (Ph.D. diss., Brown University, 1993), 245–55.

8. Jeanne Boydston, "The Woman Who Wasn't There: Women's Market Labor and the Transition to Capitalism in the United States," *Journal of the Early Republic* 16 (Summer 1996): 183–206; Amy Gilman Srebnick, *The Mysterious Death of Mary Rogers: Sex and Culture in Nineteenth-Century New York* (New York: Oxford University Press, 1995), 7–9, 45–47, 58–60. For a more general discussion of the suspicions surrounding women in public in the nineteenth century, see Mary Ryan, *Women in Public: Between Banners and Ballots, 1825–1880* (Baltimore: Johns Hopkins University Press, 1990), 130–71.

9. Sellers, *The Market Revolution*, esp. 17–21, 41–44, 152–57, 239.

10. Diane Lindstrom, "Economic Structure, Demographic Change, and Income Inequality in Antebellum New York," in John Hull Mollenkopf, ed., *Power, Culture, and Place: Essays on New York City* (New York: Russell Sage Foundation, 1988), 5.

11. Stuart Blumin, *The Emergence of the Middle-Class: Social Experience in the American City, 1760–1900* (New York: Cambridge University Press, 1989), chaps. 3, 5; Paul Johnson, *A Shopkeeper's Millennium: Society and Revivals in Rochester, New York, 1815–1837* (New York: Hill and Wang, 1978), chap. 2; Richard B. Stott, *Workers in the Metropolis: Class, Ethnicity, and Youth in Antebellum New York* (Ithaca, N.Y.: Cornell University Press, 1990), chap. 7.

12. Ronald J. Zboray, "Antebellum Reading and the Ironies of Technological Innovation," *American Quarterly* 40, no. 1 (March 1988): 65–82; Sellers, *The Market Revolution*, 369–72; Cremin, *American Education: The National Experience*, 69, 309–10.

13. Zboray, "Antebellum Reading and Technological Innovation," 74–76.

14. The clearest statement of the social control argument is Horlick, *Country Boys and Merchant Princes*; similar in emphasis is Karen Halttunen, *Confidence Men and Painted Women*; works that emphasize the self-made man message are Barker-Benfield, *The Horrors of the Half-Known Life*; Byars, "The Making of the Self-Made Man." Some authors have noted the ambivalence of these advice texts but have not sought to explore this ambivalence in relation to the basic venture of writing an advice book in this era; see Kett, *Rites of Passage*, 102–7. The best exploration of the ambivalence of Americans toward capitalism in the Jacksonian years is still Marvin Meyers, *The Jacksonian Persuasion: Politics and Belief* (Stanford, Calif.: Stanford University Press, 1957).

15. See "Burnap, George Washington," "Eddy, Daniel Clarke," "Todd, John," "Wise, Daniel" in Allen Johnson and Dumas Malone, eds., *Dictionary of American Biography* (New York: Charles Scribner's Sons, 1958), 2: 292; 3: 6–7; 18: 572; 20: 422–23. See also Halttunen, *Confidence Men and Painted Women*, 28; Kett, *Rites of Passage*, 107; Artemus Bowers Muzzey, *The Young Man's Friend* (Boston: James Monroe and Co., 1836), iv.

16. Leonore Davidoff and Catherine Hall, *Family Fortunes: Men and Women of the English Middle-Class, 1780–1850* (Chicago: University of Chicago Press, 1987), 126–30.

17. "Wise, Daniel," in Johnson and Malone, eds., *Dictionary of American Biography*, 20: 422.

18. "Alcott, William Andrus," "Arthur, Timothy Shay," in Johnson and Malone, eds., *Dictionary of American Biography* 1: 142–43, 377–79; Robert Abzug, *Cosmos Crumbling: American Reform and the Religious Imagination* (New York: Oxford University Press, 1994), 169–72.

19. In the following analysis, evidence will be culled from nine representative texts of this popular genre: William Alcott, *The Young Man's Guide* (Boston: T. R. Marvin, 1843; 1st ed., 1833); William Alcott, *Familiar Letters to Young Men* (Buffalo, N.Y.: Geo. H. Derby and Co., 1850; 1st ed., 1849); John Angell James, *The Young Man From Home* (New York: D. Appleton and Co., 1840); Artemus Bowers Muzzey, *The Young Man's Friend* (Boston: James Monroe and Co., 1836); John Todd, *The Student's Manual* (New York: Columbian Publishing Co., 1893; 1st ed., 1835); Timothy Shay Arthur, *Advice to Young Men on Their Duties and Conduct in Life* (Philadelphia: John E. Potter, 1848); George Burnap, *Lectures to Young Men on the Cultivation of the Mind, the Formation of Character and the Conduct of Life*, 2nd ed. (Baltimore: John Murphy, 1841; 1st ed., 1840); Rev. Daniel Wise, *The Young Man's Counsellor, or Sketches and Illustrations of the Duties and Dangers of Young Men* (New York: Nelson and Phillips, 1850); Daniel C. Eddy, *The Young Man's Friend: Containing Admonitions for the Erring* (Lowell, Mass.: Nathaniel L. Dayton, 1850; 1st ed., 1849). For additional texts in this genre, consult the works listed in note 7 above.

20. For a sampling of this widely dispersed commentary, see Byars, "The Self-Made Man In America," 50–53; Barker-Benfield, *The Horrors of the Half-Known Life*, 23–36; Marvin Meyers, *The Jacksonian Persuasion*, 87, 127–28; Bledstein, *The Culture of Professionalism*, 212–14; Daniel Cohen, "Arthur Mervyn and His Elders: The Ambivalence of Youth in the Early Republic," *William and Mary Quarterly* 3rd ser., 43 (July 1986): 362–80. For more general discussions of the status of youth in antebellum America, see C. Dallett Hemphill, *Bowing to Necessities: The History of Manners in America, 1620–1860* (New York: Oxford University Press, 1999), chap. 8; and Kett, *Rites of Passage*, part 1.

21. Alcott, *Young Man's Guide*, 56–57, 100, 108, 236–39; Alcott, *Familiar Letters*, 17, 191–92, 231–34; James, *The Young Man From Home*, 19–20, 58, 97; Todd, *The Student's Manual*, 116–17, 128; Muzzey, *The Young Man's Friend*, 55–56; Arthur, *Duties of Young Men*, 232; Burnap, *Lectures to Young Men*, 95–98; Eddy, *The Young Man's Friend*, 46–49.

22. Muzzey, *The Young Man's Friend*, 58.

23. Quoted from Barker-Benfield, *The Horrors of the Half-Known Life*, 156.

24. Burnap, *Lectures to Young Men*, 95–97. Burnap closely compares the "barter" economy of colonial villages to the commercial economy brought on by the transportation revolution; see 26–27.

25. Ibid., 97–98.

26. Alcott, *Young Man's Guide*, 58.

27. Cremin, *American Education: The National Experience*, 253–59.

28. For discussions of such representations in the literature of this period, see John G. Cawelti, *Apostles of the Self-Made Man* (Chicago: University of Chicago Press, 1965), chap. 2; Fred Somkin, *Unquiet Eagle: Memory and Desire in the Idea of American Freedom, 1815–1860* (Ithaca, N.Y.: Cornell University Press, 1967); Susan Kuhlmann, *Knave, Fool, and Genius: The Confidence Man as He Appears in Nineteenth-Century American Fiction* (Chapel Hill: University of North Carolina Press, 1973); Halttunen, *Confidence Men and Painted Women*, chap. 1; Barker-Benfield, *Horrors of the Half-Known Life*, 8–18; Bruce Dorsey, "City of Brotherly Love," 236–45.

29. Quoted from Halttunen, *Confidence Men and Painted Women*, 30.

30. John Angell James, *The Young Man From Home*, 94–95; for similar comments about youth possessing a roving disposition, see Muzzey, *Young Man's Friend*, 4, 47; Todd, *The Student's Manual*, 15, 42, 74–75.

31. Eddy, *The Young Man's Friend*, 65.

32. Alcott, *Familiar Letters*, 193; see also Arthur, *Duties of Young Men*, 230–32.

33. Karen Halttunen explores this theme at greatest length, see her *Confidence Men and Painted Women*, chap. 1.

34. Burnap, *Lectures to Young Men*, 110–11.

35. Ibid., 116–17; see also Wise, *The Young Man's Counsellor*, 221–25; Muzzey, *Young Man's Friend*, 74–75.

36. Wise, *The Young Man's Counsellor*, 221.

37. Eddy, *The Young Man's Friend*, 113–14; see also Wise, *The Young Man's Counsellor*, 139.

38. Eddy, *The Young Man's Friend*, 156.

39. Quoted from Alcott, *Familiar Letters*, 238; see also Muzzey, *The Young Man's Friend*, 10; Todd, *The Student's Manual*, 10; Arthur, *Advice to Young Men*, 21; Eddy, *The Young Man's Friend*, 36; Wise, *The Young Man's Counsellor*, 88–90, 18–19.

40. Wise, *The Young Man's Counsellor*, v, 17–18, 21–22.

41. Cremin, *American Education: The National Experience*, 259.

42. Alcott, *Young Man's Guide*, 19–21.

43. Ibid., 23.

44. Ibid., 25–26. On the concept of Lockean esteem, see Jacqueline Reinier, "Rearing the Republican Child: Attitudes and Practices in Post-Revolutionary Philadelphia," *William and Mary Quarterly* 3rd ser., 39 (January 1982): 150–63.

45. Alcott, *Familiar Letters*, 18; Muzzey, *The Young Man's Friend*, viii, 176–77; Todd, *The Student's Manual*, preface, 7–9; John Angell James, *The Young Man From Home*, 8; Arthur, *Advice to Young Men*, 8; Burnap, *Lectures to Young Men*, 145; Wise, *Young Man's Counsellor*, 13; Eddy, *The Young Man's Friend*, 22.

46. Muzzey, *The Young Man's Friend*, 84.

47. James, *The Young Man From Home*, 11; Todd, *The Student's Manual*, preface.

48. Halttunen, *Confidence Men and Painted Women*, 1–55; Byars, "The Making of the Self-Made Man," 24–72; Bledstein, *Culture of Professionalism*, 129–58; Horlick, *Country Boys and Merchant Princes*, 157–62; Kett, *Rites of Passage*, 105–8.

49. On the Enlightenment idea of the moral sense, see Markman Ellis, *The Politics of Sensibility: Race, Gender, and Commerce in the Sentimental Novel* (Cam-

bridge: Cambridge University Press, 1996), chap. 1; On the development of the modern usage of "conscience," see Rodney Hessinger, "Problems and Promises: Colonial American Child Rearing and Modernization Theory," *Journal of Family History* 21 (April 1996): 139–40; *Oxford English Dictionary*, 2d ed., s.v. "conscience."

50. For a description of shaming techniques in colonial America, see David J. Rothman, *The Discovery of the Asylum: Social Order and Disorder in the New Republic* (Boston: Little Brown, 1971), 45–50.

51. Arthur, *Advice to Young Men*, 99–100.

52. Muzzey, *The Young Man's Friend*, 20–21, 4–5.

53. Michel Foucault, *Discipline and Punish: The Birth of the Prison* (New York: Vintage Books, 1995), 3–31, 100–103, 195–228.

54. Muzzey, *Young Man's Friend*, 30.

55. James, *The Young Man From Home*, 42.

56. Todd, *The Student's Manual*, 153.

57. Alcott, *Young Man's Guide*, 35, 42, 108–15, 146, 156; Alcott, *Familiar Letters*, 208–9; James, *Young Man From Home*, 103–5; Muzzey, *Young Man's Friend*, 15–16, 58; Todd, *Student's Manual*, 156, 178, 184–85; Arthur, *Advice to Young Men*, 7, 236–38; Burnap, *Lectures to Young Men*, 72–74, 80, 165–66; Wise, *Young Man's Counsellor*, 55–59; Eddy, *Young Man's Friend*, 72–77.

58. Alcott, *Young Man's Guide*, 156, 110–14.

59. Arthur, *Advice to Young Men*, 237.

60. James, *Young Man From Home*, 105.

61. Muzzey, *Young Man's Friend*, 59–60.

62. Burnap, *Lectures to Young Men*, 72–73, 165.

63. Alcott, *Young Man's Guide*, 28–30, 82, 117–18; Alcott, *Familiar Letters*, 20–21, 50–60, 71–72, 104; James, *Young Man From Home*, 47–48, 102–3; Muzzey, *Young Man's Friend*, 28, 40–41; Todd, *Student's Manual*, 10–11, 60–4; Arthur, *Advice to Young Men*, 67, 69–74, 78, 119–27; Burnap, *Lectures to Young Men*, 14–17, 67; Wise, *The Young Man's Counsellor*, 23–24, 41–42, 74–75, 87–88; Eddy, *The Young Man's Friend*, 57–72. These writers in many ways seem to embody the paradoxical figure of the "venturous conservative" described by Marvin Meyers. They produced particularly exaggerated expressions of both fear and hope in the marketplace. Their strained messages reflect the contradictory impulses of their aims to both reform and sell books to young men. See Meyers, *The Jacksonian Persuasion*.

64. Arthur, *Duties of Young Men*, 69–74.

65. Alcott, *Young Man's Guide*, 29.

66. Ibid., 82.

67. Todd, *Student's Manual*, 31.

68. Arthur, *Advice to Young Men*, 31.

69. Muzzey, *Young Man's Friend*, 51; for other positive endorsements of Franklin's example, see Alcott, *Young Man's Guide*, 43; Alcott, *Familiar Letters*, 50, 71–72, 74; Muzzey, *Young Man's Friend*, 29; Todd, *Student's Manual*, 16, 17, 33, 60; Arthur, *Advice to Young Men*, 78. Burnap, *Lectures to Young Men*, 71–72. Franklin himself was posthumously competing with these authors. His *The Way to Wealth* was a popular advice book that offered a less conflicted message of upward mobility; see John G. Cawelti, *Apostles of the Self-Made Man*, 14.

70. Todd, *Student's Manual*, 156.

71. Burnap, *Lectures to Young Men*, 166.

72. Arthur, *Advice to Young Men*, 238.

73. Alcott, *Young Man's Guide*, 121.

74. Alcott, *Familiar Letters*, 204–5; James, *Young Man From Home*, 105; Arthur, *Advice to Young Men*, 66–67, 215.

75. Arthur, *Advice to Young Men*, 66–67.

76. Alcott, *Familiar Letters*, 200–201; see also ibid., 249; Arthur, *Advice to Young Men*, 230–32.

77. Muzzey, *Young Man's Friend*, 26–27; see also Alcott, *Familiar Letters*, 214; James, *Young Man From Home*, 27, 110–11, 133, 142, 144; Todd, *Student's Manual*, 154, 173–74.

78. James, *Young Man From Home*, 144; see also Wise, *The Young Man's Counsellor*, 29–30, 41–42.

79. Todd, *Student's Manual*, 154. For more commentary on the economic advantages of moral character, conscience, or dutiful behavior see James, *Young Man From Home*, 9–10, 52; Muzzey, *Young Man's Friend*, 6, 28, 33, 40–41; Alcott, *Familiar Letters*, 205; Wise, *Young Man's Counsellor*, 57–58; Eddy, *Young Man's Friend*, 75–77; Burnap, *Lectures to Young Men*, 165.

80. Thomas Augst explores the prevalent perception of competition between improving literature and urban attractions in the mid-nineteenth century in "The Business of Reading in Nineteenth-Century America: The New York Mercantile Library," *American Quarterly* 50 (June 1998): 267–305.

81. Muzzey, *Young Man's Friend*, 74–5.

82. David Reynolds, *Beneath the American Renaissance: The Subversive Imagination in the Age of Emerson and Melville* (Cambridge, Mass.: Harvard University Press, 1989).

83. Todd, *Student's Manual*, 197; see also Arthur, *Advice to Young Men*, 7; Alcott, *Familiar Letters*, 82–83.

84. Todd, *Student's Manual*, 73–74. G. J. Barker-Benfield has argued that Todd's stated fears of unethical literature can be understood as an expression of his fear that such works would inspire masturbation. Undoubtedly, this argument has some merit, but there is something more here than simply masturbation fears. Other authors, who do not seem to have been as preoccupied with sexual urges, were equally adamant about the dangers of unethical books; see Barker-Benfield, *The Horrors of the Half-Known Life*, 163–74.

85. Wise, *The Young Man's Counsellor*, 211–22. Wise later recommends the most restrained of such works, Ware's *Hints to Young Men*; see 233. For further commentaries on the need for discrimination in reading, see Burnap, *Lectures to Young Men*, 54–55, and Eddy, *The Young Man's Friend*, 93–94.

86. Alcott, *Familiar Letters*, 220–22, 261.

87. Alcott, *Familiar Letters*, 251.

88. Arthur, *Advice to Young Men*, 7.

89. Arthur, *Advice to Young Men*, 196.

Chapter 6

1. John Angell James, *The Young Man From Home* (New York: D. Appleton and Co., 1840), 36–37.

2. The original English translation was entitled *Onanism, or A Treatise upon the Disorders produced by Masturbation; or the Dangerous Effects of Secret and Excessive Venery* (London, 1766). The text mentioned here, *A Treatise on the Diseases Produced by Onanism* (New York, 1832), was not the first American edition of Tissot's work. The first, published by John Sparhawk, appeared in Philadelphia in 1771, but this edition failed to spark the interest inspired by texts published in the Jacksonian era. On eighteenth-century printings of Tissot, see Thomas Laqueur, *Solitary Sex: A Cultural History of Masturbation* (New York: Zone Books, 2003), 39, 428 n. 30.

3. Among the publications were William Alcott, *The Young Man's Guide*, 15th ed. (Boston: T. R. Marvin, 1843; 1st ed., 1833); Sylvester Graham, *A Lecture to Young Men* (Providence, R.I.: Weeden and Cory, 1834); *Solitary Vice Considered* (New York: J. N. Bolles, 1834); John Todd, *The Student's Manual* (New York: Columbian Publishing Co., 1893; 1st ed., 1835); Samuel B. Woodward, *Hints for the Young, on a Subject Relating to the Health of Body and Mind* (Boston: Weeks, Jordan, and Co., 1838); Mary S. Gove (Nichols), *Solitary Vice: An Address to Parents and Those who Have the Care of Children* (Portland, Maine: Journal Office, 1839); *An Hour's Conference with Fathers and Sons in Relation to a Common and Fatal Indulgence of Youth* (Boston: Whipple and Damrell, 1840); Eugene Becklard, *Physiological Mysteries and Revelations in Love, Courtship, and Marriage* (New York, 1842); O. S. Fowler, *Amativeness: or, Evils and Remedies of Excessive and Perverted Sexuality* (New York: Fowler and Wells, 1854; 1st ed. 1844); Frederick Hollick, *The Origin of Life: A Popular Treatise on the Philosophy and Physiology of Reproduction in Plants and Animals Including the Details of Human Generation* (New York: Nafis and Cornish, 1845); Homer Bostwick, *A Treatise on the Nature and Treatment of Seminal Diseases, Impotency, and Other Kindred Affections: with Practical Directions for the Management and Removal of the Cause Producing Them; Together with Hints to Young Men* (New York: Burgess, Stringer and Co., 1847); John B. Newman, *The Philosophy of Generation: Its Abuses, with Causes, Prevention, and Cure* (New York: Fowler and Wells, 1849); John Ware, *Hints to Young Men on the Relations of the Sexes* (Boston, 1850); Ira Mayhew, *Popular Education: For the Use of Parents and Teachers, and for Young Persons of Both Sexes* (New York: Harper and Bros., 1850).

4. Benjamin Rush, *Medical Inquiries* (Philadelphia: Kimber and Richardson, 1812), 347–56.

5. Rousseau considered the effects of masturbation in *Emile*. On the European legacy of thought about masturbation, as well as European work contemporary to that of Jacksonian America, see Laqueur, *Solitary Sex*; R. P. Neuman, "Masturbation, Madness, and the Modern Concepts of Childhood and Adolescence," *Journal of Social History* 8 (Spring 1975): 1–27; E. H. Hare, "Masturbatory Insanity: The History of an Idea," *Journal of Mental Science* 108 (January 1962): 2–25; Robert H. MacDonald, "The Frightful Consequences of Onanism: Notes on the History of a Delusion," *Journal of the History of Ideas* 28 (1967): 423–31.

6. Charles E. Rosenberg, "Sexuality, Class and Role in Nineteenth-Century America," *American Quarterly* 25 (May 1973): 131–53; Carroll Smith-Rosenberg, "Sex as Symbol in Victorian America: An Ethnohistorical Analysis of Jacksonian America," in John Demos and Sarane Spence Boocock, eds. *Turning Points: Historical and Sociological Essays on the Family* (Chicago: University of Chicago Press, 1978); G. J. Barker-Benfield, *The Horrors of the Half-Known Life: Male Attitudes Toward Women and Sexuality in Nineteenth-century America* (New York: Harper and Row, 1976), esp. part 3; Stephen Nissenbaum, *Sex, Diet, and Debility in Jacksonian America: Sylvester Graham and Health Reform* (Westport, Conn.: Greenwood Press, 1980); Ronald Walters, *Primers for Prudery: Sexual Advice to Victorian America* (Englewood Cliffs, N.J.: Prentice-Hall, 1974).

7. Robert Abzug, *Cosmos Crumbling: American Reform and the Religious Imagination* (New York: Oxford University Press, 1994), 163–66, quoted 163; Nissenbaum, *Sex, Diet, and Debility in Jacksonian America*; Dorsey, *Reforming Men and Women: Gender in the Antebellum City* (Ithaca, N.Y.: Cornell University Press, 2002), 117–20.

8. Michael Sappol, *A Traffic of Dead Bodies: Anatomy and Embodied Social Identity in Nineteenth-Century America* (Princeton: Princeton University Press, 2002), 198–208; Helen Lefkowitz Horowitz, *Rereading Sex: Battles over Sexual Knowledge and Suppression in Nineteenth-Century America* (New York: Knopf, 2002), 274–78.

9. In the late eighteenth-century, as oversight of courtship shifted away from family and toward peers, young men may have had more opportunity to encourage one another in sexual exploits. Some seduction tales—*The Coquette* and *Charlotte Temple*, for example—show such behavior, but such portrayals were intended as cautions to women, not recommendations to men (how they may have been read is another matter). Christine Stansell and John Frisch both provide some evidence of turn-of-the-century rake culture. The Jacksonian period produced more brazen celebrations of male sexual freedom. See Stansell, *City of Women: Sex and Class in New York, 1787–1860* (Urbana: University of Illinois Press, 1987), 22–30; John Frisch, "Youth Culture in America, 1790–1865" (Ph.D. diss., University of Missouri, 1970), 208–9 n. 17, 212, 231–37.

10. On the rake culture of seventeenth- and eighteenth-century England, see G. J. Barker-Benfield, *The Culture of Sensibility: Sex and Society in Eighteenth-Century Britain* (Chicago: University of Chicago Press, 1992), 37–55. Anne Lombard shows that aristocratic libertinism made headway in New England as Puritanism lost influence; see her *Making Manhood: Growing Up Male in Colonial New England* (Cambridge, Mass.: Harvard University Press, 2003), 78–79, 83–84.

11. Samuel Woodworth, "Doctor Stramonium," from *Melodies, Duets, Trios, Songs, and Ballads, Pastoral, Amatory, Sentimental, Patriotic, Religious, and Miscellaneous* (New York, 1830) in David Grimsted, ed., *Notions of the Americans, 1820–1860* (New York: George Braziller, 1970), 35–37.

12. David Reynolds, *Beneath the American Renaissance: The Subversive Imagination in the Age of Emerson and Melville* (Cambridge, Mass.: Harvard University Press, 1989), 211–24, quoted 216.

13. Horowitz, *Rereading Sex*, 32–35.

14. Ibid., 224–39.

15. Reynolds, *Beneath the American Renaissance*, 211–24, quoted 211; Horowitz, *Rereading Sex*, 210–48.

16. Timothy Gilfoyle, *City of Eros: New York City, Prostitution, and the Commercialization of Sex, 1790–1920* (New York: Norton, 1992), 92–116; Horowitz, *Rereading Sex*, 127–28, 169–72. On the Davy Crockett almanacs, which also celebrated libertinism, see Carroll Smith-Rosenberg, "Davy Crockett as Trickster: Pornography, Liminality, and Symbolic Inversion in Victorian America," *Disorderly Conduct: Visions of Gender in Victorian America* (New York: Oxford University Press, 1985), 90–108.

17. Robert Waln, *The Hermit in America on a Visit to Philadelphia: containing some account of the human leeches, belles, beaux, coquettes, dandies, cotillion parties, supper parties, tea parties, &c. &c. of that famous city, and the poets and painters of America*, 2ⁿᵈ ed., ed. Peter Atall (Philadelphia: M. Thomas, 1819), 101.

18. Ibid., *Hermit in America*, 128–29, 180–81.

19. Patricia Cline Cohen, *The Murder of Helen Jewett: The Life and Death of a Prostitute in Nineteenth-Century New York* (New York: Alfred A. Knopf, 1998), 301–29. Further evidence of a burgeoning rake culture might be the emergence of group rape as an urban crime in the years after 1830; see Stansell, *City of Women*, 96–97. Stansell sees a tempering of rake culture within the working class because of emerging protectionist attitudes toward women. Gilfoyle provides more convincing evidence, however, that a cross-class rake culture was thriving at midcentury; see *City of Eros*, 92–116.

20. Philip Howell, "Sex and the City of Bachelors: Sporting Guidebooks and Urban Knowledge in Nineteenth-Century Britain and America," *Ecumene* 8, no. 1 (January 2001): 20–50.

21. *A Guide to the Stranger, or Pocket Companion for The Fancy, Containing A List of the Gay Houses and Ladies of Pleasure in the City of Brotherly Love and Sisterly Affection* (Philadelphia, 1849), 9.

22. *A Guide to the Stranger*, 17.

23. Joseph Kett, *Rites of Passage: Adolescence in America, 1790 to the Present* (New York: Basic Books, 1977), 101–2; Gilfoyle, *City of Eros*, 92–116; Cohen, *Murder of Helen Jewett*, 10–12, 302–4, 309–10; Horowitz, *Rereading Sex*, 126–27; Srebnick, *Mysterious Death of Mary Rogers: Sex and Culture in Nineteenth-Century New York* (New York: Oxford University Press, 1995), 57–58.

24. Graham, *Lecture to Young Men*, 28–29.

25. Alcott, *Young Man's Guide*, 311–12.

26. Fowler, *Amativeness*, 45.

27. Ware, *Hints to Young Men*, 8–9.

28. Natalie Zemon Davis, "Iroquois Women, European Women," in *American Encounters: Natives and Newcomers from European Contact to Indian Removal, 1500–1850*, ed. Peter C. Mancall and James H. Merrell (New York: Routledge, 2000), 99; Kathleen M. Brown, *Good Wives, Nasty Wenches, and Anxious Patriarchs: Gender, Race, and Power in Colonial Virginia* (Chapel Hill: University of North Carolina Press, 1996), 58.

29. Their efforts in this regard was similar to those of manners writers of the

same period who looked to protect women who entered the social stage through the doctrine of "ladies first"; see C. Dallett Hemphill, *Bowing to Necessities: The History of Manners in America, 1620–1860* (New York: Oxford University Press, 1999), chap. 9.

30. Karen Halttunen, *Murder Most Foul: The Killer and the American Gothic Imagination* (Cambridge, Mass.: Harvard University Press, 1998), 14–18.

31. Woodward, *Hints for the Young*, 8, 22. For other alcohol analogies, see Alcott, *Young Man's Guide*, 323; Fowler, *Amativeness*, 55, 71.

32. *Solitary Vice Considered*, 7, 13.

33. Hollick, *The Origin of Life*, 248.

34. Ware, *Hints to Young Men*, 45–47.

35. Ware, *Hints to Young Men*, 50–51.

36. Gregory, *Facts and Important Information for Young Men*, 15–16.

37. *Solitary Vice Considered*, 11–12.

38. Hollick, *The Origin of Life*, 247. For further expressions of the fear that peer groupings, especially schools, were hotbeds for masturbation, see Woodward, *Hints for the Young*, 58; John Todd, *The Student's Manual*, 74–75 (translated from Latin in Barker-Benfield, *Horrors of the Half-Known Life*, 170); Bostwick, *Seminal Diseases*, 233; Graham, *Lectures to Young Men*, 42–43; Fowler, *Amativeness*, 17.

39. Woodward, *Hints for the Young*, 58.

40. Newman, *Philosophy of Generation*, 102.

41. Ibid., 68–69.

42. Alcott, *Young Man's Guide*, 322.

43. Fowler, *Amativeness*, 49.

44. *Solitary Vice Considered*, 7.

45. Ware, *Hints to Young Men*, 44; see also Gregory, *Facts and Important Information*, 15.

46. Isabel V. Hull, *Sexuality, State, and Civil Society in Germany, 1700–1815* (Ithaca, N.Y.: Cornell University Press, 1996), 257–80, quoted 275.

47. Gove, *Solitary Vice*, 3.

48. The only exception here is John Ware, who maintains that "promiscuous" sex with women is a greater evil. See Ware, *Hints to Young Men*, 56.

49. For an overview of the sex reformers' views toward marital sexuality, see John D'Emilio and Estelle B. Freedman, *Intimate Matters: A History of Sexuality in America, 1620–1860* (New York: Harper and Row, 1988), chap. 4.

50. Fowler, *Amativeness*, 56; Woodward, *Hints for the Young*, 12–13.

51. For those writers who maintained a concern over semen loss, semen largely represented a concentration of bodily "energies"; they simply add this fear of energy loss to a more general fear of energy depletion caused by the stimulation of both the genitals and sympathizing organs; see Woodward, *Hints for the Young*, 12–13, 30–31; Fowler, *Amativeness*, 24–25.

52. This physiological model would dominate much of medical discourse of the nineteenth-century; see Charles Rosenberg and Carroll Smith-Rosenberg, "The Female Animal: Medical and Biological Views of Woman and Her Role in Nineteenth-Century America," *Journal of American History* 60 (September 1973): 332–56.

53. On the decline of sensibility, see Andrew Burstein, *Sentimental Democracy:*

The Evolution of America's Romantic Self-Image (New York: Hill and Wang, 1999), 307–24.

54. The best overview of the various brands of sensibility writing is Markman Ellis, *The Politics of Sensibility: Race, Gender, and Commerce in the Sentimental Novel* (Cambridge: Cambridge University Press, 1996). The best account of the ascendancy of the sensibility paradigm in medicine is Christopher Lawrence, "The Nervous System and Society in the Scottish Enlightenment," in Barry Barnes and Steven Shapin, eds. *Natural Order: Historical Studies of Scientific Culture* (Beverly Hills, Calif.: Sage Publications, 1979), 19–40.

55. Graham, *Lecture to Young Men*, 20.

56. Quoted from Ellis, *The Politics of Sensibility*, 13.

57. Raymond Stephanson, "Richardson's 'Nerves': The Physiology of Sensibility in *Clarissa*," *Journal of the History of Ideas* 49 (1988): 267–85.

58. Graham, *Lecture to Young Men*, 17.

59. Ibid., 40.

60. Ibid., 47–65.

61. Ibid., 23–24.

62. Stephanson, "Richardson's 'Nerves'," 274–76; Graham, *Lecture to Young Men*, 18.

63. Ann Douglas, *The Feminization of American Culture* (New York: Knopf, 1977).

64. Graham, *Lecture to Young Men*, 25–26.

65. Ibid., 58–59, 74.

66. Newman, *Philosophy of Generation*, 52, 69.

67. Fowler, *Amativeness*, 25.

68. G. J. Barker-Benfield, "The Spermatic Economy: A Nineteenth-Century View of Sexuality," *Feminist Studies* 1 (Summer 1972): 45–74; and Barker-Benfield, *Horrors of the Half-Known Life*, part 3.

69. Hull, *Sexuality, State, and Civil Society in Germany*, 245–51, 266–69; Laura Engelstein, *The Keys to Happiness: Sex and the Search for Modernity in Fin-de-Siècle Russia* (Ithaca, N.Y.: Cornell University Press, 1992), 236–40.

70. Fowler, *Amativeness*, 28.

71. Gregory, *Facts and Important Information*, 64; Gove, *Solitary Vice*, 16.

72. Newman, *Philosophy of Generation*, 69.

73. Reynolds, *Beneath the American Renaissance*, 54–91; quoted 59, 55. In discussing the phenomenon of immoral reform, Reynolds does consider a couple of authors who wrote on masturbation. This analysis means to extend his insights, not only by expanding the number of sources for such analysis but also by showing these reformers' self-awareness of their participation in the immoral aspects of publishing.

74. Laqueur, *Solitary Sex*, 25–36.

75. Gregory, *Facts and Important Information*, 10; Fowler, *Amativeness*, 38.

76. On Foucault's notion that sex reformers were responsible for encouraging, not discouraging, sexual activity, see his *The History of Sexuality: An Introduction* (New York: Vintage Books, 1990), esp. 17–35.

77. Ware, *Hints to Young Men*, 10–11.

78. Gregory, *Facts and Important Information*, 10–11.

79. *Solitary Vice Considered*, 3.

80. Gove, *Solitary Vice*, 15.

81. Carroll Smith-Rosenberg, "Beauty, the Beast, and the Militant Woman," *Disorderly Conduct*, 109–128; Reynolds, *Beneath the American Renaissance*, 62–64.

82. Horowitz, *Rereading Sex*, 58–69. Sylvester Graham condemns "works pretending to teach how pregnancy may be avoided," most likely referring to Owen's book in the preface to his second edition; see *A Lecture to Young Men*, 2nd ed. (Massachusetts: Geo. C. Rand and Co., 1837), 22.

83. Bostwick, *Seminal Diseases*, 11–12.

84. Graham, *Lecture to Young Men*, 2nd ed., 21–22.

85. Newman, *Philosophy of Generation*, 1.

86. Ware, *Hints to Young Men*, iii.

87. Ibid., *Hints to Young Men*, iv, 50, 55.

88. Gregory, *Facts and Important Information*, 17–18.

89. "Testimonials" in Graham, *Lecture to Young Men*, 2nd ed.; Ware, *Hints to Young Men*, iii–iv.

90. Newman, *Philosophy of Generation*, 1, 48–54, 69–79.

91. M. M. Bakhtin sees interpretive mutability as characterizing the novel, in particular; see *The Dialogic Imagination*, ed. Michael Holquist, trans. Caryl Emerson and Michael Holquist (Austin: University of Texas Press, 1981), 259–422.

92. Horowitz, *Rereading Sex*, 108–14, 272–96. Horowitz additionally suggests that market considerations caused a blurring between some physiological literature and erotica. I mean to carry this analysis further by demonstrating the close connection between sensational fiction and anti-masturbation texts.

93. Graham, *Lecture to Young Men*, 62.

94. Woodward, *Hints for the Young*, iv; Bostwick, *Seminal Diseases*, 7–8.

95. Gregory, *Facts and Important Information*, 22.

96. Ware, *Hints to Young Men*, 53; Solitary *Vice Considered*, 3.

97. Horowitz, *Rereading Sex*, 274–77. Hollick reprints many documents relating to this controversy in the preface of the tenth edition of *The Origin of Life*.

98. Halttunen, "Humanitarianism and the Pornography of Pain in Anglo-American Culture," *American Historical Review* 100, no. 2 (April 1995): 303–34.

99. Graham, *Lecture to Young Men*, 23–24.

100. Gregory, *Facts and Important Information*, 35.

101. Woodward, *Hints to the Young*, 27.

102. Gregory, *Facts and Important Information*, 15–16.

103. Graham, *Lecture to Young Men*, 25–28.

104. *Solitary Vice Considered*, 12. G. J. Barker-Benfield also finds phallic imagery in John Todd's writings; see his *Horrors of the Half-Known Life*, part 3. I would like to thank Bruce Dorsey for encouraging me to highlight the phallic imagery in this literature.

105. Newman, *Philosophy of Generation*, 81–82.

106. In this respect American anti-masturbation literature departs from what Thomas Laqueur finds in Europe. The one American writer who devotes serious attention to female masturbation before 1850 is, not surprisingly, Mary Gove. If we

look at the trajectory of her career, Mary Gove may already have been moving toward her particular brand of free love, seeing sexual urges as natural impulses in both men and women. See Laqueur, *Solitary Sex*, 200–204; Horowitz, *Rereading Sex*, 105–6, 109–12.

107. Jean DuBois, M.D., *The Secret Habits of the Female Sex: Letters Addressed to a Mother on the Evils of Solitude and Its Seductive Temptations to Young Girls* (New York, 1848) [copy referenced held at Library Company of Philadelphia]; Horowitz, *Rereading Sex*, 242–43.

108. DuBois, *The Secret Habits of the Female Sex*; see also Horowitz, *Rereading Sex*, 242–43.

109. Similarly, Helen Lefkowitz Horowitz shows that some booksellers advertised physiological tracts next to erotic novels; see Horowitz, *Rereading Sex*, 273.

110. Even in their own day, there were some very conventional elements to their writings. While these reformers applied the principle of bodily sympathy to organs previously ignored and took these principles to exaggerated lengths, their basic physiological model was quite ordinary. For example, a survey of *The Journal of Health*, a magazine published by major figures in the medical establishment of Philadelphia and distributed across the country, reveals a large overlap between the sex reformers and established medicine in physiological assumptions. If sexual stimulation did not attract major attention in this periodical, other stimulating habits such as alcohol drinking, tea drinking, and consumption of stimulating foods received frequent censure. The basic principle of bodily sympathy was expressed in the discussions of both sex reformers and the established medical community. See *The Journal of Health, Conducted by an Association of Physicians*, vol. 1, no. 1 (September 1829)–vol. 4, no. 12 (August 1833); see also Charles Rosenberg, *The Cholera Years: The United States in 1832, 1849, and 1866* (Chicago: University of Chicago Press, 1962), chaps. 1–9. The attraction of these topics for the medical establishment might be expected considering the great influence of Benjamin Rush, whose ideas anticipated the place of medicine in nineteenth-century reform. On Rush's connection to body reforms, see Abzug, *Cosmos Crumbling*, chap. 1.

111. R. P. Neuman, "Masturbation, Madness, and the Modern Concepts of Childhood and Adolescence," 1–27.

112. Woodward, *Hints to the Young*, 8.

113. Bostwick, *Seminal Diseases*, 41.

114. Newman, *Philosophy of Generation*, 74.

115. Fowler, *Amativeness*, 52.

116. Ibid., 27.

117. Kett, *Rites of Passage*, 6, 217–21.

118. Foucault, *Discipline and Punish*, esp. 195–228; Hollick, *The Origin of Life*, 247.

119. Hollick, *The Origin of Life*, 268.

120. On the fear of sexual daydreams and the imaginative life of youth, especially as inspired by novels, see Barker-Benfield, *Horrors of the Half-Known Life*, 169–74; Laqueur, *Solitary Sex*, 210–22, 320–30.

121. Woodward, *Hints for the Young*, 44.

122. Bostwick, *Seminal Diseases*, 9–10.

123. Fowler, *Amativeness*, 53.

124. Bostwick, *Seminal Diseases*, 233. On surveillance and architecture, see Foucault, *Discipline and Punish*, 200–209. Foucault offers some general comments on the deployment of "technologies of power" in dealing with masturbation in particular in *The History of Sexuality*, vol. 1, 27–31. One might also rely on the threat of God's surveillance, as Todd and Alcott do; see Alcott, *Young Man's Guide*, 321–22; Todd, *The Student's Manual*, 74–75.

125. Bostwick, *Seminal Diseases*, 43–44.

126. Kett, *Rites of Passage*, Introduction, chaps. 7, 8.

127. Beyond warning against masturbation, midcentury sex reformers prohibited nonmarital heterosexual relations and placed many limits on marital sexuality; see D'Emilio and Freedman, *Intimate Matters*, chap. 4.

Conclusion

1. Alcott, *Familiar Letters to Young Men* (Buffalo: Geo. H. Derby and Co., 1850; 1st ed., 1849), 17.

2. Kett, *Rites of Passage: Adolescence in America, 1790 to the Present* (New York: Basic Book, 1977), 111–272; Howard Chudacoff, *How Old Are You?: Age Conciousness in American Culture* (Princeton, N.J.: Princeton University Press, 1989), esp. 65–91.

Bibliography

Primary Sources

Institutional Records

Philadelphia Magdalen Society (HSP)
    Annual Reports, 1819–1850
    Magdalen Society Constitution, 1800
    Minutes of the Board of Managers, 1800–1850
    White-Williams Foundation Manual Book
University of Pennsylvania (UPA)
    Archives General Collection (AG)
        Files:
            1822 Trustees
            1823 Trustees
            1824 Trustees
            1824 College Duties and Discipline
            1825 Trustees
            1825–6 Trustees and State of College
            1826–7 Trustees
            1827 Students
            1828 College Students and Activities
            1830–3 Addresses by Provost
    Correspondence:
        Frederic Beasley, 1813–20 (files 107–28)
        Paul Beck, Jr., 1820 (file 129)
    Minutes, Board of Trustees, 1813–31 (BTM)
    Minutes, Faculty, 1828–31
Harvard University (HUA)
    Reports to the Overseers, vol. 2, 1826
Philomathean Society, University of Pennsylvania
    The Journal in Four Numbers, Edited By a Senior, 1826

Princeton University (PUA)
    Ashbel Green Papers
Presbyterian Church, USA (PHS)
    Minutes of the General Assembly of the Presbyterian Church in the United States of America. Philadelphia, 1813–37
    Patterson, James. *Sermons,* 1814–37
American Sunday School Union (PHS)
    Annual Reports, 1825–50
    Seventh Report of the Philadelphia and Adult School Union, With an Account of the Formation of the ASSU, 1824

Periodicals

The American Museum. Philadelphia, 1787–92
The American National Preacher. New York, 1841
The Baltimore Weekly Magazine. Baltimore, 1800–1801
The Boston Weekly Magazine. Boston, 1802–5
The Boston Magazine. Boston, 1783–86
Columbian Magazine. Philadelphia, 1786–87
The Christian Advocate. Philadelphia, 1823–34
The Gentlemen and Ladies Town and Country Magazine. Boston, 1789–90
The Journal of Health. Philadelphia, 1829–33
The Key. Fredericktown, 1798
Lady's Magazine and Musical Repository. New York, 1801–2
Ladies Museum. Philadelphia, 1800
The Lady and Gentleman's Pocket Magazine. New York, 1796
Lady's Magazine. Philadelphia, 1792–93
The Literary Miscellany. Philadelphia, 1795
Massachusetts Magazine. Boston, 1789–96
New England Palladium. Boston, 1823
The New York Magazine. New York, 1790–97
Poulson's American Daily Advertiser. Philadelphia, 1801
Public Ledger. Philadelphia, 1843
Weekly Magazine. Philadelphia, 1798–99

Books

Adair, Robert. *Memoir of Reverend James Patterson.* Philadelphia: Henry Perkins, 1840.
Alcott, William. *The Young Man's Guide,* 15th ed. Boston: T. R. Marvin, 1843; 1st ed., 1833.

————. *Familiar Letters to Young Men*. Buffalo: Geo. H. Derby and Co., 1850; 1st ed., 1849.

An Enquiry into the Condition and Influence of The Brothels in Connection with the Theatres of Philadelphia, Intended to Awaken the Attention of Parents and Guardians, and Those Who are Opposed to the Nightly Practice of Turning our Theatres into Assignation-Houses. Philadelphia, 1834.

Arthur, Timothy Shay. *Advice to Young Men on Their Duties and Conduct in Life*. Philadelphia: John E. Potter, 1848.

Beasley, Frederic. *A Search of Truth in the Science of the Human Mind*. Philadelphia: S. Potter and Co., 1822.

Bostwick, Homer. *A Treatise on the Nature and Treatment of Seminal Diseases, Impotency, and Other Kindred Affections: With Practical Directions for the Management and Removal of the Cause Producing Them; Together with Hints to Young Men*. New York: Burgess, Stringer and Co., 1847.

Brown, William Hill. *The Power of Sympathy, or The Triumph of Nature: Founded in Truth*. 2 vols. Boston: Isaiah Thomas and Co., 1789.

Burnap, George. *Lectures to Young Men on the Cultivation of the Mind, the Formation of Character and the Conduct of Life*, 2nd ed. Baltimore: John Murphy, 1841; 1st ed., 1840.

DuBois, Jean. *The Secret Habits of the Female Sex: Letters Addressed to a Mother on the Evils of Solitude and Its Seductive Temptations to Young Girls*. New York: Sold by the Booksellers Generally, 1848.

Eddy, Daniel C. *The Young Man's Friend: Containing Admonitions for the Erring*. Lowell, Mass.: Nathaniel L. Dayton, 1850; 1st ed., 1849.

Finney, Charles G. *The Memoirs of Charles G. Finney*. Ed. Garth M. Rosell and Richard A. G. Dupuis. Grand Rapids, Mich.: Academie Books, 1989.

Foster, Hannah W. *The Coquette* ed. Cathy N. Davidson. New York: Oxford University Press, 1986; 1st ed., 1797.

Fowler, O. S. *Amativeness: Or, Evils and Remedies of Excessive and Perverted Sexuality*. New York: Fowler and Wells, 1854; 1st ed. 1844.

Gove (Nichols), Mary S. *Solitary Vice: An Address to Parents and Those who Have the Care of Children*. Portland, Maine: Journal Office, 1839.

Graham, Sylvester. *A Lecture to Young Men*. Providence, R.I.: Weeden and Cory, 1834.

————. *A Lecture to Young Men*, 2nd ed. Massachusetts: Geo. C. Rand & Co., 1837.

Gregory, Samuel. *Facts and Important Information for Young Men on the Self-Indulgence of The Sexual Appetite, Its Destructive Effects on Health, Exciting Causes, Prevention and Cure*. New York: Fowler and Wells, 1850; 1st ed. 1845.

Green, Ashbel. *Life of Ashbel Green*. Ed. Joseph H. Jones. New York: Robert Carter and Brothers, 1849.

Hollick, Frederick. *The Origin of Life: A Popular Treatise on the Philosophy and Physiology of Reproduction in Plants and Animals Including the Details of Human Generation*. New York: Nafis and Cornish, 1845.

Horatio, Nicholas J. *The New England Coquette: From the History of the Celebrated Eliza Wharton: A Tragic Drama in Three Acts*. Salem: N. Coverly, 1802.

James, John Angell. *The Young Man From Home.* New York: D. Appleton and Co., 1840.

Lieber, Francis. *The Stranger in America.* Philadelphia: Carey, Lea, and Blanchard, 1835.

Lippard, George. *The Quaker City, or The Monks of Monk Hall: A Romance of Philadelphia Life, Mystery, and Crime.* Ed. David S. Reynolds. Amherst: University of Massachusetts Press, 1995; 1st ed., 1845.

Locke, John. *Some Thoughts Concerning Education.* Ed. R. H. Quick. Cambridge: Cambridge University Press, 1913; 1st ed., 1693.

Muzzey, Artemus Bowers. *The Young Man's Friend.* Boston: James Monroe and Co., 1836.

Newman, John B. *The Philosophy of Generation: Its Abuses, with Causes, Prevention, and Cure.* New York: Fowler and Wells, 1853; 1st ed., 1849.

Onanism, or A Treatise upon the Disorders produced by Masturbation; or the Dangerous Effects of Secret and Excessive Venery. London, 1766.

Packard, Frederick. *The Teacher Taught.* Philadelphia: ASSU, 1833.

Rowson, Susanna. *Charlotte Temple: A Tale of Truth* ed. Ann Douglas. New York: Penguin Books, 1991; 1st American ed., 1794.

Rush, Benjamin. *Medical Inquiries and Observations Upon the Diseases of the Mind.* Philadelphia: Kimber and Richardson, 1812.

Solitary Vice Considered. New York: J. N. Bolles, 1834.

Tocqueville, Alexis de. *Democracy in America.* Ed. Phillips Bradley. New York: Vintage Books, 1945.

Todd, John. *The Student's Manual* . New York: Columbian Publishing Co., 1893; 1st ed., 1835.

A Treatise on the Diseases Produced by Onanism. New York, 1832.

Trollope, Frances. *Domestic Manners of the Americans.* New York: Knopf, 1949; 1st ed., 1832.

Waln, Robert. *The Hermit in America on a Visit to Philadelphia,* 2nd ed. Ed. Peter Atall. Philadelphia: M. Thomas, 1819.

Ware, John. *Hints to Young Men on the Relations of the Sexes.* Boston: Tappan, Whitemore, and Mason, 1850.

Waterbury, Jared. *Considerations for Young Men.* New York: Jonathan Leavitt, 1832.

Wayland, Francis. *Thoughts on the Present Collegiate System in the United States.* Boston: Gould, Kendall, and Lincoln, 1842.

Wise, Rev. Daniel. *The Young Man's Counsellor, or Sketches and Illustrations of the Duties and Dangers of Young Men.* New York: Nelson and Phillips, 1850.

Woodward, Samuel B. *Hints for the Young, On a Subject Relating to the Health of Body and Mind.* Boston: Weeks, Jordan, and Co., 1838.

Pamphlets

Alexander, Archibald. *Suggestions in Vindication of Sunday-Schools.* ASSU, 1832. (PHS)

Beasley, Frederic. *A Statute Recommended by the Provost.* 1824. (UPA)

Board of Trustees, University of Pennsylvania. *Laws Relating to the Moral Conduct, and Orderly Behavior of the Students and Scholars of the University of Pennsylvania.* 1801. (HSP)

———. *Report on the Existing State of Abuses in the University.* 1824. (UPA)

A Brief Appeal to the Good Sense of The University of Oxford on Classification of Merit: With Some Hints to the Rev. H. A. Woodgate on Logic by Philodicæus Oxford: H. Cooke, 1829.

Catalogue of the Officers and Students of the University of Pennsylvania. 1831. (UPA)

DeLancey, William. *Inaugural Address.* 1828. (UPA)

———. *An Address Delivered Before the Trustees, Faculty, and Students.* 1830. (UPA)

Ferris, Isaac. *An Appeal to Ministers of the Gospel in Behalf of Sunday-schools.* ASSU, 1834. (PHS)

A Guide to the Stranger, or Pocket Companion for The Fancy, Containing A List of the Gay Houses and Ladies of Pleasure in the City of Brotherly Love and Sisterly Affection. Philadelphia, 1849. (LCP)

Hall, Willard. *Defence of the American Sunday School Union, Against the Charges of Its Opponents.* ASSU, 1831. (LCP)

Henshaw, J. P. K. *The Usefulness of Sunday-Schools.* ASSU, 1833. (PHS)

Hodge, Charles. *A Sermon, Preached in Philadelphia, at the Request of the ASSU.* ASSU, 1832. (PHS)

Plans and Motives for the Extension of Sabbath Schools. ASSU, n.d. (PHS)

Reasons for the Suggestion of Certain Alterations in the Examination Statute, Lately Submitted to the Vice-Chancellor and Head of Houses by the Public Examiners. Oxford: Baxter, 1832.

Taylor, James B. *The Exigencies and Responsibilities of the Present Age.* ASSU, 1836. (PHS)

Tyng, Stephen H. *The Connexion Between Early Religious Instruction and Mature Piety.* ASSU, 1837. (PHS)

Wayland, Francis Jr. *Encouragements to Religious Effort.* ASSU, 1830. (PHS)

White, William. *An Episcopal Charge, on the Subject of Revivals, Delivered Before the Forty-Eighth Convention of the Diocese of Pennsylvania.* 1832. (LCP)

Collected Reprints

Foster, George G. "Philadelphia in Slices." Ed. George Rogers Taylor. *Pennsylvania Magazine of History and Biography* 93 (January 1969): 23–72.

Grimsted, David, ed. *Notions of the Americans, 1820–1860.* New York: George Braziller, 1970.

Hofstadter, Richard, and Wilson Smith, eds. *American Higher Education: A Documentary History.* Chicago: University of Chicago Press, 1961.

Rudolph, Frederick, ed. *Essays on Education in the Early Republic.* Cambridge, Mass.: Belknap Press, 1965.

Secondary Sources

Abzug, Robert H. *Cosmos Crumbling: American Reform and the Religious Imagination*. New York: Oxford University Press, 1994.

Allmendinger, David Jr. *Paupers and Scholars: The Transformation of Student Life in Nineteenth Century New England*. New York: St. Martin's Press, 1975.

Andrews, Dee. *The Methodists and Revolutionary America, 1760–1800: The Shaping of an Evangelical Culture*. Princeton, N.J.: Princeton University Press, 2000.

Appleby, Joyce. "New Cultural Heroes in the Early National Period." In Thomas Haskell and Richard Teichgraeber, eds., *The Culture of the Market: Historical Essays*. New York: Cambridge University Press, 1993.

Ariès, Philippe. *Centuries of Childhood: A Social History of Family Life*. Trans. Robert Baldick. New York: Knopf, 1962.

Augst, Thomas. "The Business of Reading in Nineteenth-Century America: The New York Mercantile Library." *American Quarterly* 50 (June 1998): 267–305.

Axtell, James. *The School upon a Hill: Education and Society in Colonial New England*. New Haven, Conn.: Yale University Press, 1974.

Bailyn, Bernard. "Why Kirkland Failed." *Glimpses of the Harvard Past*. Cambridge, Mass.: Harvard University Press, 1986.

Bakhtin, M. M. *The Dialogic Imagination*, ed. Michael Holquist, trans. Caryl Emerson and Michael Holquist. Austin: University of Texas Press, 1981.

Barker-Benfield, G. J. *The Culture of Sensibility: Sex and Society in Eighteenth-Century Britain*. Chicago: University of Chicago Press, 1992.

———. *The Horrors of the Half-Known Life: Male Attitudes Toward Women and Sexuality in Nineteenth Century America*. New York: Harper and Row, 1976.

———. "The Spermatic Economy: A Nineteenth-Century View of Sexuality." *Feminist Studies* 1 (Summer 1972): 45–74.

Bell, Marion. *Crusade in the City: Revivalism in Nineteenth-Century Philadelphia*. Lewisburg, Pa.: Bucknell University Press, 1977.

Bilhartz, Terry. *Urban Religion and the Second Great Awakening: Church and Society in Early National Baltimore*. Rutherford, N.J.: Farleigh Dickinson University Press, 1986.

Bledstein, Burton. *The Culture of Professionalism: The Middle Class and the Development of Higher Education in America*. New York: Norton, 1976.

Bloch, Ruth H. "American Feminine Ideals in Transition: The Rise of the Moral Mother, 1785–1815." *Feminist Studies* 4 (1978): 101–26.

———. "The Gendered Meanings of Virtue in Revolutionary America." *Signs* 13 (Autumn 1987): 37–58.

Block, Sharon. "Rape without Women: Print Culture and the Politicization of Rape, 1765–1815." *Journal of American History* 89, no. 3 (December 2002): 849–68.

Blumin, Stuart. *The Emergence of the Middle Class: Social Experience in the American City, 1760–1900*. New York: Cambridge University Press, 1989.

Boydston, Jeanne. "The Woman Who Wasn't There: Women's Market Labor and the Transition to Capitalism in the United States." *Journal of the Early Republic* 16 (Summer 1996): 183–206.

————. *Home and Work: Housework, Wages, and the Ideology of Labor in the Early Republic* (New York: Oxford University Press, 1990.

Boyer, Paul. *Urban Masses and Moral Order in America, 1820–1920*. Cambridge, Mass.: Harvard University Press, 1978.

Boylan, Anne. *Sunday School: The Formation of an American Institution, 1790–1880*. New Haven, Conn.: Yale University Press, 1988.

Branson, Susan. *These Fiery Frenchified Dames: Women and Political Culture in Early National Philadelphia*. Philadelphia: University of Pennsylvania Press, 2001.

Bratt, James. "Religious Anti-Revivalism in Antebellum America." *Journal of the Early Republic* 24, no. 1 (Spring 2004): 65–106.

Brown, Gillian. *Consent of the Governed: The Lockean Legacy in Early American Culture* Cambridge, Mass.: Harvard University Press, 2001.

Brown, Herbert Ross. *The Sentimental Novel in America, 1789–1860*. Durham, N.C.: Duke University Press, 1940.

Brown, Kathleen M. *Good Wives, Nasty Wenches, and Anxious Patriarchs: Gender, Race, and Power in Colonial Virginia*. Chapel Hill: University of North Carolina Press, 1996.

Bruce, Philip Alexander. *History of the University of Virginia, 1819–1919*. New York: Macmillan, 1920.

Burke, Colin B. *American Collegiate Populations: A Test of the Traditional View*. New York: New York University Press, 1982.

Burstein, Andrew. *Sentimental Democracy: The Evolution of America's Romantic Self-Image*. New York: Hill and Wang, 1999.

Burt, Nathaniel. *The Perennial Philadelphians: The Anatomy of an American Aristocracy*. Boston: Little, Brown, 1963.

Bushman, Richard. *The Refinement of America: Persons, Houses, and Cities*. New York: Knopf, 1992.

Byars, Ronald Preston. "The Making of the Self-Made Man: The Development of Masculine Roles and Images in Ante-Bellum America." Ph.D. diss., Michigan State University, 1979.

Carlisle, Marcia Roberta. "Prostitutes and Their Reformers in Nineteenth-Century Philadelphia." Ph.D. diss., Rutgers University, 1982.

Carwardine, Richard. "The Second Great Awakening in the Urban Centers: An Examination of Methodism and the 'New Measures'." *Journal of American History* 59 (September 1972): 327–40.

Cawelti, John G. *Apostles of the Self-Made Man*. Chicago: University of Chicago Press, 1965.

Cheyney, Edward Potts. *History of the University of Pennsylvania, 1740–1940*. Philadelphia: University of Pennsylvania Press, 1940.

Chudacoff, Howard P. *How Old Are You? Age Conciousness in American Culture*. Princeton, N.J.: Princeton University Press, 1989.

Cohen, Daniel. "Arthur Mervyn and His Elders: The Ambivalence of Youth in the Early Republic." *William and Mary Quarterly* 3rd ser., 43 (July 1986): 362–80.

————. "Introduction." *The Female Marine and Related Works: Narratives of Cross-Dressing and Urban Vice in America's Early Republic*. Amherst: University of Massachusetts Press, 1997.

————. *Pillars of Salt, Monuments of Grace: New England Crime Literature and the Origins of American Popular Culture, 1674–1860.* New York: Oxford University Press, 1993.

Cohen, Patricia Cline. *The Murder of Helen Jewett: The Life and Death of a Prostitute in Nineteenth-Century New York.* New York: Knopf, 1998.

Cooke, J. W. "The Life and Death of Colonel Solomon P. Sharp, Part 2: A Time to Weep and a Time to Mourn." *The Filson Club History Quarterly* 72, no. 2 (April 1998): 121–51.

————. "Portrait of a Murderess: Anna Cook(e) Beauchamp." *Filson Club History Quarterly* 65, no. 2 (April 1991): 209–30.

Cott, Nancy F. *The Bonds of Womanhood: "Woman's Sphere" in New England, 1780–1835.* New Haven, Conn.: Yale University Press, 1977.

————. "Passionlessness: An Interpretation of Victorian Sexual Ideology, 1790–1850." *Signs* 4 (Winter 1978): 219–36.

Cowing, Cedric. "Sex and Preaching in the Great Awakening." *American Quarterly* 20 (Autumn 1968): 625–44.

Cremin, Lawrence. *American Education: The Colonial Experience, 1607–1783.* New York: Harper and Row, 1970.

————. *American Education: The National Experience, 1783–1876.* New York: Harper and Row, 1980.

Cross, Whitney. *The Burned-Over District: The Social and Intellectual History of Enthusiastic Religion in Western New York, 1800–1850.* New York: Harper and Row, 1965.

Cutler, William W. "Status, Values, and the Education of the Poor: The Trustees of the New York Public School Society, 1805–1853." *American Quarterly* 24 (March 1972): 69–85.

Davidoff, Leonore, and Catherine Hall. *Family Fortunes: Men and Women of the English Middle Class, 1780–1850.* Chicago: University of Chicago Press, 1987.

Davidson, Cathy N. *Revolution and the Word: The Rise of the Novel in America.* New York: Oxford University Press, 1986.

Davis, Natalie Zemon. "Iroquois Women, European Women." In Peter C. Mancall and James H. Merrell, eds., *American Encounters: Natives and Newcomers from European Contact to Indian Removal, 1500–1850.* New York: Routledge, 2000.

Dayton, Cornelia Hughes. "Taking the Trade: Abortion and Gender Relations in an Eighteenth-Century New England Village." *William and Mary Quarterly* 3rd ser., 48 (January 1991): 19–49.

————. *Women before the Bar: Gender, Law, and Society in Connecticut, 1639–1789.* Chapel Hill: University of North Carolina Press, 1995.

De Cunzo, Lu Ann. "Reform, Respite, and Ritual: An Archaeology of Institutions, the Magdalen Society of Philadelphia, 1800–50." *Historical Archaeology* 29, no. 3 (1995): 1–168.

Degler, Carl. *At Odds: Women and the Family in America from the Revolution to the Present.* New York: Oxford University Press, 1980.

D'Emilio, John, and Estelle B. Freedman. *Intimate Matters: A History of Sexuality in America, 1620–1860.* New York: Harper and Row, 1988.

Ditz, Toby. "Shipwrecked; or Masculinity Imperiled: Mercantile Representations of Failure and the Gendered Self in Eighteenth-Century Philadelphia." *Journal of American History* 81, no. 1 (June 1994): 51–80.

Doherty, Robert W. "Social Bases for the Presbyterian Schism of 1837–8: The Philadelphia Case." *Journal of Social History* 2 (Fall 1968): 68–79.

Dorsey, Bruce. "City of Brotherly Love: Religious Benevolence, Gender, and Reform in Philadelphia, 1780–1844." Ph.D. diss., Brown University, 1993.

———. *Reforming Men and Women: Gender in the Antebellum City*. Ithaca, N.Y.: Cornell University Press, 2002.

Douglas, Ann. *The Feminization of American Culture*. New York: Knopf, 1977.

Doyle, Mildred, "Sentimentalism in American Periodicals, 1741–1800." Ph.D. diss., New York University, 1941.

Ellis, Markman. *The Politics of Sensibility: Race, Gender, and Commerce in the Sentimental Novel*. Cambridge: Cambridge University Press, 1996.

Engelstein, Laura. *The Keys to Happiness: Sex and the Search for Modernity in Fin-de-Siècle Russia*. Ithaca, N.Y.: Cornell University Press, 1992.

Fliegelman, Jay. *Prodigals and Pilgrims: The American Revolution against Patriarchal Authority, 1750–1800*. New York: Cambridge University Press, 1982.

Foucault, Michel. *Discipline and Punish: The Birth of the Prison*. Trans. Alan Sheridan. New York: Vintage Books, 1995.

———. *The History of Sexuality*. Vol. 1: *An Introduction*. Trans. Robert Hurley. New York: Vintage Books, 1990.

———. *Foucault Live* (Interviews, 1961–1984). Ed. Sylvère Lotringer, trans. Lysa Hochroth and John Johnston. New York: Semiotexte(e), 1996.

Freeman, Joanne B. "Dueling as Politics: Reinterpreting the Burr-Hamilton Duel." *William and Mary Quarterly* 3rd ser., 53 (April 1996): 289–318.

Frisch, John. "Youth Culture in America, 1790–1865." Ph.D. diss., University of Missouri, 1970.

Gilfoyle, Timothy. *City of Eros: New York City, Prostitution, and the Commercialization of Sex, 1790–1920*. New York: Norton, 1992.

Glenn, Myra C. *Campaigns against Corporal Punishment: Prisoners, Sailors, Women and Children in Antebellum America*. Albany: State University of New York Press, 1984.

General Alumni Society, University of Pennsylvania. *Biographical Catalogue of the Matriculates of the College*. Philadelphia: Published for the Society, 1893

Godbeer, Richard. *Sexual Revolution in Early America*. Baltimore: Johns Hopkins University Press, 2002.

Gorn, Elliott J. *The Manly Art: Bare-Knuckle Prize Fighting in America*. Ithaca, NY: Cornell University Press, 1989.

Graff, Harvey J. *Conflicting Paths: Growing Up in America*. Cambridge, Mass.: Harvard University Press, 1995.

Greven, Philip. *Four Generations: Population, Land, and Family in Colonial Andover, Massachusetts*. Ithaca, N.Y.: Cornell University Press, 1970.

———. *The Protestant Temperament: Patterns of Childrearing, Religious Experience, and the Self in Early America*. New York: Knopf, 1977.

Gross, Robert A. *The Minutemen and Their World*. New York: Hill and Wang, 1976.

Halttunen, Karen. *Confidence Men and Painted Women: A Study of Middle-Class Culture in America, 1830–1870*. New Haven, Conn.: Yale University Press, 1982.

———. "'Domestic Differences': Competing Narratives of Womanhood in the Murder Trial of Lucretia Chapman." In Shirley Samuels, ed., *The Culture of Sentiment: Race, Gender, and Sentimentality in Nineteenth-Century America*. New York: Oxford University Press, 1992.

———. "Humanitarianism and the Pornography of Pain in Anglo-American Culture." *American Historical Review* 100 (April 1995): 303–34.

———. *Murder Most Foul: The Killer and the American Gothic Imagination*. Cambridge, Mass.: Harvard University Press, 1998.

Hambrick-Stowe, Charles E. *Charles G. Finney and the Spirit of American Evangelicalism*. Grand Rapids, Mich.: William B. Eerdmans, 1996.

Hare, E. H. "Masturbatory Insanity: The History of an Idea." *Journal of Mental Science* 108 (January 1962): 2–25.

Hatch, Nathan O. *The Democratization of American Christianity*. New Haven, Conn.: Yale University Press, 1989.

Hawes, Joseph. *Children in Urban Society: Juvenile Delinquency in Nineteenth-Century America*. New York: Oxford University Press, 1971.

Hemphill, C. Dallett. "Age Relations and the Social Order in Early New England: The Evidence from Manners." *Journal of Social History* 28 (Winter 1994): 271–94.

———. *Bowing to Necessities: The History of Manners in America, 1620–1860*. New York: Oxford University Press, 1999.

———. "Middle Class Rising in Revolutionary America: The Evidence from Manners." *Journal of Social History* 30 (Winter 1996): 317–44.

Hessinger, Rodney. "'Insidious Murderers of Female Innocence': Representations of Masculinity in the Seduction Tales of the Late Eighteenth Century." In Merril Smith, ed., *Sex and Sexuality in Early America*. New York: New York University Press, 1998.

———. "'The Most Powerful Instrument of College Discipline': Student Disorder and the Growth of Meritocracy in the Colleges of the Early Republic." *History of Education Quarterly* 39 (Fall 1999): 237–62.

———. "Problems and Promises: Colonial American Child Rearing and Modernization Theory." *Journal of Family History* 21 (April 1996): 125–43.

———. "Victim of Seduction or Vicious Woman?: Conceptions of the Prostitute at the Philadelphia Magdalen Society, 1800–1850." *Pennsylvania History* 66 Special Supplement, *Explorations in Early American Culture* (1999): 201–22.

Heyrman, Christine. *Southern Cross: The Beginnings of the Bible Belt*. Chapel Hill: University of North Carolina Press, 1997.

Hobson, Barbara Meil. *Uneasy Virtue: The Politics of Prostitution and the American Reform Tradition*. New York: Basic Books, 1987.

Hofstadter, Richard. *The Development of Academic Freedom in the United States*. Vol. 1. New York: Columbia University Press, 1955.

Hogan, David. "The Market Revolution and Disciplinary Power: Joseph Lancaster and the Psychology of the Early Classroom System." *History of Education Quarterly* 29 (Fall 1989): 381–417.

Horlick, Allan Stanley. *Country Boys and Merchant Princes: The Social Control of Young Men in New York.* Lewisburg, Pa.: Bucknell University Press, 1975.

Horowitz, Helen Lefkowitz. *Rereading Sex: Battles over Sexual Knowledge and Suppression in Nineteenth-Century America.* New York: Knopf, 2002.

Howe, Daniel Walker. "Church, State, and Education in the Young American Republic," *Journal of the Early Republic* 22, no. 1 (Spring 2002): 1–24.

Howell, Philip. "Sex and the City of Bachelors: Sporting Guidebooks and Urban Knowledge in Nineteenth-Century Britain and America." *Ecumene* 8, no.1 (January 2001): 20–50.

Hull, Isabel V. *Sexuality, State, and Civil Society in Germany, 1700–1815.* Ithaca, N.Y.: Cornell University Press, 1996.

Jabour, Anya. *Marriage in the Early Republic: Elizabeth and William Wirt and the Companionate Ideal.* Baltimore: Johns Hopkins University Press, 1998.

———. "Masculinity and Adolescence in Antebellum America: Robert Wirt at West Point, 1820–21." *Journal of Family History* 23 (October 1998): 393–416.

Jackson, Leon. "The Rights of Man and the Rites of Youth: Fraternity and Riot at Eighteenth-Century Harvard." *History of Higher Education Annual* 15 (1995): 5–49.

Johnson, Allen, ed. *Dictionary of American Biography.* Vol. 2. New York: Scribner's Sons, 1929.

——— and Dumas Malone, eds. *Dictionary of American Biography.* Vol. 5. New York: Scribner's Sons, 1930.

Johnson, Paul. *A Shopkeeper's Millennium: Society and Revivals in Rochester, New York, 1815–1837.* New York: Hill and Wang, 1978.

Kaestle, Carl F. *Pillars of the Republic: Commons Schools and American Society, 1780–1860.* New York: Hill and Wang, 1983.

Kett, Joseph. *Rites of Passage: Adolescence in America, 1790 to the Present.* New York: Basic Books, 1977.

Kimmel, Michael. *Manhood in America: A Cultural History.* New York: Free Press, 1996.

Klepp, Susan E. " 'Heroines whose courage had risen superior to sex': Women, Fear, and Autobiography in the Early Republic." Paper presented to the Festive Culture and Public Ritual in Early America conference for the Philadelphia Center for Early American Studies, April 1996.

———. *Philadelphia in Transition: A Demographic History of the City and Its Occupational Groups, 1720–1830.* New York: Garland Publishing, 1989.

Knott, Sarah. "A Cultural History of Sensibility in the Era of the American Revolution." Ph.D. diss., Oxford University, 1999.

Kornblith, Gary. "From Artisans to Businessmen: Master Mechanics in New England, 1789–1850." Ph.D. diss., Princeton University, 1983.

———. "Self-Made Men: The Development of Middling Class Consciousness in New England." *Massachusetts Review* 26 (Summer–Autumn 1985): 461–74.

Kuhlmann, Susan. *Knave, Fool, and Genius: The Confidence Man as He Appears in Nineteenth-Century American Fiction.* Chapel Hill: University of North Carolina Press, 1973.

Laqueur, Thomas. *Making Sex: Body and Gender from the Greeks to Freud*. Cambridge, Mass.: Harvard University Press, 1990.

———. *Solitary Sex: A Cultural History of Masturbation*. New York: Zone Books, 2003.

Laurie, Bruce. *Artisans into Workers: Labor in Nineteenth-Century America*. New York: Hill and Wang, 1989.

———. *The Working People of Philadelphia, 1800–1850*. Philadelphia: Temple University Press, 1980.

Lawrence, Christopher. "The Nervous System and Society in the Scottish Enlightenment." In Barry Barnes and Steven Shapin, eds., *Natural Order: Historical Studies of Scientific Culture*. Beverly Hills, Calif.: Sage Publications, 1979.

Levy, Barry. *Quakers and the American Family: British Settlement in the Delaware Valley*. New York: Oxford University Press, 1988.

———. "'Tender Plants': Quaker Farmers and Children in the Delaware Valley, 1681–1735." *Journal of Family History* 3 (1978): 116–35.

Lewis, Jan. "The Republican Wife: Virtue and Seduction in the Early Republic." *William and Mary Quarterly* 3rd ser., 44 (October 1987): 689–721.

Lindstrom, Diane."Economic Structure, Demographic Change, and Income Inequality in Antebellum New York." In John Hull Mollenkopf, ed., *Power, Culture, and Place: Essays on New York City*. New York: Russell Sage Foundation, 1988.

Lockridge, Kenneth. "Land, Population, and the Evolution of New England Society, 1630–1790." *Past and Present* 39 (April 1968): 62–80.

Lombard, Anne. *Making Manhood: Growing Up Male in Colonial New England*. Cambridge, Mass.: Harvard University Press, 2003.

Lyons, Clare. "Sex among the 'Rabble': Gender Transitions in the Age of Revolution, Philadelphia, 1750–1830," Ph.D. diss., Yale University, 1996.

MacDonald, Robert H. "The Frightful Consequences of Onanism: Notes on the History of a Delusion." *Journal of the History of Ideas* 28 (1967): 423–31.

Marsden, George M. *The Evangelical Mind and the New School Presbyterian Experience: A Case Study of Thought and Theology in Nineteenth-Century America*. New Haven, Conn.: Yale University Press, 1970.

McLachlan, James. "The American College in the Nineteenth Century: Toward a Reappraisal," *Teachers College Record* 80 (December 1978): 287–306.

———. "The Choice of Hercules: American Student Societies in the Early Nineteenth-Century." in Lawrence Stone, ed., *The University in Society*, vol. 2. Princeton, N.J.: Princeton University Press, 1974.

McLoughlin, William G. "Untangling the Tiverton Tragedy: The Social Meaning of the Terrible Haystack Murder of 1833." *Journal of American Culture* 7 (Winter 1984): 75–84.

Meranze, Michael. *Laboratories of Virtue: Punishment, Revolution, and Authority in Philadelphia, 1760–1835*. Chapel Hill: University of North Carolina Press, 1996.

Meyers, Marvin. *The Jacksonian Persuasion: Politics and Belief*. Stanford, Calif.: Stanford University Press, 1957.

Moore, Kathryn McDaniel. "Freedom and Constraint in Eighteenth-Century Harvard." *Journal of Higher Education* 47, no. 6 (1976): 649–59.

Morison, Samuel Eliot. *Harvard College in the Seventeenth Century*. Cambridge, Mass.: Harvard University Press, 1936.

Mott, Frank Luther. *Golden Multitudes: The Story of the Best Sellers in the United States*. New York: Macmillan, 1947.

Neuman, R. P. "Masturbation, Madness, and the Modern Concepts of Childhood and Adolescence." *Journal of Social History* 8 (Spring 1975): 1–27.

Nissenbaum, Stephen. *Sex, Diet, and Debility in Jacksonian America: Sylvester Graham and Health Reform*. Westport, Conn.: Greenwood Press, 1980.

Noll, Mark A. *Princeton and the Republic, 1768–1822: The Search for a Christian Enlightenment in the Era of Samuel Stanhope Smith*. Princeton, N.J.: Princeton University Press, 1989.

Novak, Steven J. *The Rights of Youth: American Colleges and Student Revolt, 1798–1815*. Cambridge, Mass.: Harvard University Press, 1977.

Parker, Patricia L. "Susanna Haswell Rowson: America's First Best-Selling Author." In Kriste Lindenmeyer, ed. *Ordinary Women, Extraordinary Lives*. Wilmington, Del.: SR Books, 2000.

Perlman, Joel, and Dennis Shirley. "When Did New England Women Acquire Literacy?" *William and Mary Quarterly* 3rd ser., 48 (January 1991): 50–67.

Reinier, Jacqueline S. *From Virtue to Character: American Childhood, 1775–1850*. New York: Twayne Publishers, 1996.

———. "Rearing the Republican Child: Attitudes and Practices in Post-Revolutionary Philadelphia," *William and Mary Quarterly* 3rd ser., 39 (January 1982): 150–63.

Reynolds, David S. *Beneath the American Renaissance: The Subversive Imagination in the Age of Emerson and Melville*. Cambridge, Mass.: Harvard University Press, 1989.

Robson, David. *Educating Republicans: The College in the Era of the American Revolution, 1750–1800*. Westport, Conn.: Greenwood Press, 1985.

———. "Enlightening the Wilderness: Charles Nisbet's Failure at Higher Education in Post-Revolutionary Pennsylvania," *History of Education Quarterly* 37 (Fall 1997): 271–89.

Rodgers, Daniel T. "Republicanism: The Career of a Concept," *Journal of American History* 79 (June 1992): 11–38.

Rosenberg, Charles. *The Cholera Years: The United States in 1832, 1849, and 1866*. Chicago: University of Chicago Press, 1962.

———. "Sexuality, Class, and Role in Nineteenth-Century America," *American Quarterly* 25 (May 1973): 131–53.

——— and Carroll Smith-Rosenberg. "The Female Animal: Medical and Biological Views of Woman and Her Role in Nineteenth-Century America." *Journal of American History* 60 (September 1973): 332–56.

Roth, Randolph. *The Democratic Dilemma: Religion, Reform, and the Social Order in the Connecticut River Valley of Vermont, 1791–1850*. New York: Cambridge University Press, 1987.

Rothman, David. *The Discovery of the Asylum: Social Order and Disorder in the New Republic*. Boston: Little Brown, 1971.

Rothman, Ellen. *Hands and Hearts: A History of Courtship in America*. New York: Basic Books, Inc., 1984.

Rotundo, Anthony. *American Manhood: Transformations in Masculinity from the Revolution to the Modern Era*. New York: Basic Books, 1993.

Rousseau, G. S. "Nerves, Spirits, and Fibres: Toward Defining the Origins of Sensibility." In R. F. Brissenden and J. C. Eade, eds., *Studies in the Eighteenth Century* 3. Toronto: University of Toronto Press, 1976.

Rudolph, Frederick. *The American College and University: A History*. New York: Knopf, 1962.

Ruggles, Steven. "Fallen Women: The Inmates of the Magdalen Society Asylum of Philadelphia, 1836–1908." *Journal of Social History* 16 (Summer 1983): 65–82.

Ryan, Mary P. *Cradle of the Middle Class: The Family in Oneida County, New York, 1790–1865*. New York: Cambridge University Press, 1981.

———. "The Power of Women's Networks: A Case Study of Female Moral Reform in Antebellum America." *Feminist Studies* 5 (Spring 1979): 66–85.

———. *Women in Public: Between Banners and Ballots, 1825–1880*. Baltimore: Johns Hopkins University Press, 1990.

Salinger, Sharon V. "Artisans, Journeymen, and the Transformation of Labor in Late Eighteenth-Century Philadelphia." *William and Mary Quarterly* 3rd ser., 40 (January 1983): 62–84.

Sappol, Michael. *A Traffic of Dead Bodies: Anatomy and Embodied Social Identity in Nineteenth-Century America*. Princeton, N.J.: Princeton University Press, 2002.

Sears, Hal D. *The Sex Radicals*. Lawrence: Regents Press of Kansas, 1977.

Sellers, Charles. *The Market Revolution: Jacksonian America, 1815–1846*. New York: Oxford University Press, 1991.

Shammas, Carole. *A History of Household Government in America*. Charlottesville: University of Virginia Press, 2002.

Shepherd, Thomas James. *History of the First Presbyterian Church, Northern Liberties*. Philadelphia: n.p., 1882.

Siegel, Adrienne. *The Image of the American City in Popular Literature*. Port Washington, N.Y.: Kennikat Press, 1981.

Sinclair, Bruce. *Philadelphia's Philosopher Mechanics: A History of the Franklin Institute, 1824–65*. Baltimore: Johns Hopkins University Press, 1974.

Skemp, Sheila L. *Judith Sargent Murray: A Brief Biography with Documents*. Boston: Bedford Books, 1998

Sklar, Kathryn Kish. *Catharine Beecher: A Study in American Domesticity*. New York: Norton, 1976.

Smallwood, Mary Lovett. *An Historical Study of Examinations and Grading Systems in Early American Universities*. Cambridge, Mass.: Harvard University Press, 1935.

Smith, Billy G. *The "Lower Sort": Philadelphia's Laboring People, 1750–1800*. Ithaca, N.Y.: Cornell University Press, 1990.

Smith, Daniel Scott. "Parental Power and Marriage Patterns: An Analysis of Historical Trends in Hingham, Massachusetts," *Journal of Marriage and the Family* 35 (August 1973): 419–28.

———— and Michel S. Hindus. "Premarital Pregnancy in America, 1640–1971." *Journal of Interdisciplinary History* 5 (Spring 1975): 537–70.

Smith-Rosenberg, Carroll. *Disorderly Conduct: Visions of Gender in Victorian America.* New York: Oxford University Press, 1985.

————. "Domesticating 'Virtue': Coquettes and Revolutionaries in Young America," in *Literature and the Body,* ed. Elaine Scarry. Baltimore: Johns Hopkins University Press, 1988.

————. *Religion and the Rise of the American City: The New York City Mission Movement, 1812–1870.* Ithaca, N.Y.: Cornell University Press, 1971.

————. "Sex as Symbol in Victorian America: An Ethnohistorical Analysis of Jacksonian America." In John Demos and Sarane Spence Boocock, eds. *Turning Points: Historical and Sociological Essays on the Family.* Chicago: University of Chicago Press, 1978.

Somkin, Fred. *Unquiet Eagle: Memory and Desire in the Idea of American Freedom, 1815–1860.* Ithaca, N.Y.: Cornell University Press, 1967.

Sprague, William B. *Annals of the American Pulpit.* Vol. 4. New York: Robert Carter and Bros., 1868.

Srebnick, Amy Gilman. *The Mysterious Death of Mary Rogers: Sex and Culture in Nineteenth-Century New York.* New York: Oxford University Press, 1995.

Stansell, Christine. *City of Women: Sex and Class in New York, 1787–1860.* Urbana: University of Illinois Press, 1987.

Stephanson, Raymond. "Richardson's 'Nerves': The Physiology of Sensibility in *Clarissa.*" *Journal of the History of Ideas* 49 (April–June 1988): 267–85.

Stott, Richard B. *Workers in the Metropolis: Class, Ethnicity, and Youth in Antebellum New York.* Ithaca, N. Y.: Cornell University Press, 1990.

Thomas, Keith. "The Double Standard." *Journal of the History of Ideas* 20 (April 1959): 195–216.

Thompson, C. Seymour. "The Provostship of Dr. Beasley: 1813–1828." *General Magazine and Historical Chronicle* 33 (October 1930): 79–93.

Thompson, Roger. *Sex in Middlesex: Popular Mores in a Massachusetts County, 1649–1699.* Amherst: University of Massachusetts Press, 1986.

Tomlins, Christopher. *Law, Labor, and Ideology in the Early American Republic.* New York: Cambridge University Press, 1993.

Ulrich, Laurel Thatcher. *Good Wives: Image and Reality in the Lives of Women in Northern New England.* New York: Knopf, 1980.

University of Pennsylvania, General Alumni Society. *Biographical Catalogue of the Matriculates of the College.* Philadelphia: Printed for the Society, 1893.

Vail, R. W. G. *Susanna Haswell Rowson, the Author of Charlotte Temple: A Bibliographic Study.* Worcester, Mass.: Davis Press, 1933.

Wagoner, Jennings L. Jr. "Honor and Dishonor at Mr. Jefferson's University: The Antebellum Years," *History of Education Quarterly* 26 (Summer 1986): 155–79.

Wahrman, Dror. *Imagining the Middle Class: The Political Representation of Class in Britain, 1780–1840.* New York: Cambridge University Press, 1995.

Wall, Helena M. *Fierce Communion: Family and Community in Early America.* Cambridge, Mass.: Harvard University Press, 1990.

Wallach, Glenn. *Obedient Sons: The Discourse of Youth and Generations in American Culture, 1630–1860.* Amherst: University of Massachusetts Press, 1997.

Walters, Ronald G. *Primers for Prudery: Sexual Advice to Victorian America.* Englewood Cliffs, N.J.: Prentice-Hall, 1974.

Watt, Ian. *The Rise of the Novel: Studies in Defoe, Richardson, and Fielding.* Berkeley: University of California Press, 1967.

Wells, Robert V. "Illegitimacy and Bridal Pregnancy in Colonial America." In Peter Laslett, Karla Oosterveen, and Richard M Smith, eds. *Bastardy and Its Comparative History.* Cambridge, Mass.: Harvard University Press, 1980.

Welter, Barbara. "The Cult of True Womanhood, 1820–1860." *American Quarterly* 18 (Summer 1966): 151–74.

White, Deborah Gray. *Ar'n't I a Woman?: Female Slaves in the Plantation South.* New York: Norton, 1985.

Whiteaker, Larry. *Seduction, Prostitution, and Moral Reform in New York, 1830–1860.* New York: Garland Publishing, 1997.

Wilentz, Sean. *Chants Democratic: New York City and the Rise of the American Working Class, 1788–1850.* New York: Oxford University Press, 1984.

———. *Society, Politics, and the Market Revolution, 1815–1848,* 2nd ed. Washington: American Historical Association, 1997.

Williams, Joan C. "Domesticity as the Dangerous Supplement of Liberalism." *Journal of Women's History* 2 (Winter 1991): 69–88.

Wilson, Lisa. *Ye Heart of a Man: The Domestic Life of Men in Colonial New England.* New Haven, Conn.: Yale University Press, 1999.

Wohl, Richard. "The 'Country Boy' Myth and Its Place in American Urban Culture: The Nineteenth-Century Contribution." In *Perspectives in American History,* vol. 3. New York: Cambridge University Press, 1969.

Wolf, Stephanie Graham. *As Various as Their Land: The Everyday Lives of Eighteenth Century Americans.* New York: Harper Perennial, 1994.

Wood, Gordon. *The Radicalism of the American Revolution.* New York: Vintage Books, 1993.

Yazawa, Melvin. *From Colonies to Commonwealth: Familial Ideology and the Beginnings of the American Republic.* Baltimore: The Johns Hopkins University Press, 1985.

Zboray, Ronald J. "Antebellum Reading and the Ironies of Technological Innovation." *American Quarterly* 40, no. 1 (March 1988): 65–82.

——— and Mary S. Zboray, "Books, Reading, and the World of Goods in Antebellum America." *American Quarterly* 48, no. 4 (December 1996): 587–622.

Zuckerman, Michael. "Charlotte: A Tale of Sentiment, Seduction, and Subversion." Paper presented for the Seminar Series of the Philadelphia Center for Early American Studies, September 11, 1992.

Index

Acknowledgments

I can only hope that gratitude delayed is not like justice deferred. I have many people to thank for helping me write this book, as my interest in this topic began long ago. C. Dallett Hemphill, of Ursinus College, first piqued my interest in gender, family history, and early America. She remains to this day a mentor and a friend. Since I have known her, Dallett has faithfully read and commented on more of my work than anyone I know. When I moved to Philadelphia more than a decade ago, I found two delightfully supportive research communities. One was Temple University, which kept me intellectually and socially grounded. I found there great scholars in Margaret Marsh, P. M. G. Harris, and William Cutler. My grasp of historiography is largely due to them. Each also played an important role in shaping this project, challenging me to defend my ideas against their knowing criticisms.

My second research community in Philadelphia was the McNeil Center for Early American Studies. No one can say enough about what Richard Dunn has done for the field of early American history. I personally am indebted to Richard for providing me a home at the McNeil Center for three critical years as I researched and worked on this project. Richard's comments on my writings were also of great value. Through the McNeil Center I met many people who shaped my work. I would especially like to thank Lisa Wilson, Merril Smith, Bruce Dorsey, Sarah Knott, Susan Klepp, Roderick McDonald, Albrecht Koschnik, Seth Cotlar, Randolph Scully, Nicole Eustace, Caroline Eastman, Karim Tiro, and Michael Zuckerman for their fellowship, comments, and advice. Mike Zuckerman lavished me with attention; I cannot say I deserved it, but I certainly benefited much from it.

Over the last several years I have worked through many versions of this book. I had brilliant guides to lead me on my way. My greatest thanks must go to Kathleen Brown. Kathy intuitively grasped my project the first time she read it and pushed me to more fully realize its potential. How far it has come I will leave to others to decide, but the progress has been mostly due to her. And yet I should not slight others. Robert Lockhart, history editor at the University of Pennsylvania Press, provided great advice and feedback throughout the process. Surely he deserves much of the credit for Penn's rapidly expanding catalogue. Also at Penn, Ellie Goldberg and Erica Ginsburg both patiently answered my many questions. Bruce Dorsey was a fabulous outside reader who provided insightful advice. His expert counsel on early Philadelphia and religious reformers was a tremendous gift. I also benefited from the knowing advice of an outside reader whose probing questions strengthened this book. At a critical moment, my dear and longtime friend Julie Berebitsky provided very helpful feedback as I worked my way through thorny theoretical issues. Lee Braver advised me on Foucault, while Reneé Sentilles lent her sharp critical eye to my Introduction. Dee Andrews gave helpful feedback on Chapter 4.

Since I arrived at Hiram College, friends and colleagues have provided much support and insightful readings of my work. My chair, Glenn Sharfman, and my dean, Michael Grajek, have supported me in many ways. I am especially grateful for their financial support, and even more for the sabbatical they granted that helped me finish this project. Glenn, along with Vivien Sandlund, Janet Pope, Ericka Thomas, and Robert Sawyer, has made life at Hiram very rewarding. As my colleagues in crime in the History Department, they have taught me much about a profession that keeps expanding like the horizon before me. Friends and colleagues in other departments were also of great assistance. Ellen Summers organized a faculty writing group whose members ripped through my writing with great abandon. I would especially like to thank Ellen, as well as Joyce Dyer, Janet Pope, Don Fleming, Gwen Fischer, and Debra Rodriguez, for their helpful feedback on my Introduction. Kirsten Parkinson has been a good friend and equally good sounding board for ideas. My commute has been the richer for her being in the car with me. Hiram student Ian Dixon worked faithfully on my index, while Sarah Woodford offered her sharp copyediting skills.

I also must thank the archivists who faithfully retrieved, no matter how hidden, the documents I used in writing this book. I am grateful for the assistance I received at the Historical Society of Pennsylvania, the College of Physicians of Philadelphia Library, the University of Pennsylvania Archives, the Library Company of Philadelphia, Princeton University Archives, Harvard University Archives, and the Presbyterian Historical Society. Linda Stanley and Terry Snyder, formerly of HSP and Penn Archives, respectively, made trips to the archives both fun and intellectually gratifying.

Parts of Chapter 1 appeared in Merril Smith, ed., *Sex and Sexuality in*

America (NYU Press, 1998), while portions of Chapter 2 were published in *Pennsylvania History* 66, special supplement, *Explorations in Early American Culture* (1999): 201–22. An earlier version of Chapter 3 appeared in *History of Education Quarterly* 39 (Fall 1999): 237–62 (copyright by History of Education Society; reprinted by permission). I would like to thank the publishers for allowing me to reprint the material appearing in their publications.

To really serve justice I should also thank those who gave me rest from my work. My parents, Frank and Dorothy; my brothers, Greg and Glen, and their families; and my sister, Chrissa, would have supported me with or without a book contract. They have brought laughs and good cheer to my life. My grandparents, including my grandfather Frank Hessinger, Jr. (known as Pappy to me), to whose memory this book is lovingly dedicated, believed in me long before I believed in myself. My family by marriage, the Feeny clan, has also sustained me. Bill, Peg, Ted, Catherine, Julie, and Gerry have always been great company. Our journeys together have been delightful. My partner, Norah, deserves more than anyone. Not only has she read many more drafts of chapters than I care to count, but she has been my best friend and confidant. Words cannot repay the debt I owe her; nonetheless, I offer up my gratitude as a token of love.